LAW FOR K–12 LIBRARIES
AND LIBRARIANS

LAW FOR K–12 LIBRARIES AND LIBRARIANS

LEE ANN TORRANS

U N L I M I T E D

A Member of the Greenwood Publishing Group

Westport, Connecticut • London

Library of Congress Cataloging-in-Publication Data

Torrans, Lee Ann, 1952–
    Law for K–12 libraries and librarians / Lee Ann Torrans.
        p. cm.
    Includes bibliographical references and index.
    ISBN 1–59158–036–6 (alk. paper)
    1. School libraries—Law and legislation—United States. 2. Fair use
(Copyright)—United States. 3. Librarians—Legal status, laws,
etc.—United States. I. Title.
KF4219.T67 2003
344.73'092—dc21   2003002592

British Library Cataloguing in Publication Data is available.

Library of Congress Catalog Card Number: 2003002592
ISBN: 1–59158–036–6

First published in 2003

Libraries Unlimited
A Member of Greenwood Publishing Group, Inc.
88 Post Road West, Westport, CT 06881
www.lu.com

Printed in the United States of America

The paper used in this book complies with the
Permanent Paper Standard issued by the National
Information Standards Organization (Z39.48–1984).

10 9 8 7 6 5 4 3 2 1

Dedicated to
Emily

and

"Miss Dixie" Splawn
who loves children

CONTENTS

1

INTRODUCTION

A law is valuable not because it is the law, but because there is right in it.
　　　　　　　　　　　　　　　　　　—Henry Ward Beecher

Welcome! If you are reading this, you probably have stolen a few moments from your job, your family, your errands, or some other aspect of your life. If you are a school librarian, your most precious commodity is your time. The tools of your trade were at one time books and a few periodicals. Your domain was finite and consisted of walls, doors, and windows. Your patrons were visible bodies, and your circulation records were kept in a sturdy wooden box. News that directly affected your library was infrequent and had little to do with the United States Supreme Court or the FBI. Welcome to the new millennium!

The United States Supreme Court is at perennial odds with the United States Congress and continues to strike down laws that directly impact libraries. We have become so jaded when it comes to federal laws that impact the library that we await a Supreme Court ruling before we take them seriously. The FBI can surveil our students' computer activities unbeknownst to the librarians. Even with the best filters, students can access not only adult pornography but also contraband child pornography that lurks within it. But wait—is that virtual pornography or real pornography? Now there is a legal distinction brought to us courtesy of the United States Supreme Court!

Anyone who has watched the United States Supreme Court reverse congressional laws understands that the law is fluid and not fixed. It changes and develops to reflect the changes and developments in society.[1] As our fluid laws develop in our complex society so does the duty of the librarian to understand these laws as they affect the library's activities and service. The study of the law for the K–12 librarian is not just the study of laws as they impact the library, but also how they affect the school systems, their faculties, their students, and their community. It is not uncommon for the librarian to have a deeper understanding of the laws that affect the library than the principal, superintendent, or even the school district's lawyer.

The Copyright Act of 1976, U.S. Code Volume 17, recently has been modified twice by Congress. The Digital Millennium Copyright Act (DMCA) and the Sonny Bono Copyright Term Extension Act both impacted libraries and their duties and rights, and now a ruling from the United States Supreme Court indicates this term extension is valid.

The laws of both the federal and state governments attempt to balance the rights of the individual with the rights of society. The more complex our society becomes the more complex our laws become. The World Wide Web has created new legal issues not wholly addressed by the laws related to print communications. These laws, ranging from employment issues to Internet access issues, affect the library, for the library is not only a window upon the world but a window of the world. The librarian is the guide and the keeper of the law within the library, a sheriff in a modern day Dodge, for all can enter the library through the Internet—the good, the bad, the legal, and the illegal. Child pornography is contraband, as illegal as heroin, and its presence in the library can bring liability for the library and the librarian. It is contrary to our laws for any child to view pornography and the courts have deemed we have a societal "compelling interest" in protecting the innocence of our children.

The Unabomber used the library to research his victims' identities. The terrorists of September 11 used the library and a Kinko's shop for e-mail communications. Copyright violations are federal crimes.

Libraries are still noble repositories of information and dedicated to learning, however, their scope of services has broadened. Maryland's Supreme Court view of a library and its purpose, found in a seventy-five-year-old case, *Johnston v. Baltimore*, provides a majestic interpretation of the function of a library. In this case the court stated:

At the present time it is generally recognized and conceded by all thoughtful peoples that such institutions form an integral part of a system of free public education and are among its most efficient and valuable adjuncts. An enlightened and educated public has come to be regarded as the surest safeguard for the maintenance and advancement of the progress of civilized nations. More particularly is this true in republican forms of government, wherein all citizens have a voice. It is also true that education of the people ought not and does not stop upon their leaving school, but must be kept abreast of the time by almost constant reading and study. It would therefore seem that no more important duty or higher purpose is incumbent upon a state or municipality than to provide free public libraries for the benefits of its inhabitants.[2]

Libraries have historically been accorded a high position by the courts in our society. At the turn of the nineteenth century, only 6 percent of seventeen-year-olds were high school educated, and the high schools were college preparatory institutions at that time. It wasn't until World War II that half of all Americans had a high school diploma. In the 1950s, the schools were segregated in the South. Many Mexican Americans did not have access to quality secondary education. Children with disabilities were excluded in large part from regular classrooms and public schools. However, education has progressed and the function of the library as a source of education has been modified.

Schools are now confronted by an immense amount of data that was historically inaccessible but is now available from the media and the Internet. The librarians are the first to filter these vast resources of information. Libraries may retain television news broadcasts, but not television news magazines. When a school librarian creates a bibliography of Web sites, that librarian makes value judgments on behalf of the library and the school about the quality and appropriateness of the information found on those sites. Once the Web sites are winnowed for bias, age appropriateness, curricular relevance, and quality, it is the librarian's task to organize this information in such a way that it makes sense so that students (and their parents) may be confident in its accuracy and objectivity.

As libraries face difficulties associated with the Internet, a familiar theme in our culture of "technology out of control" surfaces. This concept stretches back at least to Mary Shelley's *Frankenstein*, a novel of tragedy and warning published in 1818. The Frankenstein story, still popular throughout the world, is a cautionary tale about the dangers of experimenting with technologies we don't fully understand. This approach grabs attention and makes headlines, but perhaps the better perspective is that of Henry David Thoreau: "All our inventions are wont to be pretty toys, which distract our attention from serious things. They are but improved means to an unimproved end."[3]

As long as our attention is diverted to the method of access, it is diverted from our true goal, which is the education of our children. Our society has determined that there is a compelling interest in protecting our children from information that is deemed harmful. In reaching this goal then, the complexities of our society, and therefore the complexities of our laws, must be respected.

SCOPE OF THIS BOOK

The law is a technical business. Thousands and thousands of law review articles exist covering the issues raised in this book. A typical law review article consists of 40,000 to 75,000 words, the length of this entire book, and covers an issue that may have been addressed by no more than a sentence in this book. Entire courses are taught in law school on many of these chapters. Students spend a semester on one issue and often that is simply an introductory course. More-detailed courses are also offered. Weeklong seminars are held for attorneys who practice in these areas to educate them on less than half a chapter found in this book. Judges who sit on the United States Supreme Court and those judges who preside in the smallest counties of this country do not agree on what the current status of the law truly is on some of these topics. There are thousands of laws and thousands of cases that interpret the issues covered in this book. Few are in agreement.

This book is not intended to create lawyers from librarians nor is its purpose to give legal advice. Always consult an attorney if there is a legal question. This book is intended to alert the school librarian to the mere existence of legal issues. In some instances librarians are unaware that federal and/or state statutes exist covering topics they deal with each day.

Some chapters go into more detail than any librarian should be required to endure. Details supporting broad topics found in this text can be extensive. You may choose to do no more than read the first sentence describing a broad topic and skim the details. With this approach you will at least become familiar with the legal concept. The goal is that you will understand the relevance of such an issue and understand that such a topic exists in the law. Should the issue surface in your library, you can then refer to the chapter for a more detailed understanding and to better enable you to address your school's attorney and superintendent.

DEVELOP POLICIES AND PROCEDURES THAT REFLECT THE LAW

Developing policies and procedures for your library will serve the library well and this book is designed to enable you to begin to address legal issues with formal policies and procedures in the library. In developing library policies and supporting procedures the opportunity will be presented to think through new issues and determine precisely which policies are best for your faculty, students, community, and administration. This text is intended to present legal issues that can be addressed by policy and managed by procedure.

For example, it is important to have a policy that makes the library accessible by people with disabilities. You might go a step further and create a policy that includes student workers with disabilities in the library. Your procedures supporting these policies will vary but might include an effort to purchase fiction works about people with disabilities, or to state a preference for student workers with disabilities, to have aisles of at least forty-two inches between bookshelves even though the federal requirement is thirty-six inches, and consideration of the need for quiet distraction-free carrels for students with attention deficit disorder.

Also, for example, because Web page building is becoming the domain of the media center and of the librarian, it might be the school policy to create bibliography Web pages for specific areas of study. Your procedures supporting these duties might include a library-created criteria for inclusion of specific Web sites in the library Web page bibliography. Your procedure might also include an education program for both the faculty and the students on the laws of copyright, trademark, and the means for tracing the ownership of a copyright.

When students are building Web sites, it should be the policy of the school that material subject to copyright cannot be used unless it is protected as a "fair-use" exception to the law of copyright. However, it might be the procedure of the library to educate the students that exact reproductions of two-dimensional works of art, such as paintings and drawings, may not be subject to copyright if the original work has exceeded copyright protection. The students are free to adorn their Web sites with the works of Monet, Manet, or the fantasy watercolor paintings of William Blake (of "The Tyger"[4] fame), who many students would find rivals any modern-day video game graphic designer.

Your library policy might be to educate students on correct bibliographic format. To reduce unscheduled class visits, the procedure could include the implementation of a sign-up sheet located on the library bulletin board, which teachers would be required to use as a prerequisite to obtaining the librarian's direct time and attention. The new library policy also may provide for an annual presentation to the faculty during in-service meetings. This presentation could detail library procedures to implement the library policies and could be a wonderful opportunity to obtain feedback from the faculty.

Although some matters are best dealt with informally, take the opportunity to review your library's policies and procedures. Ask yourself: If I were gone unexpectedly for a year, could a temporary librarian take these policies and procedures and manage the library? Could my substitute modify the procedures as necessary and maintain the purpose of the policies? Do the policies truly reflect the essence of the library? Are the library policies flexible enough to accommodate changes and are the procedures specific enough to guide the functioning librarian? It is the goal of this book to guide you to develop policies and procedures that will govern your library both when it is under direct public assault and when things are running smoothly.

Librarians must be able to defend their decisions, whether they concern the selection of material on a library Web site bibliography page or the protection of a student's privacy by refusing to turn over a student's circulation record. If, for example, as the librarian, you are called to the school board to face an angry group of parents, would you be able to justify your position based upon library and school policies? Are you prepared to turn to a teacher over lunch and tell him or her that you cannot disclose whether Suzy checked out *The Catcher in the Rye* because it is policy to respect the privacy of student records, oh, and by the way, it is also against the law!

Thinking through these issues in advance may make the librarian's life simpler when inevitable conflicts arise. Admittedly, it is not fair to put the librarian in the position of fully understanding these many complex legal issues, but if you are reading this, you already understand that life is not fair!

NOTES

1. Kermit L. Hall, *The Magic Mirror: Law in American History* (New York: Oxford University Press, 1990), 336.

2. *Johnston v. Baltimore*, 158 Md. 93 (1930).

3. Henry David Thoreau, *Walden,* originally published in 1854.

4. Blake's work can be accessed online via deep linking, a legal issue addressed in this text. Deep linking occurs when a link bypasses the main page of a Web site and goes straight to the subject matter of relevance. A link straight to the *William Blake Exhibition* Web site of the Metropolitan Museum of Art would be an example of a deep link. At the Metropolitan Museum of Art Web site, available at http://www.metmuseum.org, you may link to Special Exhibitions. From there you may link to Past Exhibitions, June, 2001. From there you may link to the artwork of William Blake or browse the various other works of art. Exact replications of two-dimensional works of art that have an expired copyright may be incorporated in the Web pages of students without violation of copyright. However, photographs of three-dimensional objects such as statues do not have the same protection. They are deemed to be an original creation because there is an amount of subjectivity in the angle, the lighting, and the size of the statute in relation to the size of the photo.

However, the Fair Use Exception of the Copyright Act of 1976 will enable the student to use some copyrighted works. Without deep linking some searching may be required, but if the Web site is as wonderful as the Metropolitan Museum of Art's, this search could be an act that enhances the experience. In an attempt not to deep link I have provided the home page of the Metropolitan Museum of Art with "directions" to the *William Blake Exhibition* there in June of 2001.

2

—◆•••◆—

COPYRIGHT

The primary objective of copyright is not to reward the labor of authors, but to promote the Progress of Science and useful Arts.
—The United States Supreme Court

The rights conferred by copyright are designed to assure contributors to the store of knowledge a fair return for their labors.
—*Twentieth Century Music Corp. v. Aiken,*
422 U.S. 151, 156 (1975)

All librarians have some working knowledge about copyright, and most have developed their favorite resources to support their research needs when questions arise concerning the topic. This chapter is intended to simply give the librarian an understanding of the road the United States has taken in arriving at its current laws of copyright, which is helpful in understanding the purpose of copyright. It is important to understand the foundation and roots of our copyright laws, which originated with our founding fathers, are an important principle on which our Constitution is based. The concept of the right of copy, or of ownership of the product of the creative process, was influenced by the British history of the law of copyright. This is a history of both the benefit and the detriment to public good that copyright laws bring to our society. Copyright is a legal creation, and it exists solely because our society believes these laws serve to enhance the progress of our society. The laws of copyright exist for a legally defined purpose and within legally defined limits. The legally defined purpose is not to enrich the creator of the work, but to benefit society. The enrichment of the creator of the work is a byproduct of the benefit to society.

This chapter will cover the following topics:

U.S. and British View of Copyright

The Purpose of Copyright

History of United States Copyright Law

Current Copyright Law

Sonny Bono Copyright Term Extension Act

What Does Copyright Protect?

Violation of Copyright Results in an Infringement

Rights Granted to Owners of Copyright

Works of Faculty or Works for Hire

International Copyright Law

What materials can be the subject of a copyright? Justice Oliver Wendell Holmes defined that which might be subject to copyright as follows: "Personality always contains something unique. It expresses its singularity even in handwriting, and a very modest grade of art has in it something irreducible, which is one man's alone. That something he may copyright unless there is a restriction in the words of the act."[1]

The idea of progress has a central place in copyright law. The idea of progress is the belief that humankind is on an inevitable course of betterment, and that knowledge is a product of an ongoing cumulative effort that is secular in nature. Often the importance of the betterment of our society as it relates to copyright law is overlooked. The knowledge process, which is at the core of copyright law, is best understood through the idea of progress for our society.[2] This is the cornerstone of education and a concept familiar and embraceable by all school librarians. Our fundamental purpose is to enhance the knowledge process and the product of this purpose is progress for our society.

The legal protection of copyright does not invoke a symbol of quality or merit. Congress explicitly stated that its standard for copyright protection did not include any requirement of "aesthetic merit." It also specified that the "term 'literary works' does not connote any criterion of literary merit or qualitative value."[3] Consequently, the fact that a work is copyrighted does not import merit or value to that work.

FIRST SALE DOCTRINE

The basic understanding everyone has, almost intuitively, is that the laws of copyright do not prohibit the loaning of materials by the library. The loaning of materials by a library is accomplished pursuant to the "First Sale" doctrine. The doctrine of First Sale is not found specifically in the Copyright Act. This doctrine is found in case law interpreting the copyright statute and is known as "common law," as opposed to "statutory law." The doctrine allows purchasers of tangible products containing copyrighted information, such as books, to dispose of those works in any way they wish. They may sell them, give them away, loan them, rent them, or use them for doorstops. Libraries, which purchase works and loan them to users, accomplish this process by employing the First Sale doctrine. The grants of powers to the owner of copyright found in 17 U.S. Code Section 106 do not prohibit any of the activities associated with the First Sale doctrine. However, license agreements, which are contractual agreements between parties, may limit these rights.[4]

U.S. AND BRITISH VIEW OF COPYRIGHT

The Constitution granted to Congress the power "to promote the Progress of Science and useful Arts" by securing copyrights and patents "for limited Times." The founding fathers were suspicious of "monopolies," a word used in Britain to define the right of copy (copyright) with a definitively negative connotation and a concept that was ultimately found to hinder the progress of society rather than enhance it.

Legal monopolies pervaded the rights of copy of Britain for many years. This monopoly served to limit public access to information for the sole purpose of enriching those to whom these monopolies had been granted. A review of legal arguments regarding copyright in the nineteenth century could have been made in our country, today.

In 1834, it was determined that in the United States, as it had previously been determined in England, the right of copy was not a natural right, but a right given to the creator by the State. This concept was contrasted to the position held by the proponents of perpetual copyright who argued that "securing copyright" meant the affirmation of preexisting rights. However, the proponents of the opposing view, and the view ultimately adopted by the United States as had been adopted in Britain, argued that "securing copyright" meant nothing more than "to obtain" or "to provide" something that did not already exist. Copyright was in their view a legal creation, not a natural state.

These same issues were at the forefront of the law of copyright. In the Supreme Court challenge to the Sonny Bono Copyright Term Extension Act (CTEA), history repeated itself. The struggle between the powerful members of our society who own copyrights facing expiration, such as movie studios, music publishers, and the heirs of the creators, argued for lengthy terms for rights of copy. Challenging them were those who would reprint or otherwise reproduce classic works and circulate them more widely. At the hearings on the Copyright Term Extension Act it was once again, hundreds of years later, argued that fairness required U.S. copyrights to last for the lives of the author and two generations of descendants. This argument was supported by the fact that the European Union allowed such a lengthy term for copy. In the House and Senate hearings on the CTEA, heirs of copyrighted material presented both oral testimony and written requests for more lengthy terms of copyright. Included were the written testimony of Marsha Durham, daughter of composer Eddie Durham; the written testimony of Mary Ellin Barrett, daughter of composer Irving Berlin; and the prepared statement of Shana Alexander, author and daughter of composer Milton Ager.[5] The Supreme Court ruled in January 2003 that Congress could extend the term of copyright.

THE PURPOSE OF COPYRIGHT

The United States Constitution clearly states that the purpose of copyright is "to promote the progress of Science and useful Arts." Always keeping the constitutional purpose of copyright in mind is helpful in understanding the role copyright plays in education.

The fundamental and essential importance of education in building a better world is universally recognized. Using copyrighted material in education greatly expands students' accomplishments in their studies and research, and the faculties' ability to educate the students. Valid instructional use of copyrighted materials is important for the educators to understand and for the students to learn. No student should enroll in college without a clear understanding of copyright laws, and it is unlikely that an educator would be found by the courts to have acted in "good faith" should they not attempt to understand copyright laws and guidelines and implement them in their daily activities.

The court has the authority and the discretion to release an educator from a lawsuit brought for copyright infringement. This authority is found in the Copyright Act and case law supporting it. Prior to releasing the educator from the lawsuit the court must find the educator acted in "good faith." This finding of "good faith" by the court is essential; without it the educator cannot be released from the suit.

The court must find that the educator made a "good faith" effort to understand copyright law and did in fact comply with the law as understood by the educator. If the court finds that the educator did not make a good faith effort to both understand and apply copyright law, the court does not have the statutory discretion to release the educator.

The burden will be on the educator to first present evidence to the court of his or her history of studying copyright law as it applies to the education system. Evidence could include documentation of attendance at seminars regarding copyright and conventions at which copyright was discussed, as well as copies of the school's, or even the library's, policies and handbook on copyright. The educator also could present evidence of all college courses taken that addressed the issue of copyright. Secondly, the educator must explain to the court his or her understanding of copyright in the instance over which the lawsuit has been brought, and their rationale in application of law to their specific factual situation. Without this presentation the educator will remain a party to the suit and liability may attach.

The "Classroom Guidelines," which are implemented in many libraries as binding policies, are considered by some authors to be overly restrictive and not consistent with the true spirit of the copyright law. However, it is the constant threat of litigation for the infringement of the right of copy that has created a legitimate concern at most educational institutions. This apprehension over copyright infringement and the possible ensuing litigation requires most educational institutions simply to adopt the "Classroom Guidelines" as their one and only guide to the use of copyright material. (See chapter 4, "Fair Use in Education of Material Protected by Copyright," for a full discussion of this topic.)

Do not be deterred from using copyrighted information. Simply educate yourself as to the quantity of material from a particular source that is usable before the act of copyright infringement occurs. This mental exercise can become second nature for the educator and the college-bound student. Balancing valid, critical, and acceptable educational needs with the creator's rights as accorded by statute is the issue. While you are balancing rights, it would be a good idea to keep up with the news. The opponents to copyright extension have vowed to continue their efforts to reduce the term of copyright.

WORLD'S OLDEST COPYRIGHT

We all know that the works of Shakespeare have long lost their right of copy, so certainly the Dead Sea Scrolls have lost their right of copy. Right? Well, not exactly. Some of these scrolls date back to the third century B.C., whereas others are more recent, relatively speaking. On the western shores of the Dead Sea in the region of Judea, Pliny the Elder described "a solitary race . . . remarkable beyond all the other tribes in the whole world," called the Essenes.[6] This tribe would be unremarkable and forgotten outside this small reference had it not been for eleven caves above the Wadi Qumran, which contained the remnants of this civilization. Khirbet Qumran is the excavation site for the Dead Sea Scrolls, which represent the remains of the library of the Essenes. The surviving fragments of this library represent over six hundred books, which were saved from advancing armies by being hidden in the caves.

After years of painstaking study, hundreds of parchment fragments found in a cave near the Dead Sea were pieced together to form a 2,000-year-old missive from the leader of a Jewish sect to a Jewish leader in Jerusalem. In 1992, three scholars included this missive in a book they published and edited, *A Facsimile Edition of the Dead Sea Scrolls*, without the permission of the scholar who pieced together and translated this missive. When challenged, a unanimous

Israeli three-judge panel agreed that the scholar who pieced the missive together could not claim copyright on the scroll fragments, nor on those fragments that were pieced together by physical resemblance. However, the court noted that 40 percent of the text was missing from the parts that had been pieced together and this 40 percent came from the author's "creative depths." The court found the scholar was therefore entitled to the copyright protection of the entire missive. This is the oldest known copyright in the history of man. While no one really believes the work of the Essenes was the work that was the subject of a copyright the creative portion of the work entitled the scholar to the protection of Israeli copyright law. The copyright bestowed upon these works by the State of Israel was found to be valid.[7]

Here two lessons are to be learned. First, an old story, long out of copyright, can be modified, and the result can be copyrighted. Behold the Disney presentation of the familiar tale of "Beauty and the Beast." The origins of the tale itself are from 1757—it was written in France by Jeanne-Marie le Prince de Beaumont—and yet the tale is known to most. There can be no question but that Disney enhanced de Beaumont's tale with their own "creative depths" just as the scholar enhanced the missive found in the Dead Sea Scrolls with his own "creative depths."

The second lesson is one that is reinforced daily as we watch twenty-four-hour cable news or log on to the Internet: the scope of our world is now worldwide. Each country has its own copyright laws. We are participants in treaties that require the citizens in the United States to observe the copyright laws of other participating countries.

HISTORY OF UNITED STATES COPYRIGHT LAW

The soul and source of the right of copy or copyright in the United States resides in our Constitution. "The Congress shall have Power . . . To promote the Progress of Science and useful Arts, by securing for limited Times to Authors and Inventors the exclusive Right to their respective Writings and Discoveries."[8] The original copyright statute of 1790 granted copyright terms of fourteen years with a fourteen-year renewal period.

In 1831, the initial terms of the 1790 law were extended to twenty-eight years, renewable for fourteen years. For nearly eighty years (1831 to 1909), the term of copy remained at forty-two years. Our Constitution empowers Congress to enact copyright law and defines a policy for the objectives of any laws the Congress may take to further this right of copy. Historically, Congress has extended the period of copyright for the benefit of the creator of the work, which in turn has limited the public's access to the copyrighted material.

Included in the concept of "monopolies" is the concept of copyright. Thomas Jefferson believed that each generation should start fresh and not be overly burdened with legal and financial obligations inherited from the previous generation. Jefferson believed all debts, patents, copyrights, and even laws, should expire "when a majority of those of full age shall be dead."[9] Jefferson computed nineteen years to be the period of time in which these patents and copyrights should expire. However, the span of life has increased in the last two hundred years. Factoring in the lengthened lifespan of Americans, today Thomas Jefferson's original concept of copyright would allow the copyright to expire after 30 years.

The effort in Congress that led to passage of the Copyright Act of 1976 began in 1955 when Congress authorized the U.S. Copyright Office to conduct studies of various copyright issues.[10] The Copyright Office delivered those studies in 1960 and 1961, which began in earnest the process of legislation producing the Copyright Act of 1976, which in turn became effective on January 1, 1978.

In one interpretation of the Copyright Act of 1976, the Supreme Court focused on the importance of social goods and public purpose derived from the copy of materials and referred to the rights of an author to control the copy of their works as a "monopoly." One of the greatest social goods and public purposes of protected works is education. The Court stated: "The monopoly privileges that Congress may authorize are neither unlimited nor primarily designed to provide a special private benefit. Rather, the limited grant is a means by which an important public purpose may be achieved." [11]

In 1994 in another important interpretation of the Copyright Act of 1976, the Court made a more direct statement about the Fair Use serving constitutional purposes: "From the infancy of copyright protection, some opportunity for fair use of copyrighted materials has been thought necessary to fulfill copyright's very purpose, '[t]o promote the Progress of Science and useful Arts.'"[12] The courts are sensitive to the needs of society to use the works of others to promote progress and the good of all men, and balance these needs with the rights of the creators.

Our resulting law of copyright permits the educational fair use of copyrighted materials; it can be found in 17 U.S.C. 107 (1994). Our copyright laws permit a right to copy the works of another for educational fair-use purposes, that is "for purposes such as criticism, comment, news reporting, teaching (including multiple copies for classroom use), scholarship, or research." Also included in the exclusion from the protection of copyright is a writer's or a publisher's right to parody the copyrighted work of another.

A recent parody that withstood an appellate review of an injunctive challenge was the work of Alice Randall, *The Wind Done Gone,* published by Houghton Mifflin.[13] In this novel, the story of *Gone with the Wind* is told from the diary entries of Scarlett's half sister, Cynara, the mistress of Rhett Butler and the daughter of Scarlett's planter father and Mammy. The book jacket to *The Wind Done Gone* describes the novel as "[a] provocative literary parody that explodes the mythology perpetrated by a Southern classic."

The Mitchell heirs claimed Randall infringed their copyright. The trial court agreed claiming *The Wind Done Gone* was "unabated piracy" of *Gone with the Wind* and the district court granted Suntrust's motion for a prelimi-nary injunction, enjoining Houghton from "production, display, distribu-tion, advertising, sale or offer for sale" of *The Wind Done Gone*. The appellate court, however, disagreed and lifted the injunction prohibiting the publica-tion of *The Wind Done Gone*, creating a great deal of publicity for the work. The Eleventh Circuit held that the novel's publisher was entitled to a fair-use defense because the book was a defensible parody of Margaret Mitchell's *Gone with the Wind* and as such was not protected by the laws of copyright. Ultimately the publisher and the Mitchell heirs reached an agreement per-mitting the publication of the work; Houghton Mifflin agreed to make a financial contribution to Morehouse College in Atlanta at the request of the Mitchell estate. (See chapter 3, "Scope and Terms of Copyright," and chap-ter 4, "Fair Use in Education of Material Protected by Copyright," for fur-ther discussion of parody and copyright.)

The recent extensions of copyright have extended the original right granted to authors and publishers. For example, *Gone With the Wind* was published in 1936. In accordance with the copyright term in force under the 1909 Copyright Act, which prevailed in 1936, Mitchell's novel would have gone into the public domain in 1992. In fact it would have gone into the public domain in 1964 if the copyright holder had not duly renewed the copyright that year. However, subsequent copyright extension laws have extended the period of copyright far beyond those envisioned by many authors and publishers at the time of the creation of the original work. This exemplifies the argument many have against the extension of the term of copyright. This extension, when applied retroactively, does not serve as a motivation for the creation of copyrighted works because the works have already been created. The argument against retroactive extensions is that it benefits the heirs of the creators and not the impetus for creation, which is the constitutionally defined purpose of copyright.

CURRENT COPYRIGHT LAW

The Copyright Revision Act of 1976,[14] codified as Title 17 of the United States Code, is the main legal text that governs copyright policy. It has been revised by both the Sonny Bono Copyright Term Extension Act and the Dig-ital Millennium Copyright Act.

In 1978, guidelines for the application of Title 17 were developed by the National Commission on New Technological Uses of Copyright Works (CONTU), which dealt with issues raised by photocopiers and computers. Expectations were that the document would be reviewed and updated peri-odically. These guidelines, however, have never been revised. They are avail-able at: http://www.cni.org/docs/info.policies/CONTU.html (accessed January 29, 2003).

The Conference on Fair Use (CONFU), convened by the Working Group, brought together copyright owner and user interests to discuss fair-use issues and to develop guidelines for fair uses of copyrighted works by librarians and educators. After four years of meetings, 1994–1998, a final report was issued, but it does not include guidelines for fair-use copying. It contends that widely supported guidelines will be complicated by the competing interests of the copyright owner and user communities.

The Digital Millennium Copyright Act (DMCA) was passed in October 1998 to address the law's five titles, which implement the World Intellectual Property Organization (WIPO) Internet Treaties; establish safe harbors for online service providers; permit temporary copies of programs during the performance of computer maintenance; make miscellaneous amendments to the Copyright Act, including amendments that facilitate Internet broadcasting; and create sui generis protection for boat hull designs. Of particular interest to libraries was a controversial title establishing database protection, which was omitted by the House-Senate Conference. Fair use was not addressed by this act.

The United States Code is not difficult to access. It is a relatively easy matter to consult Title 17 regarding questions about copyright coverage of a particular work. The Library of Congress also maintains records of copyright applications.[15]

SONNY BONO COPYRIGHT TERM EXTENSION ACT

In 1995, a bill regarding copyright was introduced in the House and the Senate, and both chambers held hearings. The bill never exited the committee because restaurant and bar owners lobbied Congress for a broader exemption on paying royalties for music broadcast in their establishments. It took three years for the restaurateurs to be successful with their lobbying and win an exemption from the proposed copyright act. In March 1998, the bill passed in the House of Representatives but stalled in the Senate. In October 1998, a similar version of the bill reached the Senate floor and passed by unanimous consent. The bill quickly passed in the House with a voice vote so that no members who voted yea or nay could be identified. The Sonny Bono Copyright Term Extension Act (CTEA) became the law, and suddenly works that were expected to become part of the public domain were frozen under continued copyright for another twenty years.

The lobbyists' most effective argument was that American copyright law should be made to conform to that of the European Union. American culture is an important component of European consumption. The lobbyist's argued that copyrights in the United States would expire sooner than they did in Europe, unfairly penalizing American corporations and creators. One critic responded to this position that Europe was more interested in the current works of American culture such as *Jurassic Park*, not in the relatively few works from the 1920s and 1930s whose copyright owners benefit from term extension. He noted that the greatest market for these older works are Americans interested in scholarship and research and that locking these works away would limit their interpretation, access, and impact to benefit society. This amendment was reviewed by the United States Supreme Court, which found the twenty-year extension to be a valid exercise of congressional authority. To read the briefs of the parties, go to the *Eldred v. Ashcroft Legal Document Archive* sponsored by Harvard University.[16]

PUBLIC DOMAIN WORKS DERAILED BY CTEA

Porgy and Bess was published by George and Ira Gershwin in 1935. Prior to the Copyright Term Extension Act it was set to become public domain material in 2015. Now it will not be public domain material until 2035. Because it is protected by copyright, permission must be obtained from The Estate of George and Ira Gershwin to perform this play. Representatives of the Estate have stated: "The monetary part is important, but if works of art are in the public domain, you can take them and do whatever you want with them. For instance, we've always licensed 'Porgy and Bess' for the stage performance only with a black cast and chorus. That could be debased. Or someone could turn 'Porgy and Bess' into rap music."

Critics of copyright extension respond that that is just the point. It is time to do something new and original with *Porgy and Bess*. They believe the lengthy copyright terms stifle artistic innovation and the creation of new works based on the old. A rap version of *Porgy and Bess* would breathe new life into this classic and with it would come a new audience. It is argued that whole new generations would become familiar with *Porgy and Bess* if it were made a part of the public domain and society would benefit from this "mainstreaming" of an American classic tale in music.

Showboat, written by Hammerstein, Kern, and Ferber, was published in 1927. Prior to the Copyright Term Extension Act, it was set to become public domain material in 2007. Now it will be public domain material in 2027. It, too, could become embraced by the mainstream if it could be interpreted in a modern fashion.

SCOPE OF COPYRIGHT LAW AS DEFINED BY THE U.S. SUPREME COURT

Neither the United States Constitution nor the United States Supreme Court holds the primary purpose of copyright protection to be to provide reimbursement to the creator. The Supreme Court routinely invokes the concept of promotion of the progress of science and useful arts in explaining the scope of the copyright laws. The Supreme Court repeatedly reminds lower courts that "[t]he primary objective of copyright is not to reward the labor of authors, but '[t]o promote the Progress of Science and useful Arts.'"[17] However, in sanctioning the Sonny Bono Copyright Term Extension Act, the Supreme Court noted, "The wisdom of Congress' action, however, is not within our province to second guess. [We are] satisfied that the legislation before us remains inside the domain the Constitution assigns to the First Branch." Clearly, the Supreme Court desires both to remind the courts of the purpose of the law of copyright, to promote the progress of science and the useful arts, but believes Congress can interpret how this can best be promoted by its statutory authority.

WHAT CAN YOU COPYRIGHT?

You cannot copyright an "idea." Rather you copyright the expression of that idea. Einstein could not copyright his theory of relativity: $E = mc^2$. However, he could and did copyright his expression of that idea found in his text, *Relativity: The Special and General Theory*.

One of the more famous photographs of our time was of the Afghani girl on the cover of *National Geographic* in June 1985. Her identity was unknown until the photographer returned to Afghanistan in 2002 to locate her. That image is clearly copyrighted and has been reproduced thousands of times since the original photo was taken in 1983 when Sharbat Gula was twelve years old. The right to photograph Sharbat Gula is not protected by copyright. It is the very expression or the photograph itself that is protected.

During the Academy Awards designers sit glued to their television with sketch pads in hand. Their purpose is to copy the most popular dresses and reproduce them and sell them as soon as possible. This activity is not an infringement of copyright. The dress is the "idea." An image or drawing of the dress can, however, be protected by copyright.

The design found on fabric is protected by copyright. The method in which the fabric is made is not protected by copyright, however, it very well could be protected by patent. Malden Mills, who recently emerged from bankruptcy, invented Polartec but failed to patent the process, to their everlasting regret, although they did trademark the name Polartec.

A play can be protected by copyright but the blocking of that play cannot be protected. Choreography can be protected, if it is not extemporaneous. Titles, names, short phrases and slogans, mere listings of ingredients or contents, ideas, procedures, methods, systems, processes, concepts, principles, discoveries or devices, and works that consist entirely of information that is common property and contain no original authorship cannot be copyrighted. For example, standard calendars, height and weight charts, tape measures and rules, and lists of tables taken from public documents or other common sources cannot be copyrighted.

For example, the Supreme Court's opinion in *Eldred v. Ashcroft* (the challenge to the Copyright Term Extension Act) cannot be copyrighted and could be reproduced here as a public document in full or in part. The title *Beauty and the Beast* cannot be copyrighted. I could write a book about my dog, the beast, and my cat, the beauty, and title it *Beauty and the Beast,* or I could even name it after my cat, The Great Gatsby, notwithstanding the fact that F. Scott Fitzgerald's novel preempts any story I might share about my cat. L'Oreal's slogan, "Because I'm worth it," or BMW's slogan for the "ultimate driving machine" may not be copyrighted although they are both registered trademarks that can be found in the online registration of the U.S. Patent and Trademark Office at http://www.uspto.gov. A common device such as a lawn chair cannot be copyrighted, although a unique design may be patented. The procedure for building an atomic bomb cannot be copyrighted although the book in which it is published may be copyrighted. The dual-entry system of bookkeeping cannot be copyrighted, nor can the rules for a game of bridge or tennis, although the books in which they are published may be copyrighted. The facts of Laura Bush's life may not be copyrighted, but the biography in which they are found may be.

WHAT DOES COPYRIGHT PROTECT?

Copyright protects five rights in areas where the author or the owner of the work retains exclusive control. The sixth right is a redundant right that limits the right of public performance to not only live performance but also to digital transmissions of the public performance. These rights are:

1. The right of reproduction (i.e., copying),
2. The right to create derivative works,
3. The right to distribution,
4. The right to public performance,
5. The right to public display, and
6. The digital transmission performance right.

The law of copyright protects the first two rights of reproduction and creative derivative works in both private and public contexts. An owner of a copyright can restrict the last four rights in the public sphere, but not in the private sphere. For example a family can perform for their family members a play that is copyrighted without liability for copyright infringement. Your children may perform *The Cat in the Hat* in your home for your family without a violation of copyright.

Claims of infringement must show that the defendant exercised one of these rights in the context of a public or private violation of the first two rights, reproduction or creation of a derivative work, or the public violation of the last four rights.

THE RIGHT OF REPRODUCTION

The right of reproduction is perhaps the most important right granted by the Copyright Act. Under this right, no one other than the copyright owner may make any reproductions or copies of the work. Examples of unauthorized acts that are prohibited under this right include copying a computer software program, copying a fifty-page book for students, or copying a workbook for class use. It is not necessary that the entire original work be copied for an infringement of the reproduction right to occur. All that is necessary is that the copying be "substantial and material." What is substantial and material is determined on a case-by-case basis.

Perhaps one of the best-known copyright cases that evaluated a "substantial and material" copying involves a university practice of creating coursepacks.[18] Kinko's copied the coursepacks as prescribed by professors and sold them directly to the students. Kinko's was found to have infringed copyrights when it photocopied book chapters for sale to students as "coursepacks" for their university classes. The court found that the copying conducted by Kinko's was for commercial purposes and not for educational purposes. The court also found that most of the works were factual—history, sociology, and other fields of study—a factor that weighed in favor of fair use. However, it looked at other elements of the copying and found that copying 5 to 25 percent of the original full book was excessive. The court found a direct effect on the market for the books because the coursepacks directly competed with the potential sales of the original books as assigned reading for the students. The court specifically refused to rule that all coursepacks are infringements, requiring instead that each item in the "anthology" be individually subject to fair-use scrutiny.

PHOTOS OF REPRODUCTIONS OF OLD MASTERS OR ARTWORK IN THE PUBLIC DOMAIN

Many of us know and love the artwork of Georgia O'Keefe. Ms. O'Keefe was wildly successful both artistically and financially very early in her life. Her earliest works remain some of her most famous and are currently becoming public domain works. Private collectors own many works created prior to 1922 and some can be found in museums and galleries around the world. Does this mean that any photograph of any of her works that were published prior to 1922 are public domain? Can we use these works in our Web pages, and even on the cover of this book? Yes.

This same issue was addressed in 1999 in a Southern District of New York case, *The Bridgeman Art Library, Ltd. v. Corel Corp.* This case confirmed that the marketing of photographic copies of public domain master artworks, without adding anything original, does not constitute copyright infringement when the underlying work is in the public domain.

In this case Bridgeman claimed to have exclusive ownership rights to photographic transparencies and digital images of works of art located in various museums. Corel, the defendant in the case, markets CDs containing photographs of some of the same artworks. Bridgeman could not prove that Corel had copied its images, and Corel claimed it had independently created these images. Bridgeman alleged Corel "must have" copied Bridgeman's images.

It was undisputed that Bridgeman "strives to reproduce precisely those works of art" that are in the public domain. The significance here is that Bridgeman, by its own admission, did not meet the originality requirement of the law of copyright. The court found the act of exact photography of a painting was not protected under the law of copyright because "skill, labor or judgment merely in the process of copying cannot confer originality."

Bridgeman did claim that it added a color bar to each image, and that this transformed the works into something that was protected. However, the court found that because the reproductions were all of public domain images, no infringement could have occurred. The court held that British law applied to the copyright issues, but because the United States Copyright Act and British copyright law were substantially the same in the relevant areas, the result would have been the same under either law. The case has been given *de facto* precedential value by many in the art world and is generally considered by commentators to be a well-reasoned case.

However, use caution! The same reasoning does not apply to architecture or sculpture. There is an argument that more creativity is possible when photographing a three-dimensional object, such as a building. Here subjective considerations such as the angle of the photographed subject, the lighting, and the framing of the subject matter are all subjective decisions that rely on the creators' subjective decisions. The result is consequently, a creative material and subject to copyright. As such, it would be safest to assume that copyright protection applies to just about all photographs of three-dimensional objects.

When digitizing images of three-dimensional works, such as buildings, a public domain analysis similar to that for fine art is required, with a few considerations unique to architectural images. Title 17 U.S.C. §120 deals with the scope of exclusive rights in architectural works. The law in relevant part, at 17 U.S.C. §120(a), states, "Pictorial representations permitted. The copyright in an architectural work that has been constructed does not include the right to prevent the making, distributing, or public display of pictures, paintings, photographs, or other pictorial representations of the work, if the building in which the work is embodied is located in or ordinarily visible from a public place."

Note that architectural plans, three-dimensional models, and other two-dimensional works related to architecture are protected under copyright law as pictorial, graphic, or sculptural works, and the statutory provision does not apply to images other than those of constructed buildings visible from a public place.

Given this statutory exemption for architectural works, when digitizing images of buildings visible from a public place, one does not need to be concerned about whether the building itself is subject to copyright, as would be the case with a work of fine art created after 1923. However, copyright must still be considered in terms of the slide or photograph of the building (if one is not the author or copyright owner of the image in question). If clear rights to use the image do not exist, permission should be sought from the photographer, unless making a copy of the image is permitted under a fair use analysis. The photographer is deemed to have put that "something special" or that "something of him" in the work. The angle of the shot, the play of the sun and shadow on the building of the night skyline, and the frame of the object within the photo are all elements of artistic creation and render the photo of the object protected by copyright.

Because you see a reproduction of the work of Georgia O'Keefe on the cover of this book, it can be understood that this work was created prior to 1922 (and in fact was created in 1919) and that the photograph is an exact replication of the original work, adding nothing new to her original painting. This photograph is now in the public domain and after 2019 more and more of her art will become public domain works. Once the CTEA passed, her works were no longer part of the public domain, with the exception of the few that were created before 1922.

THE RIGHT TO CREATE A DERIVATIVE WORK

A derivative work may not be made from an original work without being considered an infringement of a copyright. A derivative work usually involves a type of transformation. It is a work based upon one or more preexisting works, such as a translation, musical arrangement, dramatization, fictionalization, motion picture version, sound recording, art reproduction, abridgment, condensation, or any other form in which a work may be recast, transformed, or adapted. A work consisting of editorial revisions, annotations, elaborations, or other modifications that, as a whole, represent an original work of authorship is a "derivative work."

Infringing on a work or creating a derivative work occurs when someone other than the copyright holder makes a change to the work. To change even one pixel in an online image that is subject to copyright is to infringe upon that copyright. By taking this action, a derivative work has been created. It doesn't matter if you think it looks better or sounds better; the copyright holder is the only one that can legally make changes to his or her original work.

For a derivative work to be copyrightable, it must be "different enough" from the original works that it can be considered a new work in its own right. Minor alterations are not "different enough" to create a new work. John

Fogerty was found to have created a new work, but he had to go to the United States Supreme Court to enforce his right to do that.

John Fogerty was the lead singer of Creedence Clearwater Revival in the late sixties and early seventies. He was sued by Fantasy Records for allegedly plagiarizing his own riff from "Run Through the Jungle"—to which Fantasy owned the copyright—in his new song "The Old Man Down the Road." Fogerty won the case after bringing his guitar up to the witness stand and showing the jury how he wrote his songs.

It is a common practice for art students to make collages. They take magazine photos from beautifully colored magazines or art catalogs and create new works. This is not typically different enough to create a new work and is an infringement upon copyright unless permission is obtained from the copyright holder of those works, or unless the taking is of such an amount to be a fair use for an educational purpose. Copyrighted material can be used in a derivative work without permission, if only a minimal amount of the original work or a *de minimus* amount is used.

Making a derivative work violates copyright. Making something new is acceptable. Using a *de minimus* amount of a work protected by copyright is acceptable. Clearly, you cannot publish a screenplay based on the works of Anne Rice. Only Anne Rice can do that, and the 1994 adaptation of Anne Rice's novel *Interview with the Vampire* is an example of a derivative work that required the author's permission. However, one might be inspired by Anne Rice to write of a modern-day, all-powerful but confused vampire. The estate of Margaret Mitchell claimed *The Wind Done Gone* was a derivative work, while the publisher claimed it was a parody. As a derivative work it violated the law of copyright, but as a parody it did not. The estate of Margaret Mitchell sued in federal district court and then encountered an appeal before they ultimately settled their claim, and the district court and the appellate court did not agree in their decisions. John Fogerty was able to ask the Supreme Court to decide his case.

Librarians in their role as creators of bibliographies or in the supervision of student and even faculty bibliographies must make these copyright decisions without the benefit of attorneys presenting their case and judges deciding the issue. These are not easy calls to make. Each time a faculty creation is put on reserve in the library, the librarian should review the work for copyright infringement. This is neither a gracious nor simple act. The most political course of action would be to create a committee for review for copyright infringement.

PUBLIC DISTRIBUTION RIGHTS

Distribution Rights grant to the copyright holder the exclusive right to make a work available to the public by sale, rental, lease, or lending. This right allows the copyright holder to prevent the distribution of unauthorized copies of a work. In addition, the right allows the copyright holder to control the first distribution of a particular authorized copy. However, the distribution right is limited by the First Sale doctrine, which states that after the first sale or distribution of a copy, the copyright holder can no longer control what happens to that copy.

After a book has been purchased at a bookstore (the first sale of a copy), the copyright holder has no authority over how that copy is further distributed. Thus, the book could be rented, resold, or even burned without the permission of the copyright holder. Used-book stores routinely accept books for resale. What you cannot do with the book, however, is copy it. It is yours to burn, yours to sell, and yours to read, but it is not yours to copy.

Congress has enacted several limitations to the First Sale doctrine, including a prohibition on the rental of software. If you could simply rent Microsoft Windows, their purchase would never be necessary. You could simply rent the software from Blockbuster and pay $3.00 each time it was needed. The legal landscape with regard to technology and software is rapidly changing. The next chapter provides detailed information on this issue, arriving in various states in the form of model legislation known as the Uniform Computer Information Transactions Act (UCITA).

PUBLIC PERFORMANCE RIGHTS

Public performance rights allow the copyright holder to control the public performance of certain copyrighted works. The scope of the performance right is limited to the following types of works:

- Literary works,
- Musical works,
- Dramatic works,
- Choreographic works,
- Pantomimes,
- Motion pictures, and
- Audio-visual works.

Purchasing the text of a play does not give the purchaser the right to perform that play publicly. That right must be obtained from the holder of the copyright.

Under the public performance right, a copyright holder is allowed to control if the work is performed "publicly." A performance is considered "public" when the work is performed in a "place open to the public or at a place where a substantial number of persons outside of a normal circle of a family and its social acquaintances are gathered." A performance is also considered to be public if it is transmitted to multiple locations, such as through television and radio.

"Happy Birthday to You," protected until 2031, technically cannot be performed in public without a license; waiters aren't supposed to sing it unless their restaurants pay royalty fees, but the good news is you may sing it in your home. Otherwise, everyone would be sending in royalty fees every birthday . . . in a perfect world. "Happy Birthday" was sold to Warner Communications, for an estimated price of $25 million; at the time Warner purchased the song, the expected copyright expiration was 2010.[19]

A violation of the public performance right would occur if a motion picture or a video were shown in a public park or theater without obtaining a license from the copyright holder. In contrast, the performance of the video on a home television where friends and family are gathered would not be considered a public performance and would not be prohibited under the Copyright Act. Your children could perform all or parts of *Cats* for their family, but not at their recital. This right has been expanded to include digital transmissions. Videos from home or rented from Blockbuster generally cannot be shown in a classroom on a rainy day to entertain students. (See chapter 4 for further information.)

The public performance right is generally held to cover computer software, which is considered a literary work under the Copyright Act. In addition, many software programs fall under the definition of audio-visual works. The application of the public performance right to software has not been fully developed, except that it is clear that a publicly available video game is controlled by this right. However, UCITA may be rapidly changing these laws.

PUBLIC DISPLAY RIGHTS

Public display rights are similar to the public performance rights, except that this right controls the public "display" of a work. This right is limited to the following types of works:

- Literary works,
- Musical works,
- Dramatic works,
- Choreographic works,
- Pantomimes,
- Pictorial works,
- Graphical works,
- Sculptural works, and
- Stills (individual images) from motion pictures and other audio-visual works.

The definition of when a work is displayed "publicly" is the same as that described above in connection with the right of public performance; that is, it may not be performed in a "place open to the public or at a place where a substantial number of persons outside of a normal circle of a family and its social acquaintances are gathered."

No author may copyright facts or ideas.[20] The copyright is limited to those aspects of the work—termed "expression"—that display the stamp of the author's originality. Creation of a nonfiction work, even a compilation of pure fact, entails originality.[21] The use of facts, however, presents a gray area in the law, because even though facts cannot be copyrighted, the decision of which facts to use entails a mental process involving the copyrightable concept of "compilation." Justice Sandra Day O'Connor noted: "In the realm of factual narrative, the law is currently unsettled regarding the ways in which uncopyrightable elements combine with the author's original contributions to form protected expression."

Ideas belong to the public at large and are protected by the First Amendment of the United States Constitution.

VIOLATION OF COPYRIGHT RESULTS IN AN INFRINGEMENT

If one of the enumerated protections of the law of copyright is violated or infringed upon there can be both civil and criminal consequence. Under United States copyright law today copyright protection attaches to every creative work as soon as the work is created and "fixed in any tangible medium of expression."[22] Copyright infringement occurs when someone with access to a copyrighted work creates a substantially similar work; and uses it in a way that violates one or more of the copyright owner's five exclusive rights—the rights of reproduction; distribution; adaptation; performance; and public display.[23] An individual who has been afforded a certain degree of copyright protection in the United States is not guaranteed protection against copyright infringements that may occur abroad; even though the copyright holder and the copyright infringer are U.S. citizens.

In addition to the person who directly infringes someone's copyright, others who assist in the infringement may face derivative liability under two theories.

First, one who induces, causes, or materially assists in the infringement may be guilty of contributory infringement.[24] Courts generally require that the plaintiff prove that the contributory infringer knew or had reason to know of the direct infringer's infringement and materially contributed to it.[25] It is this theory of the law that has the potential to create problems for libraries and that places specific duties upon a library to afford it protection from the actions of its patrons.

Secondly, the doctrine of vicarious liability, derived from the doctrine of *respondeat superior*, or the doctrine of responsibility by the master, may create liability when one has the right and the ability to supervise the infringing activity and derives financial interest from those activities.[26] It is this theory of the law that has the potential to create problems for libraries and that places specific duties upon a library to afford it protection from the actions of its patrons. Some copying may be permissible as personal use or fair use; or for "transformative" uses such as parody and commentary. *Saturday Night Live* is probably the most familiar source of parody, and it is this exception to the copyright law that allows the familiar and wonderful parodies we all enjoy. Most everyone who watches the news has observed that they freely take small portions of other's work for a news report about that work. It has become a common practice.

Finally, copyright protection has a limited term, and works for which the copyright term has expired, or which never had copyright protection, are in the public domain and are free for anyone to reproduce or imitate. Many United States publications are also an example of public domain work.[27]

The First Sale doctrine as supported by copyright law is the fundamental legal basis that permits a school library to lend materials. The limitations imposed upon this doctrine by the law of copyright are important both for the librarians and the students to understand. The limitations upon copying can be learned. With the aide of technology and the ease of access to information it is tempting to "cut and paste." It must be the librarian who presents the guidelines to the students. Just as balancing a checkbook is a real-life skill the students will use for the remainder of their lives, understanding copyright is becoming a real-life skill students will call upon for the remainder of the lives.

WHO RECEIVES THE PROTECTION OF COPYRIGHT?

Generally authors sell their right of copy to publishers. When this happens the author no longer has control over the ultimate rights of the work. John Fogerty is a successful musician, who, in the late 1960s, was the lead singer and songwriter of a popular music group known as Creedence Clearwater Revival. In 1970, he wrote a song titled "Run Through the Jungle" and sold the exclusive publishing rights to Fantasy, Inc. The music group disbanded in 1972 and Fogerty subsequently published under another recording label. Although clearly "Run Through the Jungle" is a rock-and-roll tune, it could conceivably be remixed for children, for orchestras, or for a country version. All rights to reproduce this tune belong to Fantasy Inc.

"God Bless America" is owned by the Girl Scouts of America. "Yesterday" by Paul McCartney is owned by Michael Jackson and Sony Corporation, but "That'll be the Day" by Buddy Holly is owned by McCartney Productions Ltd.

George Gershwin published songs alone and with his brother, his lyricist, Ira Gershwin. George Gershwin died of surgical complications from a brain tumor in 1937 at the age of forty-eight. *Rhapsody in Blue* would have become public domain material in 2005 had Congress not passed the CTEA. Commercials feature George Gershwin's music regularly. United Airlines used *Rhapsody in Blue* for years as its theme. H&R Block recently encouraged their clients to think of their services as "Someone to Watch over Me." "I Got Rhythm" has been adopted by Visa to inform the public that the Tony awards don't take "other" credit cards.

The Gershwin heirs are still enjoying the benefits of the labors of George and Ira Gershwin. Fifteen years ago, the license fee for using a Gershwin song in a television commercial for one year could be $45,000 to $75,000. The same song might now go for $200,000 to $250,000, to which George and Ira would no doubt respond, "'S wonderful, 's marvelous, that you belong to me . . . or at least my heirs." Or would they? Well certainly their heirs have "Someone to Watch over Me" so they do not have to "Do, Do, Do" like George and Ira did, did, did because receiving the royalties is "Nice Work If You Can Get It" and because "They Can't Take That Away from Me" because the Supreme Court decided "Let's Not Call the Whole Thing Off!" and ruled "My One and Only" still belongs to the Gershwin heirs, who have their royalties for twenty additional years rather than "Plenty of Nothing." So they can sing "Strike Up the Band (and thank you, Justice Ginsburg, for your opinion extending the term of copyright)," while Laurence Lessig only sighs "Isn't It a Pity." But the rest of the world "On a Foggy Day" can still play "Rhapsody in Blue" for a fee! (You cannot copyright a title!)

RIGHTS GRANTED TO OWNERS OF COPYRIGHT

The U.S. Copyright Act grants certain exclusive rights to the owner of a copyright in a work. These exclusive rights are different from the rights given to a person who merely owns a copy of the work. For example, when a person purchases a video, they have received a property right in a copy of a copyrighted work, the video. The video owner may then resell the video. However, the purchaser of the video did not provide any rights of copyright when they purchased the video. Federal Law does govern the uses to which a purchased video may be put. These are in addition to the copyright laws. The Copyright Act grants five rights to a copyright owner.

The rights are not without limit, however, as they are specifically limited by fair use and several other specific limitations set forth in Title 17 of the United States Code. Infringement of copyright can occur when the infringer is knowledgeable of the laws of copyright and when the infringer is not knowledgeable. The familiar adage, "Ignorance of the law is no excuse," applies to copyright just as it applies to the failure to notice a posted speed limit sign.

The concept that "ignorance of copyright law is no excuse" serves to explain why it is important for the educator to study and attempt to understand the laws of copyright as a pre-requisite for the release by the court of the educator for statutory damages for the infringement upon a copyright.

Not only can copyright be deliberately violated or violated without knowledge of the laws of copyright, copyright can be subconsciously violated.

After George Harrison left the Beatles, he released a triple album, *All Things Must Pass,* filled with songs including the hit "My Sweet Lord." He lost a copyright infringement lawsuit because of the song's similarity to the 1962 Chiffons hit "He's So Fine." The court in *Bright Tunes Music Corp. v. Harrisongs Music, Ltd.,*[30] acknowledged that Harrison may have unconsciously copied the tune. The court stated:

His subconscious knew it already had worked in a song his conscious did not remember . . . That is, under the law, infringement of copyright, and is no less so even though subconsciously accomplished.

COPYRIGHT OF CHARACTERS

Although the 1976 Copyright Act does not mention the protection of "characters" in its list of specifically protected works, courts have found a right of copy does exist in "sufficiently developed characters."

Harry Potter and the *Goosebumps* series have drawn preteens and teens to the library and reading. It is not uncommon for libraries to associate themselves with these characters. Publishing companies may offer posters or cutouts, and libraries gladly adorn their premises with advertising that lends an air of excitement and a contemporary feeling. However, the characters of Harry Potter and of Goosebumps are both copyrighted and trademarked, as are most characters such as Snoopy, Spiderman, and even James Bond. This means these images may not be reproduced independently by the library. A muralist may not be hired to adorn the walls with Mickey Mouse or Barbie. Using a famous fictional character in ads or products may be copyright infringement (and it may also be trademark infringement). To avoid being sued, don't use these characters without permission, known as a "merchandise license."

There are mixed opinions about what constitutes a "sufficiently developed character," ranging from whether an author who develops a character and sells the work also sells the character to arguments that turn on whether the visual image of the character is supported by a storyline, words, action, and personality or whether there is simply a visual image. Opinions are mixed on some close calls. There, however, many instances in which the calls are not close. Harry Potter is not a close call. An example of a litigated close call was James Bond, a suave, dynamic, Englishman who liked martinis, fast women, and fast cars. Protection was ultimately found to exist for James Bond, and Honda was not allowed to advertise its cars with an "imitation" James Bond. (*Metro-Goldwyn-Mayer, Inc. v. American Honda Motor Co., Inc.,* 900 F. Supp. 1287 (C.D. Ca. 1995)).

Who was your favorite character? These characters are all sufficiently developed to be protected by copyright and there are thousands more: Barney, Minnie Mouse, Winnie the Pooh, Batman, or sweet little Bambi. These characters have impacted our culture and our economy. These are by anyone's standard "sufficiently developed characters," and they are also trademarked. Link to the U.S. Patent and Trademark Office (http://www.uspto.gov), where you will find an online registry for "wordmarks." A trademark can be used to protect a new product name or other indication of a product's source. A trademark can be registered with the U.S. Patent and Trademark Office. The registration can be renewed every ten years and provides perpetual protection for the trademark. The cost for registering a trademark is significantly higher than the cost of registering a copyright.

Harry Potter is protected by both a copyright and various trademarks. He is "sufficiently developed" to be afforded copyright protection. He has a series of books, he has a line of products, and he has his own movies. We know the character Harry Potter. Many characters are licensed by different companies for different purposes and have different owners in different countries. A cursory search of trademark information indicates that some *Harry Potter* rights in the United States belong to Time Warner Entertainment Company; L.P. American Television and Communications Corporation, a Delaware corporation; and Warner Communications Inc., a Delaware Corporation Limited Partnership Delaware 75 Rockefeller Plaza New York New York 10019. Scholastic Press, Inc., is the U.S. publisher of *Harry Potter* books and retains the right of copy for Harry Potter.

WORKS OF FACULTY OR WORKS FOR HIRE

Typically faculty members who create works in the course of their employment have created works for hire. However, many school districts have contractual exceptions to this concept, and those that do not have that exception may be open to the implementation of this exception.

In a work made for hire situation, the "author" of the work is no longer the individual who created the work. Instead, the author is considered to be the entity that hired the creators of the work (such as a corporation for whom the author works as an employee). Why are works for hire so important? Faculty members like to retain ownership of their works and often do. The issue then becomes: Is this a work for hire? This is particularly relevant to the ownership of Web sites created by librarians. Unless you agree with the school that these are subject to joint ownership, you can't take them with you. (See chapter 8, "Library Web Sites.")

Also works that were made "for hire" or by an employee have a ninety-five-year copyright protection term for the owner of the copyright. Karey Mullis, recipient of the 1993 Chemistry Nobel Prize for inventing polymerase chain reaction (PCR), invented a way to replicate large amounts of DNA from infinitesimal amounts of DNA.[31] Since 1986, PCR has literally changed the world—making DNA fingerprinting and even cloning possible. The lab that employed Mullis paid him a $10,000 bonus for his discovery and later sold the patent for a reported half billion dollars.

The Copyright Act limits the work made for hire doctrine to two specific situations:

1. Work prepared by an employee within the scope of his or her employment; or
2. Work specially ordered or commissioned for use, including
   - Contributions to a collective work,
   - Part of a motion picture or other audiovisual work,
   - Translations,
   - Supplementary work,
   - Compilations,
   - Instructional text,
   - Tests,
   - Answer material for a test, and
   - Atlases.

It is recommended that parties agree in writing that a work is a work made for hire. More importantly to the educator, if the work is to be considered to be created for the educational institution *and* for the creator/educator, it is recommended that this agreement be in writing in the educator's contract, specifically allowing the educational institution to retain the work and permitting the educator to take the work with them.

INTERNATIONAL COPYRIGHT LAW

The World Intellectual Property Organization (WIPO) in 1980 and the Paris Convention for the Protection of Industrial Property in 1984 serves to protect the copyright laws of each signatory nation to the various treaties. With headquarters in Geneva, Switzerland, WIPO is one of the sixteen specialized agencies of the United Nations system of organizations. It administers twenty-three international treaties dealing with different aspects of intellectual property protection.

A "fake" Harry Potter book was released in China in June of 2002. This book had a distinctive Chinese flavor and was titled, *Harry Potter and Leopard Walk Up to Dragon*. This version includes Chinese ghosts, magic, and kung fu. Harry turns into a grotesque dwarf after a sweet-and-sour rain and encounters many of the typical Harry Potter challenges and adventures.

The Agreement on Trade Relations of 1979 between the United States of America and the People's Republic of China ("1979 Agreement") marked the beginning of Western intellectual property protection in China. This agreement has been largely ignored. However, when the Chinese themselves have a monetary stake in the protection of intellectual property these agreements have become more significant. Zhang Deguang of the People's Literature Publishing House has the *Harry Potter* publishing rights in China and believes the fake has made a negative impact on their book sales. This Chinese company is quickly promoting the rights of ownership of Mr. Harry Potter.

Unfortunately, not all countries have copyright treaties with the United States and not all intellectual property that is stolen in other countries has an agent in that country with a vested interest in protecting the rights of copy, as Harry Potter had in China. Copyright is not the subject of universal protection. Recently proposed Egyptian copyright legislation "stipulates that copyright material in a foreign language becomes public domain if it is not translated into Arabic within a given period."[32] It is important to remember Chapter 17 of the United States Code addressing copyright issues refers to actions of infringement that occur in the United States and extend to other countries by treaty agreement.

CONCLUSION

Copyright is a legal creature, technical and artificial in its creation, with a ferocious bark and a bite that can be no more than a nip or as deadly as a shark attack. In reality, few works merit the extended protection given to them by Congress. There are precious few truly great works. However, all works are protected equally. Many works have meaning to but a few members in our society. Mark Twain was a staunch supporter of the extensions of the federal term of copyright and he noted in *Eruption:* "In a century we have produced two hundred and twenty thousand books; not a bathtub-full of them are still alive and marketable."[35]

There is no financial incentive in reproducing these works notwithstanding the fact that they could benefit society as a foundation for new works. Congress could provide financial incentives to give works to the public domain rather than cloistering them for what is a lifetime times two or three for many.

Few want to incur the potential wrath of copyright infringement, few want to be troubled to learn the details, and most want to find someone to handle this issue for them. Too often it is the librarian who is called upon to make decisions as to what is and is not the subject of a copyright. The first step is to understand what is subject to copyright; the second is to understand the term of copyright. Interpreting and applying copyright law is a leap from the choice to become a librarian but in many ways it has become one of a librarian's tools of the trade. Librarians are finding themselves squarely in the center of much of the free speech litigation of this country. It is essential to learn and to stay informed and in some instances become involved.

NOTES

1. *Bleistein v. Donaldson Lithographing Co.*, 188 U.S. 239, 250 (1903).

2. Michael D. Birnhack, "The Idea of Progress in Copyright Law," *Buffalo Intellectual Property Law Journal* 1 (summer 2001): 3.

3. H.R. Rep. No. 94–1476, at 51 (1976).

4. For insight into both library and publishing media positions on the doctrine of first sale, review the Library of Congress's postings of " Initial Comments: Joint Study Required by Section 104 of the Digital Millennium Copyright Act," April 2002. *Federal Register Notice 65 FR 35673*. Available: http://www.loc.gov/copyright/reports/studies/dmca/comments/. (Accessed September 1, 2002).

5. See, for example, *1995 Senate Hearing* at 1–4 (statement of Senator Hatch); *1995 House Hearing* at 268 (prepared statement of Marsha Durham, widow of Eddie Durham).

6. *Historia Naturalis*, Loeb Classical Library (London: 1942), 2: 276–277.

7. Wojciech Kowalski, "Legal Aspects of the Recent History of the Qumran Scrolls: Access, Ownership Title and Copyright," in *On Scrolls, Artefacts and Intellectual Property*, ed. T.H. Lim, H.L. MacQueen, and C.M. Carmichael (Sheffield: Sheffield Academic Press, 2001). Nimmer, David. 2001. Copyright in the Dead Sea Scrolls. Houston Law Review 38:5–217.

8. U.S. Constitution, art. 1, §8, cl. 8.

9. Thomas Jefferson, Letter to James Madison, September 6, 1789, in *The Portable Thomas Jefferson*, ed. Merrill D. Peterson (New York: Penguin Books, 1977).

10. Paul J. Heald and Suzanna Sherry, "Implied Limits on the Legislative Power: The Intellectual Property Clause as an Absolute Constraint on Congress," *University of Illinois Law Review* 1119 (2000).

11. *Sony Corp. of Am. v. Universal City Studios, Inc.*, 464 U.S. 417, 429 (1984).

12. *Campbell v. Acuff-Rose Music Inc.*, 510 U.S. 569, 575 (1994) (quoting U.S. Constitution, art. 1, §8, cl. 8).

13. *Suntrust Bank v. Houghton Mifflin Co.*, 268 F.3d 1257 (11th Cir.), reh'g en banc denied, 275 F.3d 58 (table) (11th Cir. 2001).

14. Public Law 94–553.

15. Cornell Legal Information Institute provides online access to the United State Code and other legal references. Available: http://www.law.cornell.edu.

16. Harvard Law, "Open Law, *Eldred v. Ashcroft*." Available: http://eon.law.harvard.edu/openlaw/eldredvashcroft/legal.html.

17. *Feist Publications, Inc. v. Rural Telephone Service Co.*, 499 U.S. 340, 349 (1991). See *Fogerty v. Fantasy, Inc.*, 510 U.S. 517, 526–27 (1994); *Sony Corp. of America v. Universal City Studios, Inc.*, 464 U.S. 417, 428–29, 431–32 (1984); *Twentieth Century Music Corp. v. Aiken*, 422 U.S. 151, 156 (1975). Accord *Harper & Row v. Nation Enterprises*, 471 U.S. 539, 546 (1985).

18. *Basic Books, Inc. v. Kinko's Graphics Corp.*, 758 F.Supp. 1522 (S.D.N.Y. 1991).

19. *Time*, January 2, 1989, 88.

20. 17 USC §102.

21. See, for example, *Schroeder v. William Morrow & Co.*, 566 F.2d 3 (CA7 1977) (copyright in gardening directory); *cf. Burrow-Giles Lithographic Co. v. Sarony*, 111 U.S. 53, 58 (1884) (originator of a photograph may claim copyright in his work).

22. 17 U.S.C.102 (1994). Copyrightable works are broadly construed to include not only books, paintings and sculptures, but also movies, plays, musical compositions, recordings, photographs, computer software code, architectural designs, and even routine business writings.

23. 17 U.S.C. 501 (Supp. V 1999); see also *Nichols v. Universal Pictures Co.*, 45 F.2d 119 (2d Cir. 1930) (stating test for infringement). 17 U.S.C. 106 (Supp. V 1999).

24. The doctrine of contributory copyright infringement originated with Justice Oliver Wendell Holmes' decision in *Kalem Co. v. Harper Bros.*, 222 U.S. 55 (1911).

25. *Gershwin Publ'g Corp. v. Columbia Artists Mgmt., Inc.*, 443 F.2d 1159, 1162 (2d Cir. 1971).

26. See *Polygram Int'l Publ'g, Inc. v. Nevada/TIG, Inc.*, 855 F. Supp. 1314, 1325–26 (D. Mass. 1994).

27. 17 U.S.C. 105 (1994) (stating that federal government works are never subject to copyright).

28. *Fogerty v. Fantasy, Inc.*, (92–1750), 510 U.S. 517 (1994).

29. *Bleistein v. Donaldson Lithographing Co.*, 188 U.S. 239 (1903).

30. *420 F.Supp. 177 (1976)*

31. Polymerase Chain Reaction (PCR) Hot Start was first mentioned in the literature in 1991 by the inventor of PCR, Karey Mullis. Hot Start is a PCR refinement that suppresses mis-priming artifacts and results in a more sensitive, consistent reaction with concomitantly higher yields. The technique works by either physically separating or chemically inactivating one or more of the reaction components until high temperature triggers mixing or reactivation to give a complete reaction mixture. Although the technique can be accomplished manually, the advent of high through-put PCR demands the convenience of a temperature-triggered delivery. The last ten years have seen a wide variety of Hot Start technologies become commercially available through a number of different vendors.

32. Amr Ahmed Hassabo, *The Protection of Liberties Versus Information Systems* (Cairo: Dar Al Nahda Al Arabia, 2000).

33. *Eruption,* ed. Bernard De Voto (New York: Harper & Brothers, 1940).

3

SCOPE AND TERMS
OF COPYRIGHT

Upon the whole, I see no Reason for granting a further Term now, which will
not hold as well for granting it again and again, as often as the Old ones Expire;
so that should this Bill pass, it will in Effect be establishing a perpetual Monopoly, a Thing deservedly odious in the Eye of the Law; it will be a great Cramp
to Trade, a Discouragement to Learning, no Benefit to the Authors, but a general Tax on the Publick.

> —A letter to a Member of Parliament 1735
> on the topic of the extension of the term of copyright

In this chapter the following topics will be covered:

The Purpose and Scope of Copyright Protection

Public Domain

What If I Infringe upon a Copyright?

Are Educators Protected from Copyright Infringement?

What If Someone Infringes upon My Copyright?

Works Protected by Copyright

Compilations Are Protected by Copyright

Works That Cannot Be Protected by Copyright

Works for Hire

U.S. Supreme Court and Public Domain—The Case of Eric Eldred and
Eldritch Press

THE PURPOSE AND SCOPE OF COPYRIGHT PROTECTION

Copyright is intended to increase, and not to impede, the harvest of knowledge.

—Sandra Day O'Connor

The purpose of copyright as envisioned by the United States Constitution and interpreted by the Supreme Court is to promote the progress of science and the useful arts. This purpose is much broader than the rights of the creator of the protected work for remuneration. The purpose of the statutorily ordained right of copy is to benefit society and remuneration to the creator has been determined to be an intrinsic element of reaching that purpose. Public benefit has been balanced with the rights of the creators of the material. The United States Constitution refers to copyright as follows:

The Congress shall have Power . . . To promote the Progress of Science and useful Arts, by securing for limited Times to Authors and Inventors the exclusive Right to their respective Writings and Discoveries.

—Patent and Copyright Clause—
United States Constitution, art. 1, §8, cl. 8

One commentator noted that there is no finite definition of promoting progress. She stated: "Whatever the meaning of 'promote the progress of science and useful arts,' it cannot be either (i) raising the economic value of American copyright-protected goods, or (ii) providing a wealth transfer to certain individuals."[1]

The issue here is a balance between remuneration to the author and promoting the public good. The Supreme Court reminds us of this fact. After referring to the constitutional provision for copyright the Court states:

[This] limited grant is a means by which an important public purpose may be achieved. It is intended to motivate the creative activity of authors and inventors by the provision of a special reward, and to allow the public access to the products of their genius after the limited period of exclusive control has expired.[2]

Keeping these two concepts in harmonious balance to both provide incentive to create works for the public good and the release of those works to the public domain is the goal.

Copyright does permit an income, or as the Supreme Court put it, a "special reward" and "exclusive control" of the work to the creator for a set period of time and after the expiration of that statutorily defined period, the work belongs to the public through a concept known as the right of "public domain."

Very few works actually remain in print from 1927 until recently. Most of the works created during this time are no longer commercially viable works.

However, in many instances these works are needed for educational purposes and research, and have commercial appeal in niche markets. The cost of searching the copyright owners and often the impossibility of finding the copyright owners of obscure works that are out of print make many materials unavailable to the public during the period of copyright.

Mark Twain, whose real name was Samuel Clemens, was born in 1835 as Halley's comet was visible; when he was 12, his father died, leaving the family in a difficult financial condition. Mark Twain sought desperately not to impact his children in that manner and wanted to leave them an enduring income. *Tom Sawyer* was published in 1876, and *Huck Finn* was published in 1884. As a result of some poor business decisions associated with his printing company, Mark Twain found himself essentially bankrupt in 1894 and began a world lecturing tour to repay his creditors. The copyrights on his books began to expire during his period of financial crisis. In 1904 he began dictating an autobiography that was to be published in serial excerpts so that his family would have an inheritance. In December 1906, Mark Twain donned his white suit to testify before a congressional committee on the new copyright bill. Twain explained his vision of copyright, which was to be expanded from mere expressions to ideas and to be extended in perpetuity. This Congress refused to do. In 1910, just as Halley's comet returned, Mark Twain passed on. Clearly, his books would find a home in that bathtub.

It is also ironic that during the time Twain testified before Congress, David Wark Griffith, the father of American film, was reading a short story by Twain called "The Death Disk," a fable set in the time of Cromwell's rule of England. The young actor made unauthorized use of Twain's story (which Twain himself had borrowed from Thomas Carlyle) to make a short silent film in 1909 for the American Mutoscope and Biograph Company—and so film production was born with the violation of copyright.

According to *Books in Print*[3] the number of books in print for the past three years exceeds 600,000 while all the titles in print from 1920 to 1950 do not exceed 6,000.[4] Most older books do not have sufficient commercial appeal to warrant republication as indicated in Table 3.1.

Arnold Lutzker, in his amici curiae brief to the Supreme Court, which challenged the Copyright Term Extension Act, noted that RCA demolished a warehouse in Camden, New Jersey, which housed four floors of cataloged recordings including "alternate takes, test pressings, master matrix books, and session rehearsal recordings." Although some materials were saved, the majority were dynamited and bulldozed into the Delaware River.[5] These recordings could have served as a rich repository of research for music scholars and could have been reproduced in niche markets to enhance the appreciation and love of music.

The scope of copyright is extensive and it applies to obscure works just as it applies to works still in print. Many argue that this scope is extensively broad

Table 3.1
Comparison: Books Registered to Books Remaining in Print

Years	Books Registered	Books Remaining in Print	Remaining in Print (%)
1927–1931	66,947	646	1.0
1932–1936	56,723	682	1.2
1937–1941	59,192	929	1.6
1942–1946	41,261	911	2.2
1947–1951	52,530	1,720	3.3

Source: Arnold P. Lutzker and Carl H. Settlemeyer III, amici curiae brief filed supporting *Eric Eldred et al. v. John D. Ashcroft,* U.S. Supreme Court (2002).

and suppresses the use of works that could benefit society with release into the public domain. Here is a simple outline of the scope and terms of copyright.

GENERAL U.S. COPYRIGHT DURATION

a. For works created after January 1, 1978 (applies regardless of publication), copyright exists from the moment of creation for the duration of the author's life plus fifty years. Joint authors are covered through the last surviving author's life plus fifty years. Corporate authorship or works for hire are covered for seventy-five years from publication or one hundred years from creation, whichever is shorter.

b. Works published between 1964 and 1977 have automatically been given seventy-five years of coverage from the date first published with a copyright notice.

c. Works published between seventy-five years ago and 1963 have a copyright duration of twenty-eight years, with option of renewal for an additional forty-seven. If not so renewed, they are now in the public domain.

d. Works published more than seventy-five years ago are now in the public domain.

e. Unpublished works created before January 1, 1978, are protected at least until December 31, 2002, or for the author's life plus 50 years, whichever is greater.

f. Works created before January 1, 1978, but published between then and December 31, 2002, are protected until Dec. 31, 2027.

COPYRIGHT TERM EXTENSION ACT (CTEA)—SONNY BONO ACT

The Copyright Term Extension Act was signed into law October 27, 1998. The suggestion has been made that President Clinton was inhibited from vetoing this legislation because of his deep involvement in the Monica

Lewinsky scandal. There was no argument on the floor over this amendment. It was quickly and quietly signed into law. This act extends the term of copyright an additional 20 years. This makes the term of copyright for most works the life of the author plus 70 years and the life of works for hire 95 years.

A Disney movie would be an example of a work for hire. Now these movies will enjoy copyright protections for ninety-five years. An objection many have to this act is that it makes these rights retroactive.

MATERIALS IN THE PUBLIC DOMAIN

a. Many but not all U.S. government publications.

b. Works copyrighted before January 1, 1978, and published in the United States more than seventy-five years ago unless the Copyright Term Extension Act is revoked.

c. All works copyrighted in the United States before September 19, 1906.

FOREIGN COPYRIGHT REGULATIONS

a. The United States has copyright treaties with many countries, protecting works published in other countries.

b. Title 17, Section 104 specifies that some foreign works may have the protection of U.S. copyright law.

TANGIBLE MEDIUM OF EXPRESSION REQUIREMENT FOR A COPYRIGHT

A tangible medium of expression is required in order for a work to be subject to copyright protection. A work is considered fixed when it is stored on some medium in which it can be perceived, reproduced, or otherwise communicated. For example, a song is considered fixed when it is written down on paper or recorded in any fashion. A computer program is fixed when stored on a computer hard drive. Copyright protection exists the moment an original work of authorship becomes fixed. An extemporaneous speech or dance is not a fixed work although the state of California has enacted laws to protect certain categories of extemporaneous works not covered by the federal statute.

WORKS THAT CANNOT BE PROTECTED BY COPYRIGHT

Some types of material are ineligible for copyright protection. Generally, these materials are either protected by some other intellectual property, or have been considered inappropriate for protection. These are: unfixed works; titles and short phrases; ideas; and useful articles.

Works that have not been fixed in a tangible form of expression are not protected under the Copyright Act, because fixation is one of the prerequisites for copyright protection.

For example, both choreographic works that have not been notated or recorded and improvisational speeches or performances that have not been written or recorded are ineligible for copyright protection. For many years, unrecorded music concerts were also unprotected by copyright law because they were not fixed. This caused problems when bootleg tapes of rock concerts would appear because was no cause of action under the Copyright Act (there was often protection under certain state statutes and common law). However, the Uruguay Round Agreement Act has provided copyright protection for these works,[6] and now 17 U.S.C. 1101 protects live musical performances. However, it is important to note the unauthorized fixation and trafficking in sound recordings and music videos is protected only since 1994 and state laws also provide protection in this area of copyright law; it is not preempted by federal law.

Also, works that consist entirely of information that is common property and containing no original authorship cannot be copyrighted. Standard calendars, height and weight charts, tape measures and rules, and lists of tables taken from public documents or other common sources cannot be copyrighted, nor can titles, names, short phrases and slogans, mere listings of ingredients or contents, ideas, procedures, methods, systems, processes, concepts, principles, discoveries, or devices. However, it should be noted that some devices and discoveries may be protected by patent.

PUBLIC DOMAIN

Works that are in the "public domain" are not copyright protected. All works created by individual authors (and created "for hire" such as newspaper articles) before 1923 are in the public domain. All copyrights eventually expire; expiration dates vary and the list above can help you determine whether the copyright has expired. Once the copyright expires, the owner has no exclusive rights to the work. Some composers and creators renounce their copyright and give their work to the public, either during their lifetime or at their death. All works that are not protected under copyright law are said to be in the public domain.[7]

Creative Commons is a licensing organization founded by fellows and students at the Berkman Center for Internet and Society at Harvard Law School. It is now housed at and receives support from Stanford Law School, where Creative Commons shares space, staff, and inspiration with the Stanford Law School Center for Internet and Society. Offering work under a Creative Commons license allows an author to offer some rights to any taker, and only on certain conditions. The author is allowed to mix and match conditions from eleven Creative Commons licenses. Although this is not precisely public domain, it does allow copyright works to be used generally by giving credit to the actual author.

Frances Hodgson Burnett's *The Secret Garden* was published in 1911. It became part of the public domain on January 1, 1997. This was the year before the passage of the CTEA of 1998. This work was safely in the public domain upon the passing of the CTEA and there it will safely remain for all time. However, upon the passage of the CTEA of 1998, the door was firmly shut on new material entering the public domain until the year 2019.

New and creative derivative works, including plays, musicals, video and audio cassettes, and even cookbooks have been created as a result of the end of the copyright of *The Secret Garden*. Warner Brothers released their movie version of *The Secret Garden* in 1993, and many audio-cassette versions have been created, as have shortened easy-to-read picture book versions. As a result of the expiration of copyright this old tale has been revived and lives a new life in the public's experience in various forms, formats, interpretations, and languages.

In 1993, *My Antonia* by Willa Cather entered the public domain and new editions immediately appeared making the story more universally appealing in its various formats, each competing with one another to entice the reader to "their" version. *The Velveteen Rabbit* reached classic status once it passed into the public domain available in book, CD, play format, and animated character format.

Thomas Nast's works are in the public domain and are the basis of Santa Claus and Uncle Sam as we know them. Nast himself based his Santa Clause on a public domain figure. Disney does not want the same fate for Mickey Mouse. They do not want to see Mickey in the public domain selling used cars and buying state lottery tickets. They do not want to see Mickey sporting a Yankee's baseball hat, drinking his favorite beer, or frequenting his favorite restaurant, and more importantly they do not want to see him endorsing anything for free—not even reading.

Steamboat Willie, the first appearance of the character now known as Mickey Mouse, debuted in 1928. Without the CTEA, Mickey would and could appear in movies, on Broadway, in your local pizza parlor, as a suave international mouse of mystery, or even in X-rated films (perish the thought). However, it is important to note, that Mickey has changed since Steamboat Willie. Subsequent design changes will keep Mickey Mouse—as we typically visualize him—safe for a long time to come. The *Steamboat Willie* Mickies and Minnies are a more primitive version of the famous mice. However, it is interesting to note that *Steamboat Willie* was borrowed by Disney from the Buster Keaton's movie, *Steamboat Bill*. Thanks to the Sonny Bono Copyright Term Extension Act the original Minnie and Mickey will be safe from public domain for quite a while.

Books that would have become public domain in 2002, without the Sonny Bono Copyright Extension Act are *The Sun Also Rises* by Ernest Hemingway,

The Little Engine That Could, by Watty Piper (Mabel C. Bragg), and *Winnie the Pooh* by A.A. Milne.

The creator of the honey-loving bear Winnie the Pooh, A.A. Milne, left in his will the copyright to five beneficiaries who license Winnie the Pooh for commercial use. In 1920, Milne and his wife, Daphne, had their only child, Christopher Robin Milne. They gave him stuffed toys, including a bear, a tiger, a kangaroo, and a donkey whose neck grew limp from the boy's affection. Mother and child would play together, creating stories and voices for the animals. Milne used this as inspiration for a 1924 poem about a boy and his teddy bear, and he later created the cast of *Winnie the Pooh*, published in 1926. The book's hero is a boy named Christopher Robin.

Because the Pooh books had been favorites of Walt Disney's daughters, Disney brought Pooh to film in 1966. In 1993, the Walt Disney Company acknowledged that Pooh Bear is second only to Mickey Mouse in their portfolio of the most-loved and trusted characters. By 1996, after the second release of *The Many Adventures of Winnie the Pooh*, Winnie the Pooh was considered to be more popular than any other Disney character.

In 1998, conditioned upon the passing of the CTEA, the members of the London society Garrick Club sold Winnie the Pooh rights to Walt Disney for another twenty years. Disney paid approximately sixty million dollars for the right to make Winnie the Pooh films until 2026.

Pooh has become a $1-billion-a-year industry for Walt Disney Co., which acquired rights to the Milne characters in 1961. Disney paid $352 million to buy the remaining Pooh rights from various Milne heirs in England. In 2001 Disney bought all future rights from the Milne estate for $352 million. A Milne family trust distributed the money to four principal beneficiaries.

A London men's club to which A.A. Milne once belonged received $88 million; the members decided to set up a scholarship fund for actors and writers. An additional $88 million went to the British boarding school that Milne attended as a boy. The Royal Literary Fund for struggling writers was given $132 million. The $44 million remaining was put in a trust named for Clare Milne, the author's granddaughter, who has cerebral palsy; the trust pays benefits to her and other disabled people.

In 1988, before the copyright expired on Maurice Ravel's "Mother Goose Suite," it cost $540 in rights fees to perform the piece twice publicly. Now that the work is in the public domain, the only cost is for its sheet music, which can be purchased on Amazon.com for $5.95.

BOOK MOUSE CAUSES QUITE A STIR

In Flint, Michigan, Walt Disney Co. officials requested a formal extension of time to consider challenging the Genesee District Library's mascot for an alleged similarity to Mickey Mouse. The library submitted a trademark registry request with the U.S. Patent and Trademark office for their version of a mouse character named "Book Mouse." Book Mouse is a blue mouse with big ears who sports giant round reading glasses, the better to read with, see. He will soon be one year old. Book Mouse is a full-blown mascot for the library. He (at least I think it's a he) appears on the library's bookmarkers and bumper stickers, and in library-sponsored coloring books. Book Mouse routinely makes scheduled advertised personal appearances at various library branches and he marches in local parades.

The latest word from Book Mouse, himself, indicates that he is in fact *not* Mickey Mouse. He does not now, nor has he ever had an identity crisis. He respects Mickey's illustrious career, but Book Mouse states that he is pleased with his career choice, to be a mascot for the Genesee District Library. Book Mouse has no intention of leaving Genessee for Hollywood. While Book Mouse is significantly younger than Mickey Mouse, who first appeared in 1928 in *Steamboat Willie*, he believes he can even at his young age be an approachable, charismatic, and fun representative for Genesee District Library.

Attorneys for Mickey have not yet taken Book Mouse's deposition. Because Book Mouse is the only six-foot blue mouse in Genessee, he admits to having natural curiosity regarding other animated characters of an allegedly similar species and would be glad to meet with Mickey personally to discuss this issue.

Book Mouse is openly available to discuss this issue with all who attend his presentations. The attorney for Book Mouse and the library does not believe Book Mouse has cut into Disney's profits. Still Disney requested additional time to study the similarities between Book Mouse and Mickey Mouse. Maybe it's just an honest mistake, or maybe they are mouse cousins like the City Mouse and the Country Mouse, but a true meeting of the mice might put this issue to rest once and for all. Disney will get back to Genesee District Library on that one! Mickey is not only protected by copyright but he, as an animated figure, is trademark protected, and like the slogan says "trademarks are diamonds, and diamonds are forever" and so is Book Mouse, or least that's what the residents of Genesee and its surrounding areas are hoping. They all agree on one thing, the love of their Book Mouse, and they are willing to testify that their love of Book Mouse in no way diminishes their love of Mickey.[8]

Disney has historically been a significant "recycler" of works that were in the public domain. The company has freely based its characters and stories on public domain stories such as the *Little Mermaid*, the *Hunchback of Notre Dame*, *Cinderella*, *Pocahontas*, and *Beauty and the Beast*. Disney successfully defended a challenge to its rights to *Bambi* in appellate court after loosing in District Court. *Bambi* is based on a work originally titled *Bambi, a Life in the Woods* and properly copyrighted in Germany. Disney released the first *Bambi* animated movie in 1942, and has subsequently re-released it seven times.[9]

WHAT IF I INFRINGE UPON A COPYRIGHT?

The consequences of copyright infringement can be very real. For this reason many school districts have adopted the Classroom Guidelines with no exceptions. In some districts, each school has a designated person who can make exceptions and in others, there is a designated person in the district office who can make exceptions to the Classroom Guidelines. (See "Guidelines" in chapter 4, "Fair Use in Education of Material Protected by Copyright.")

The authors of intellectual property have a property right in their creations that is protected within the copyright law. This property interest is subject to abuse by those who attempt to use the ideas of others for commercial gain without permission of the copyright owner. Under these circumstances, copyright owners may file a civil action for copyright infringement seeking damages for the infringement upon their copyright.

What are the actual financial damages incurred by Disney in the showing of *Lady and the Tramp* to a class in Houston? At most the cost of the videotape, perhaps even if one were to stretch the damages to the maximum, the cost of the videotape times the number of viewers. This would not pay for the filing fee for the lawsuit. Because the actual damages can be minimal, statutory damages also may be allowed. Disney has, however, historically found that there is no need to bring a lawsuit for the showing of its movies to second graders on a rainy day. They typically send what is known as a "cease and desist letter," asking the school to respect their right of copy or their ownership rights as defined by the law of copyright. Every parent and every teacher understands the concept of "cease and desist." In simple language it is known as, "Stop that or else. . ."

An example of a cease and desist letter followed by a lawsuit would be found in the case of Bill Nye the "Science Guy." Bill Nye sued Disney for more than half a million dollars for using his likeness on attractions at EPCOT Center.[10] Usually it is Disney who sends the cease and desist letters when their movies are viewed in schools. What's good for the mouse is good for the . . . Science Guy.

Although a warning is all that is necessary, in many cases the consequences of copyright infringement can be both civil and criminal. Civil statutory damages for copyright infringement can be extensive. In a copyright infringement lawsuit, a plaintiff may elect to pursue either actual damages and lost profits or statutory damages as defined by the copyright statute 17 U.S.C. §504(c)(1). Statutory damages range from $750 to $30,000 per act of infringement as the court considers just. These damages can increase to a maximum of $150,000 per infringed work if the infringement is found to be willful. A recent decision by the Supreme Court held that the parties, either the copyright owner or the infringement defendant, have a right to a trial by jury on the amount of statutory damages recoverable in an action against an infringer.[11]

The relevant federal statute states that "the copyright owner may elect, at any time before final judgment is rendered, to recover, instead of actual damages and profits, an award of statutory damages for all infringements involved in the action, with respect to any one work . . . of not less than $750 or more than $30,000 as the court considers just."[12]

The statute continues, "In a case where the copyright owner sustains the burden of proving, and *the court finds,* that infringement was committed willfully, *the court in its discretion* may increase the award of statutory damages to a sum of not more than $150,000" (emphasis added).[13]

Where a case involves infringement of several works, a multiplier effect takes hold. In *Feltner v. Columbia Pictures, Inc.,* 523 U.S. 340 (1988), the trial judge found 440 separate acts of infringement—one for each airing by Feltner of a syndicated television episode for which license fees to Columbia went unpaid. The judge also found the infringements willful, but assessed only $20,000 per infringement, resulting in an award to Columbia of $8.8 million (plus attorney's fees). These numbers can far exceed actual damages.

Criminal sanctions for the violation of copyright are also provided by Title 17, Section 506 with penalties that include fines and prison terms.[14] Criminal infringement of a copyright occurs *(a)* when any person infringes a copyright willfully, either for purposes of commercial advantage or private financial gain or *(b)* by the reproduction or distribution, including by electronic means, during any 180-day period, of one or more copies or phonorecords of one or more copyrighted works, which have a total retail value of more than $1,000. The statute indicates evidence of reproduction or distribution of a copyrighted work, by itself, shall not be sufficient to establish willful infringement.

ARE EDUCATORS PROTECTED FROM COPYRIGHT INFRINGEMENT?

The statute does allow the Court to remit statutory damages for an educator from suits for copyright infringement where there is a finding by the court that the infringer believed and had reasonable grounds to believe that the use of the copyrighted work was a fair use as prescribed by 17 U.S.C. Section 107. 17 U.S.C. Section 504(c)(2)(i) allows:

The court shall remit statutory damages in any case where an infringer believed and had reasonable grounds for believing that his or her use of the copyrighted work was a fair use under section 107, if the infringer was:

(i)

An employee or agent of a nonprofit educational institution, library, or archives acting within the scope of his or her employment who, or such institution, library, or archives itself, which infringed by reproducing the work in copies or phonorecords.

The court is statutorily bound and guided by the duty to inquire as to the *whether an infringer who is an employee of a nonprofit education institution, library or archive believed [had] reasonable grounds for believing that his or her use of the copyrighted work was a fair use under section 107.* In order for an educator, including a librarian, to be released from a copyright infringement suit, the court must be presented with convincing evidence that the educator or librarian had a reasonable basis for believing they were engaging in a fair use of copyrighted material. Simply saying "I thought the use was fair" will not be adequate; rather, they must state to the court the foundation for their belief that the use was fair. This must include a history of an effort to understand the fair use of copyrighted material and an analysis of the application at issue.

This is an affirmative burden the educator must meet and it would be wrong to believe that the court would dismiss any educator who made no effort to learn the laws of copyright and further made no effort to search for an answer to their questions prior to the infringement upon the copyright of another.

WHAT IF SOMEONE INFRINGES UPON MY COPYRIGHT?

The great advantage of registering a copyright is that the act of registration entitles the registrar to statutory damages and attorney's fees. If a copyright has not been registered, a suit for actual damages can still be brought, though no suit can be brought for statutory damages. The current filing fee for copyright protection is $30 per application. Generally, each work requires a separate application. The work must be deposited with the Copyright Office. A deposit is usually one copy of an unpublished work or two copies of a published work to be registered for copyright. In certain cases such as works of the visual arts, identifying material such as a photograph may be used instead. It can take up to six months to have a work registered. Minors can register for copyright protection.

WORKS PROTECTED BY COPYRIGHT

Copyright is the right of the author of the work or the author's heirs or assignees, not of the individual who only owns or possesses the physical work itself. If you have been left the diary of your grandmother you may register such a work if you are the lawful heir.

The phrase "works of authorship" is used in the Copyright Act to describe the types of works that are protected by copyright law. Works of authorship covers a broad domain and a vast scope of mediums in which the work may be fixed. It may include mediums not yet discovered or known. For example CDs were at one time unknown but music placed on a CD will be subject to the same copyright as music placed on a 45 rpm record. "Works of authorship" is a purposefully broad phrase specifically chosen by Congress to avoid the need to rewrite the Copyright Act with each new medium technology provides. Although Congress deliberately omitted defining the mediums in which works would be protected, it clarified the substance of works of authorship. The eight works of authorship Congress referred to in its Act are:

- Literary works;
- Musical works, including any accompanying words;
- Dramatic works, including any accompanying music;
- Pantomimes and choreographic works;
- Pictorial, graphic, and sculptural works;
- Motion pictures and other audiovisual works;
- Sound recordings; and
- Architectural works.

COMPILATIONS ARE PROTECTED BY COPYRIGHT

Almost any work that is created by an author will meet the originality requirement. Compilations can be copyrighted by virtue of the selection process that goes into the compilation and even recognition of the order in which the selections are placed. This compilation of materials is deemed to require some original thought.

Compilation copyrights are defined by the Copyright Act as a work that is formed by the "collection and assembling of preexisting materials or of data that are selected in such a way that the resulting work as a whole constitutes an original work of authorship." An example of a compilation would be an anthology of American poetry. The individual poems would not be subject to copyright protection because the copyright would have expired. However, the selection of the poems and their ordering and location in the anthology involves original, creative expression and as such is subject to copyright protection.

A grouping of facts can also be protected as a compilation. Compiling Web links can be a compilation and subject to copyright protection. The creative, original expression that is being protected is the sorting, selecting, and grouping of all the Web sites into the list. Thus, the library's collection of approved Web pages for science students is subject to the protection of copyright.

The white pages telephone directory is an example of an unprotected grouping of facts. The individual facts (name, address, and telephone number) are not protected under the copyright law. In addition, the compilation in this case consists solely of gathering all available telephone numbers in a particular area and sorting them alphabetically. The U.S. Supreme Court has held that this minimal level of selecting and arrangement does not involve enough originality to be protected by copyright.

WORKS THAT CANNOT BE PROTECTED BY COPYRIGHT

Narratives Present a Gray Area in Copyright

No author may copyright facts or ideas.[15] The copyright is limited to those aspects of the work—termed "expression"—that display the stamp of the author's originality. Creation of a nonfiction work, even a compilation of pure fact, entails originality.[16] The use of facts, however, presents a gray area in the law, because while facts cannot be copyrighted, the decision of which facts to use entails a mental process involving the copyrightable concept of "compilation." Justice Sandra Day O'Connor noted: [I]n the realm of factual narrative, the law is currently unsettled regarding the ways in which uncopyrightable elements combine with the author's original contributions to form protected expression."[17]

Titles and Slogans Are Not Subject to Copyright

Titles and slogans are not subject to copyright protection. In theory they are too short or lacking in originality to qualify for copyright protection.[18] An example would be the slogan: "If you build it; they will come." An Internet search of this phrase indicates it was in use long before the movie that made it famous and is employed by everyone from Web site developers to senior citizen centers.

Of course, brand names, slogans, and phrases that are used in connection with a product or service may be protectable under trademark law. SimCity is a trademark-protected game. As a game SimCity will remain protected. Names cannot be protected across various industries. The classic example is "Delta." Delta Air Lines is entitled to control the name Delta with regard to the airline industry. However, in the area of plumbing supplies Delta Faucet is king.

Ideas Not Subject to Copyright

Ideas and principles, among other conceptual entities, are specifically excluded from copyright protection. The Copyright Act states: "In no case does copyright protection for an original work of authorship extend to any idea, procedure, process, system, method of operation, concept, principle, or discovery, regardless of the form in which it is described, explained, illustrated, or embodied in such work." The exclusion of ideas and principles maintains the distinction between copyright protection and patent law. Ideas and inventions are the subject matter for patents, whereas the expression of ideas is governed by copyright law. The expression of ideas includes the expression itself, which is found in the wording. Many commentators may reflect on the implications of a newsworthy event. The implications may be identical, but the wording and the narrative is copyrightable. There were thousands of ways to describe the events of September 11, 2001, but each unique description, attributable to writers all delivering identical sentiments, is individually copyrightable.

In the fiction arena of copyright, a cat who solves mysteries is a good idea and several mystery writers center their plots on mystery-solving cats; several even name their books, "The Cat Who. . ." although clearly, Lillian Jackson Braun is the most prolific "Cat Who" author.

A second, less expected result of the idea and expression dichotomy is the inability to obtain copyright protection for blank forms. Although graphical or literary elements that might be found on a form (such as a photograph or a detailed explanation of a term) would be subject to copyright protection, there is no copyright in the blank form itself. The blank form is considered to be a type of idea, a conclusion that stems from an old Supreme Court decision in which ledger forms were held to not be subject to copyright.

Useful articles may not be subject to copyright protection. A useful article is one that has a utilitarian function. Useful articles are things such as ice cream, a shovel, a chair, a pencil, or a hammock. The only elements of the useful article that can be protected by copyright are those "features that can be identified separately from, and are capable of existing independently of, the utilitarian aspects of the article." However, the unique design of a useful article can make that useful article eligible for trademark protection. A Franklin stove, while a useful article, was unique enough in its design to qualify for trademark protection.

Benjamin Franklin wrote in his *Autobiography* (on which the copyright has expired):

Governor Thomas was so pleased with the construction of this stove [i.e., the Franklin stove] . . . that he offered to give me a patent for the sole vending of them for a term of years; but I declined it from a principle which has ever weighed with me on such occasions, viz.: That, as we enjoy great advantages from the inventions of others, we should be glad of an opportunity to serve others by any invention of ours; and this we should do freely and generously.[19]

The beautiful prints found on Ben and Jerry Ice Creams are images that are protectable under copyright law even though the container is a useful article. The image is clearly separable from the ice-cream container. Another commonly considered example is that of clothing. The print found on the fabric of a skirt or jacket is copyrightable because it exists separately from the utilitarian nature of the clothing. The design of the clothing is not subject to copyright protection, consequently the designers who copy the runway designs of prominent designers infringe upon no rights of copy. A unique portable folding chair may certainly be subject to trademark protection.

Anticircumvention and the DMCA

The DMCA (Digital Millennium Copyright Act) prohibits circumvention of technology that prevents access to a work. Copyright management devices that protect the work from infringement may not be removed. The library community postponed the enactment of this clause pending a study on this issue by the Library of Congress. The concern was that the freedom of access and an intrinsic right to read would be inhibited. The belief is that users will be adversely affected in their ability to make noninfringing use of copyrighted works. The published findings of the Library of Congress are available online at: http://www.loc.gov/copyright/1201/anticirc.html (accessed January 31, 2003).

The Librarian of Congress, on the recommendation of the Register of Copyrights, announced the classes of works subject to the exemption from the prohibition on circumvention of technological measures that control access to copyrighted works. The two classes of works are:

1. Compilations consisting of lists of Web sites blocked by filtering software applications; and
2. Literary works, including computer programs and databases, protected by access control mechanisms that fail to permit access because of malfunction, damage, or obsolescence.

These exemptions are in effect from October 28, 2000, to October 28, 2003. For these two categories of works circumvention of devices designed to protect their data will be valid.

WORKS FOR HIRE

On January 1, 2003, unpublished works made for hire created in 1882 and those by authors who died by 1932 will be available. Unpublished works were included in the Sonny Bono Copyright Term Extension Act and twenty years of copyright protection were added.

For a work made for hire, such as a work by an employee, copyright lasts for 120 years after the date of creation. For a work by a personal author, copyright expiration dates are tied to the death of the author, because the term lasts for his/her lifetime plus 70 years. If the work is anonymous or by a personal author for whom there is no record of a death date, it can enter the public domain after 120 years from its creation date.

FEDERAL PREEMPTION AND STATES' RIGHTS

Prior to 1976 in the United States, violations for copyright were addressed by the individual states and by the federal statute. That dual jurisdiction was abolished with the 1976 Copyright Act for most rights of copy, with a few limited exceptions. Congress saw the need for consistency and uniformity for copyright. However, when the history of copyright in this country is reviewed in its totality, the states' interpretations of copyright played a role in developing current law.

Live musical performances constitute an important exception to the federal preemption of the law of copyright. There was a time when there was no federal copyright protection for live musical performances; the 1976 Copyright Act did not provide protection for them. Prior to 1996 you could tape this music without violating federal copyright law (note: there were state copyright laws that might have governed this issue). Title 17, Section 1101 *et seq.* of the United States Code now provides copyright protection for live musical performances concurrently with the continued states' rights of copy that had historically existed for live musical performers. This right has not been preempted by federal statute, and the two rights co-exist.

Some states, such as California, have enacted statutory copyright laws that govern live musical performances. California's statute clearly grants copyright protection to improvisational performers and provides that "the author of any original work of authorship that is not fixed in any tangible medium of expression shall receive exclusive ownership in the representation or expression thereof." See Cal. Civ. Code 980 (a)(1) (West. Supp. 1997).

It was the Uruguay Round Agreements Act (URAA), enacted on December 8, 1994, and effective January 1, 1996, that impacted the General Agreement on Tariffs and Trade (GATT) and included an agreement on the Trade-Related Aspects of Intellectual Property (TRIPS); amends the U.S. Copyright Law, Title 17, sections 104A, 109(b); and adds a new Chapter 11 to Title 17 and a new Section 2319a to Title 18. In summary, the changes restored international copyrights to various "improper" or "incomplete" copyright works prior to 1978 (this was before the United States became a member of the Berne Convention treaty). It modified the computer program rental provisions and added new civil and criminal remedies for "bootlegged" recordings of live musical performances and music videos, something the United States had not previously had.

To read the Uruguay Round Treaty Agreement, you may link to the U.S. Copyright Office at http://www.copyright.gov/title17/92appiii.html. The entire World Trade Organization (WTO) Agreements are summarized at its Web site.

U.S. SUPREME COURT AND PUBLIC DOMAIN—THE CASE OF ERIC ELDRED AND ELDRITCH PRESS

"I think I can I think I can," said the little red engine; "I think I can I think I can, reach the Supreme Court," said Eric Eldred. Out of the 7,852 cases filed in the U.S. Supreme Court in 2002, there were seventy-seven signed opinions. The Court agreed to hear 86 cases. Getting to the Supreme Court is a feat itself. Many people were shocked when Eric Eldred's case challenging the Sonny Bono Copyright Term Extension Act was accepted by the U.S. Supreme Court for review and scheduled for argument in the fall of 2002.

Eric Eldred created a Web site to encourage his triplet teenage daughters to read more. Eldred found many classics were sponsored on the Web by several nonprofit sites. But Eldred felt these electronic editions were inferior to their print versions; they had typos, or relied on outdated texts, or were difficult to read. He created his own online edition, sprucing it up with a glossary, a time line, illustrations, and a biography of the author. He envisioned a global electronic library that would make unusual and out-of-print books available for people who couldn't find them in libraries or used-book stores. His e-library would be accessible to the blind through text-to-speech generators. Getting permission from publishers wouldn't be a problem, he thought, because the works he wanted were all in the public domain, and their copyrights expired.

Eldred's daily hit count grew to 20,000. In 1997, the National Endowment for the Humanities recognized his Eldritch Press as one of the 20 best humanities sites on the Web. More recognition came when both the Nathaniel Hawthorne Society and the William Dean Howells Society endorsed Internet links to his pages. He began looking forward to scanning rare works with copyrights that were scheduled to expire.

On October 27, 1998, as the nation was preoccupied by the impeachment scandal, President Clinton quietly signed into law the Sonny Bono Copyright Term Extension Act. The act extended protection by twenty years for cultural works copyrighted after January 1, 1923. Works copyrighted by individuals since 1978 got "life plus seventy" rather than the existing "life plus fifty"; works made by or for corporations, known as "works made for hire," got ninety-five years. Works copyrighted before 1978 were shielded for ninety-five years, regardless of how they were produced. Eldred's plans and hopes were dashed. The works he had been watching closely were now well out of his reach. *The Great Gatsby* would never grace his Web site. An out-of-print collection of stories by Sherwood Anderson, *Horses and Men*, and an edition of Robert Frost's poetry collection *New Hampshire* were not to see new life on the Web. Many books have no mass-market value but are valuable to individual researchers. The Bono Act shields those works, too. When the original copyright holders cannot be found, the books cannot be published.

Harvard Law School professor Lawrence Lessig (now at Stanford) came to Eldred's aid and took the case pro bono. He filed a complaint against the government on Eldred's behalf with the U.S. District Court for the District of Columbia. He believed public access to artworks was at stake. The claim is based in a violation of Eldred's freedom of speech: "The extension takes works that would have entered the public domain and privatizes them improperly; the result is like a tax on freedom of expression. Eldred can't publicly utter these words now without paying a penalty imposed by the government."

Further, he claimed the copyright clause's "incentive" requirement was destroyed by the Act. He argued that incentive to a corpse is meaningless and that is precisely what the Act does because the copyright extension protection is retroactive. It goes to works created by authors now dead. Lessig claimed, "Extensions can't be retroactive, because the Constitution gives Congress the right to grant exclusive rights only if those rights create incentives to produce more speech. Extending these benefits retroactively doesn't serve any purposes the copyright clause was designed for."

Lessig's former Harvard Law School colleague Arthur Miller weighed in on the opposite side. He argued that copyrights were still limited and that Bono is consistent with past copyright extensions, which all covered preexisting works. "Congress's repeated extensions reflect a consistent congressional judgment that yesterday's works should not enjoy lesser protection than tomorrow's simply because new copyright legislation was passed today."

Eldred lost in district court. He lost in the appellate court. But out of the dark and against all odds, the U.S. Supreme Court agreed to hear his case. Justice Stephen Breyer, as a Harvard professor in 1970, wrote an article for his school's law review in which he raised the question of scrapping copyrights altogether. "Authors in ancient times, as well as monks and scholars in the middle ages, wrote and were paid for their writings without copyright protection," said Breyer. "Taken as a whole . . . the evidence now available suggests that, although we should hesitate to abolish copyright protection, we should equally hesitate to extend or strengthen it." It appears that Justice Breyer may have telegraphed his opinion on copyright in his historical publications. He appears to have been, at least in 1970, squarely aligned to Eric Eldred's position.

In January 2003, Justice Ruth Bader Ginsburg wrote for the majority in the Eldritch Press case, "Congress acted within its authority and did not transgress constitutional limitations. . . . We are not at liberty to second-guess congressional determinations and policy judgments of this order, however debatable or arguably unwise they may be."

In a twenty-two-page dissent that chronicled the development of intellectual property law since the 1790 act, Justice John Paul Stevens said that by declining to review the copyright extension, the Court has ceded to Congress "its principal responsibility in this area of the law." Justice Stephen Breyer's analysis was consistent with his early writings in the area of copyright law. He focused on the economic impact, and in his opinion he referred to research performed for Congress that concluded that CTEA will cost U.S. consumers "several billion" dollars in additional royalty payments to copyright holders. "The economic effect of this 20-year extension—the longest blanket extension since the Nation's founding—is to make the copyright term not limited, but virtually perpetual. . . . Its primary legal effect is to grant the extended term not to authors, but to their heirs, estates or corporate successors."

You may reach Eric Eldred's site, titled "Eldritch Press," at http://www .eldritchpress.org (accessed January 30, 2003), where his greeting is: "Here are free, accessible books. Read them and go in peace."

CONCLUSION

The purpose of copyright is often viewed to be the method by which authors are compensated and this is widely understood to be its essential purpose. That is neither the Constitutional purpose nor the purpose the United States Court has historically chosen to emphasize. The Supreme Court has repeatedly defined the purpose of copyright as one necessary to enhance society by "promoting the progress of science and the useful arts."

Many of the elegantly drafted briefs filed in the Supreme Court in the Eldritch case noted that copyrights that now have been extended in time to benefit authors long departed do not serve that purpose. Works that could benefit authors and scholars and form the basis of new insights into history are now shut away for another twenty years, which are all the years that some scholars have left. Eisenhower's papers will not be available to this generation of scholars and students.

Many works that are protected by copyright do not have a vast commercial appeal. Unless persons willing to preserve those works can somehow obtain financial incentive for their preservations, they will continue to be unavailable to the public.

The Library of Congress's *American Memory* and The University of North Carolina at Chapel Hill's program *Documenting the American South* are limited in their abilities to include important works from the 1920s and 1930s. They do not have the funds to find the copyright holders and obtain releases. It is the public that is deprived from these severe limitations. One project provides Web access, through digital scanning and descriptive indexing, to a unique collection of rare American music material in the UNC-Chapel Hill Music Library.

If we are to share our humanity and understand our strengths and limitations, we must review our past and interpret it for the future. The Copyright Term Extension Act inhibits our ability to do just that in many instances and does not promote the progress of science and the useful arts.

NOTES

1. See Julie Cohen, "Copyright and the Perfect Curve," *Vanderbilt Law Review* 53 (2000): 1799–1800.

2. *Harper & Row v. The Nation Magazine,* 471 U.S. 539 (1985). See also: *Sony Corp. of America v. Universal City Studios, Inc.,* 464 U.S. 417, 429 (1984).

3. *Books in Print Online (2002).* Available: http://www.booksinprint.com. (Accessed July 8, 2002).

4. Arnold P. Lutzker and Carl H. Settlemeyer III. Amici Curiae brief filed supporting *Eric Eldred et al v. John D. Ashcroft*, U.S. Supreme Court (2002) representing fifteen library associations: American Association of Law Libraries, American Historical Association, American Library Association, Art Libraries Society of North America, Association for Recorded Sound Collections, Association of Research Libraries, Council on Library and Information Resources, International Association of Jazz Record Collectors, Medical Library Association, Midwest Archives Conference, Music Library Association, National Council on Public History, Society for American Music, Society of American Archivists, and Special Libraries Association.

5. Ibid. Arnold P. Lutzker and Carl H. Settlemeyer III are quoted from Bill Holland, "Labels Strive to Rectify Past Archival Problems," *Billboard*, July 12, 1997.

6. In December 1994, Congress changed the law of unrecorded music performances when it passed The Uruguay Round Agreements Act. This act prohibited the recording of live musical performances (that is, bootleg copies) even when there was no other "fixation" of the work. This provision includes separate prohibitions against the distribution and transmission of bootleg copies. In fact, the prohibition against transmission does not even require that a physical copy of the performance ever be made. This is an independent act that provides a right similar to a copyright but must be looked to individually for statutory damages.

7. Lolly Gasaway, "When Works Pass Into the Public Domain." Available: http://www.unc.edu/~unclng/public-d.htm. (Accessed March 23, 2002.)

8. Copyright protection for literary characters has become far more common, requiring only that the characters be sufficiently developed and finely drawn. See Melville B. Nimmer and David Nimmer, *Nimmer on Copyright* 2.12 (2001).

9. *Twin Books v. Disney*, 83 F. 3d 1162 (9th Cir. 1996).

10. Emily Flinn, *Austin American Statesman*, 20 February 2000, sec. B8.

11. *Feltner v. Columbia Pictures Television, Inc.*, 140 L.Ed. 2d 438 (1998).

12. 17 U.S.C. §504(c)(1).

13. 17 U.S.C. §504(c)(2).

14. See 18 U.S.C. §2319.

15. 17 U.S.C. §102.

16. See, for example, *Schroeder v. William Morrow & Co.*, 566 F.2d 3 (CA7 1977) (copyright in gardening directory); *cf. Burrow-Giles Lithographic Co. v. Sarony*, 111 U.S. 53, 58 (1884) (originator of a photograph may claim copyright in his work).

17. *Harper & Row v. The Nation*, 470 U.S. 539 (1985).

18. 17 U.S.C. §102(b) (1994).

19. Benjamin Franklin, "Autobiography," in *The Works of Benjamin Franklin*, ed. John Bigelow (New York: G. P. Putnam's Sons, 1904), 237–38.

REFERENCES

Berkman Center for Internet and Society, Harvard Law School. "Open Law, Eldred et al v. Ashcroft." Available: http://eon.law.harvard.edu/openlaw/eldred vashcroft/legal.html. (Accessed January 31, 2003). This is an archive of the pleadings filed in the *Eldred et al. v. Ashcroft* challenge to the Sonny Bono Copyright Term Extension Act.

The Library of Congress. *American Memory.* Available: http://memory.loc.gov /ammem/ammemhome.html. (Accessed January 31, 2003). An important library resource.

The Legal Information Institute, Cornell Law School. Available: http://www4.law .cornell.edu/uscode/17/. (Accessed January 31, 2003). Provides online access to Title 17 United States Code. This is an excellent resource for primary legal sources. It is always helpful to review the actual statute when studying that statute, no matter how many times you have read it. Reading it with a new issue in mind may open new applications for consideration.

Lolly Gasaway. "When Works Pass into the Public Domain." University of North Carolina, Chapel Hill. Available: http://www.unc.edu/~unclng/public-d .htm. (Accessed January 31, 2003). This is an excellent chart of periods of copyright.

The University of North Carolina at Chapel Hill. *Documenting the American South.* Available: http://memory.loc.gov/ammem/amhome.htm. (Accessed January 31, 2003). Another important library resource.

4

FAIR USE IN EDUCATION OF MATERIAL PROTECTED BY COPYRIGHT

Copyright is intended to increase, and not to impede, the harvest of knowledge.

—Sandra Day O'Connor

This chapter will cover:

Fair Use Doctrine Is a Legal Defense

The Four-Prong Test

The Guidelines

Damages for Infringement and the Concept of Good Faith

What Can We Copy Pursuant to the Law?

What Can We Copy Pursuant to the Guidelines?

THE RIGHTS OF COPY OR COPYRIGHTS

There are five exclusive rights of the copyright owner: the rights to copy, perform, adapt, distribute, and display the work. The acronym here is: Don't Copy, don't PADD with copyrighted work (Perform—Adapt—Distribute—Display). Permission from the copyright owner to use the work in the capacity of one of these five rights is required.

New works build to one degree or another on the previous works of others. It can be difficult to determine when something new is created or when there is simply an adaptation. Ideas are not subject to copyright. Adaptation of facts and style do not infringe upon a copyright. Ideas, facts, and style are elements of a work that are not protected by copyright and can be reused. They may give life to a new original expression. The line is not always an easy one to draw. Also, works that consist entirely of information that is common property and containing no original authorship cannot be copyrighted. For example, standard calendars, height and weight charts, tape measures and rules, and lists of tables taken from public documents or other common sources cannot be copyrighted.

THE HISTORY OF FAIR USE

Fair use in American copyright law originated in the nineteenth century as a judicial doctrine that excused certain uses of copyrighted works, particularly if those uses embraced only a small portion of the original work and were for socially beneficial purposes.[1] Education is the chief socially beneficial purpose. Fair use remained a judicially created and applied doctrine until 1978 when the Copyright Revision Act of 1976 took effect and included the first American fair-use statute. This statute, titled "Limitations on Fair Use, Exclusive Rights," can be reviewed at 17 UAC 107. Through nearly two decades of earlier debate, every proposed revision bill included at least some acknowledgment of fair use.[2] The bill that Congress finally passed in late 1976 affirmed that fair-use rights existed, especially for teaching, research, scholarship, and news reporting, and it offered four factors for evaluating whether a use was "fair."

The fair use of a copyrighted work, including such use by reproduction in copies or phonorecords or by any other means specified by that section, for purposes such as criticism, comment, news reporting, teaching (including multiple copies for classroom use), scholarship, or research, is not an infringement of copyright.

The old adage that "ignorance is no excuse" holds true for copyright. We are all responsible for knowing the rules and abiding by them. Knowing the rules and taking some reasonable steps to apply them can go a long way toward avoiding a claim of infringement.

FAIR USE DOCTRINE IS A LEGAL DEFENSE

Fair use is a doctrine of legal defense that allows someone other than the copyright owner to use the copyrighted material in a reasonable manner without the owner's prior consent.[3] The most important fact to understand in this simple sentence is that "fair use" is a defense. A defense is used by a defendant who is actively involved in a lawsuit. It is employed as a legal strategy after suit is brought. The doctrine of fair use gives preference to nonprofit educational uses of copyrighted material. It does not, however, by any means give the educational community *carte blanche*.

The prerequisite necessary to avail oneself of the legal defense of fair use is to have and to demonstrate an understanding of copyright laws. The courts have resolutely stated in the case of *Basic Books v. Kinko's* that simply ignoring copyright laws and having no guidelines by which to evaluate what is an educational fair use of an author's work is not a basis from which an educator or a librarian may claim the fair use defense.[4]

The doctrine of fair use of material protected by copyright is a legal defense against claims of copyright violation. Those charged with the infringement of a work subject to the protection of the copyright laws offer the Fair Use Doctrine as a defense or justification for the alleged infringement. In order to determine whether an alleged infringement of copyrighted work constitutes a fair use rather than an unlawful one, the courts have applied a four-factor test as mandated by federal law.

THE FOUR-PRONG TEST

In determining whether the use made of a work in any particular case is a fair use, the factors to be considered shall include the following:

1. the purpose and character of the use, including whether such use is of a commercial nature or is for nonprofit educational purposes;
2. the nature of the copyrighted work;
3. the amount and substantiality of the portion used in relation to the copyrighted work as a whole; and
4. the effect of the use upon the potential market for or value of the copyrighted work.

Despite congressional intent to consider other factors and to keep fair use flexible for diverse and changing circumstances, most analyses and court rulings have relied extensively, if not exclusively, on these four statutory factors. A useful acronym is to remember that the four factors are a PANE: purpose, amount, nature, and effect.

The fair-use formula calls for some balance of these factors, with courts generally assessing the number of factors that militate in favor of each party in an infringement lawsuit. The factors are not necessarily weighed equally; the effect on the value of the original often receives greatest weight, particularly when a court concludes that the use may have obviated a potential sale of the original work.[5] Providing an income for the creator is an important purpose of the copyright law.

Because there is no congressional guidance in our federal law on how to weigh the four factors of fair use, the courts have employed a case-by-case approach to interpreting fair use. In a case-by-case approach the court will look at the facts of each individual case and decide whether or not there has been a fair use of the work or there has been an infringement upon the rights of copy; the Supreme Court, however, has stated that the last two factors are the most important factors in making the determination of copyright infringement.

In no statute and in no case is there an articulation of a bright line rule to determine what is a fair use of a copyrighted material. The fact is there are no hard-and-fast rules to follow, no legislatively or judicially approved rules, and no guidelines set in legal stone. The guidelines we have are set in clay, and they are not law. As each application of the doctrine of fair use is applied to each unique situation, it is very difficult to determine what is and what is not a fair use of a work.[6] The nine members of the Supreme Court cannot always agree on a determination of what is and is not a fair use of a copyrighted work, and yet librarians, who are not attorneys, must make these decisions for the benefit of their library. An understanding of the four factors below will help.

The Purpose and Character of the Use to Be Considered in Fair Use

Where the purpose and character of the use of the copyrighted material is to create or produce a new work or a work that is different from the original work, the Fair Use Doctrine will be applied for nonprofit educational purposes but not for commercial gain. This use of material subject to copyright is considered to be transformative and is protected by the Fair Use Doctrine.[7] A transformative work takes a portion of one work, incorporates it into another and creates a new work. Quoting a source in a paper is a transformative use, as is any commentary or criticism of the original.

The Nature of the Copyrighted Work in Fair Use

The Fair Use Doctrine examines the nature of the copyrighted work in relation to its established purpose. The use of factual material is more susceptible to fair use.[8] Historical and geographical data are examples of factual materials that are more likely to be considered within the realm of fair use. Works of fiction as found in novels, poetry, or short stories are less likely to be considered to be the subject of fair use and more likely to be the subject of copyright protection.

Private, unpublished research and creative works are much more likely to be protected than published works. In private and unpublished works the author still retains the right to control the final tangible expressions before publication.

The Amount and Substantiality of the Material Used

The third factor of the Fair Use Doctrine evaluates the quantity of the work in proportion to the total work of the copyrighted material. This sounds simplistic, and it is, but there are secondary tests in this analysis. Quantity may not always be the controlling factor. Case law interpreting this element of fair use analysis has determined extensive portions of the work may be used if these portions are not the "heart of the work" or the "essence" of the work and the use of these portions that exceed the guideline quantity creates no adverse market impact for the original work The overall importance of the portion copied to the work from which it was copied will be analyzed. The copying of entire works for use in the classroom will not be considered a fair use. This includes out-of-print material. However, it is important to note that a library may make a copy of an out-of-print material for preservation purposes. This is quite different from a publisher producing an out-of-print material for sale. Copying that would not be considered fair use for educational purposes may be acceptable pursuant to section 108 of DMCA.

The Effect of the Use on the Work's Market Value

The U.S. Supreme Court has characterized the effect of the use of the work on its market value as the most important element in fair-use analysis. The Court has generally held that "fair use . . . is limited to copying by others which does not materially impair the marketability of the work which is copied."[9] The other three factors remain elements of consideration in the doctrine of fair use, notwithstanding the focus of the court on the fourth factor. A showing of widespread use that would negatively affect the potential market of the copyrighted material would preclude a fair-use defense.[10]

THE GUIDELINES

We have all heard of "The Guidelines." Where did these guidelines come from? Are these guidelines the law? Do we have to follow the guidelines? Generally, when people in education refer to "The Guidelines" they are referring to the "Classroom Guidelines." These guidelines are not the law, though the publishing industry wishes that they were and many educational institutions treat them as such. It is essential that librarians have guidelines that govern the use of copyrighted material. The "Classroom Guidelines" are only recommendations. In law they are known as a safe harbor—a place of legal protection to be used to shelter the user from a lawsuit. A library cannot have anyone and everyone in the library making a good faith effort to conform to copyright law. A library can have a designated person who can, on a case-by-case basis, make exceptions to the guidelines. Exceptions are made one at a time, on an individual basis applying the law to the facts.

Should the students themselves be able to make case-by-case decisions on the fair use of a copyrighted work? Well how about just the straight-"A" students, or students on the student council, or students with brown eyes? Of course, not.

Should the head of each department be able to make case-by-case decisions? Should faculty members who have taken a recent course in copyright be able to make this decision? Typically not even in universities have these parties been given the right to make these decisions. Then how about any librarian? Probably not.

Based on historical legal precedent, every school district and every library should have guidelines. The fair-use guidelines for the school district do not have to be identical to the fair-use guidelines for the library, though they typically are. Guidelines are just that—guidelines. Even more importantly they are the minimum amount a party may copy without (probably) being in violation of copyright law; they are not the maximum amount.

Conjointly, if your school adopts the "Classroom Guidelines" without exception under any circumstance it may be shortchanging itself even though this wholesale adoption of the guidelines is clearly an attempt at protection. If your school adopts these guidelines without putting a librarian or at least a copyright officer in a position to permit exceptions, the school is definitely shortchanging itself. The Classroom Guidelines provide guidance as to the minimum that may be borrowed from a copyrighted material before the act of copyright infringement occurs. In many, many instances, however, more material than the amount prescribed may be "fairly used," which is the reason copyright infringement is determined on a case-by-case basis. If your school district does not allow exceptions to be made under certain circumstances on a case-by-case basis as opposed to the rigid guidelines, your faculty and your students may not be benefiting from the fair use exception to the law of copyright as intended by Congress and the courts. However, many schools and universities have done just that: they have adopted the guidelines across the board, which makes the publishing industry quite happy, but it may not be best for education.

Before being placed in the position of making exceptions to the guidelines, a person should clearly understand the limits of the guidelines and understand the law of copyright. The guidelines are not the law of copyright. (This point is redundantly made because it is so significant. So many librarians believe the guidelines are the law.) The law of the fair use of copyrighted material is based on a four-pronged test, which is examined above.

GUIDELINES FOR EDUCATIONAL FAIR USE EXCEPTIONS TO THE COPYRIGHT LAWS

While Congress has codified the four enumerated fair-use principles, it has never adopted any of the guidelines into legislation. These guidelines remain simply that, guidelines. No court has adopted them as a legal precedent, so they do not have even that appearance of usefulness and legitimacy. To the contrary, Congress and the courts have acted deliberately to not create a lawfully binding standard from these guidelines.

It would, however, be disastrous to have nothing to guide individual libraries and librarians in developing policy for copyright protection in their libraries. The guidelines are simply proposed guidance. Many argue that these guidelines destroy the legitimate purpose of copyright exceptions, which is to honor the spirit of the right of copy as balanced with the right of education. However, in the real world, where decisions must be made every day, these guidelines created by no legislature and endorsed by no judiciary affect education and library activities in a significant manner. The open question is, should they be wholly accepted and endorsed in every library as *the* guidelines to govern the library?

The Guidelines for Classroom Copying are the guidelines that have the greatest impact on K–12 education. However, it would be much too simple to have just one set of guidelines. There are many. The following guidelines can be found online at http://www.musiclibraryassoc.org.

Classroom Guidelines are formally known as the Agreement on Guidelines for Classroom Copying in Not-for-Profit Educational Institutions with Respect to Books and Periodicals, H.R. Rep. No. 94-1476, at 68–70 (1976). The Music Guidelines are formally known as: Guidelines for Educational Uses of Music, H.R. Rep. No. 94- 1476, at 70–71 (1976).

The Off-Air Guidelines are formally known as Guidelines for Off-Air Recordings of Broadcast Programming for Educational Purposes, H.R. Rep. No. 97–495, at 8–9 (1982). These guidelines first appeared in 127 Cong. Rec. 18, at 24,048–49 (1981).

CONTU Guidelines on Photocopying Under Interlibrary Loan Arrangements, in National Commission on New Technological Uses of Copyrighted Works, Final Report of the National Commission on New Technological Uses of Copyrighted Works, July 31, 1978 can be found online at http://www.chi.org/docs/infopols/CONTU.html.

The Digital Imaging Guidelines are formally known as Proposal for Educational Fair Use Guidelines for Digital Images, in Information Infrastructure Task Force, Working Group on Intellectual Property Rights, Conference on Fair Use: Final Report to the Commissioner on the Conclusion of the Conference on Fair Use, November 1998, and found in the CONFU Final Report 33–41. The Distance Learning Guidelines are formally known as the Proposal for Educational Fair Use Guidelines for Distance Learning, and found in the CONFU Final Report 43–48.

The Multimedia Guidelines are formally known as the Proposal for Fair Use Guidelines for Educational Multimedia, in CONFU Final Report 49–59. A slightly different version of the Multimedia Guidelines was the subject of a "nonlegislative report" issued by a congressional subcommittee in December 1996. See Staff of House Subcomm. on Courts and Intellectual Prop. of the House Comm. on the Judiciary, 104th Cong.

GOOD FAITH COMPLIANCE WITH GUIDELINES

Guidelines are essential for the working librarian. There must be some articulated principle to which actions and behavior can adhere and on which policies can be based. It is important for the library and its personnel to have some sense of confidence that their policies comply with the law and that, with the understanding that guidelines are flexible, their compliance with guidelines is an indication of good faith This flexibility should be monitored by a single source and authority within the library rather than modified by every employee of the library on a case-by-case basis. This wholesale, across-the-board modification could result in a de facto non-application of guidelines.

The guidelines have evolved from the principles codified in the Copyright Act of 1976, and the case law on which this statute was based. This sword cuts both ways: The guidelines are considered to be the "minimum" intrusions permissible on the rights of copy, yet there is room for exception and interpretation. However, the farther the action of copy deviates from the guidelines, the less likely the action will be considered to have been taken in good faith. Good faith is an important fact the court considers in its assessment of damages and penalties. Because Congress never enacted the guidelines and no court ever has read them into law in a legal decision, the guidelines are not themselves binding on the public as a rule of law.

BURDEN OF PROOF IN INFRINGEMENT OF A COPYRIGHT

The plaintiff has the burden of proof. The one who claims that an infringement upon their copyright has been made must prove prima facie a case of infringement before the doctrine of the fair use of a copyrighted material is presented for review.[11] Fair use has been called "the last resort of scoundrels." After the complaining party has proven ownership of the work copied, that the work has been registered for copyright, and that the defendant(s) have copied or infringed upon the work, fair use as an affirmative defense is presented in a trial for copyright infringement. It is the defendant (the claimed infringer) who claims the portions copied were used fairly and invokes the Fair Use Doctrine.

DAMAGES FOR INFRINGEMENT AND THE CONCEPT OF GOOD FAITH

Damages for infringement upon a copyright come in two forms: statutory, incurred as a result of the act of infringement upon copyright; and actual damages in the form of lost profits. It is extremely unlikely that damages will be sought from a school library. Indeed, their very existence will serve as a deterrent to an overzealous faculty and even students. However, it is not unreasonable to advise the faculty of these damages in the event the right of copy is infringed upon.

A more likely case scenario is that a "cease and desist" letter will be sent by the owner of the copyright and the educational institution will be able to seek legal counsel regarding the alleged violation of copyright and take appropriate action. However, even this course of conduct is extremely undesirable.

Statutory damages are available to copyright owners who successfully prove infringement. Although a work need not be registered to collect damages in the form of lost profits, it must be registered to collect the statutory damages,[12] or those damages articulated in the statute itself.[13]

Statutory damages will be preferred by the copyright holder when the actual damages are minimal, such as showing a Disney movie in a classroom on a rainy day. Statutory damages allow the court to award up to $30,000 per work infringed.[14] Statutory damages may reach as high as $150,000 if the infringement is "willful."[15] Should the court find that the infringer is "innocent" or acted in good faith, the statute directs: In a case where the infringer sustains the burden of proving, and the court finds, that such infringer was not aware and had no reason to believe that his or her acts constituted an infringement of copyright, the court in its discretion may reduce the award of statutory damages to a sum of not less than $200. This decision to impose damages lies solely within the discretion of the court.

These damages are guaranteed to scare a faculty into compliance and create a situation in which virtually no one wants the duty of deciding when exceptions to the guidelines should be made.

THE COURT HAS THE POWER TO DISMISS A FACULTY OR LIBRARIAN DEFENDANT

An "employee or agent" of a nonprofit educational institution, library, or archives may be eliminated as a defendant, if the infringer can demonstrate that he or she "believed and had reasonable grounds for believing that his or her use of the copyrighted work was a fair use under Section 107 of the Copyright Act."[16]

The decision of a court to eliminate the employee or agent will be determined on the good faith action of the employee. Because what is and is not a fair use of the work of another is vague and often decided on a case-by-case basis, Congress has given the court the discretion to eliminate one of the largest financial consequences of infringement for educators and librarians who apply fair use in a reasonable manner. It is of utmost important to note this is not an automatic immunity for educators. The provision in no fashion exonerates educators. It simply allows the court to make a determination as to the good faith actions of the educator.

It is extremely likely that the courts will presume that educators understand copyright law and the guidelines and have made their best effort to apply them before any educator is dismissed from a suit. The educator will have to prove to the court that they are "innocent infringer[s]." Although this proof is only necessary after the case of infringement is made prima facie, this is clearly the reason strict applications of guidelines are encouraged. (See chapter 3 for a more detailed discussion of dismissal of an educator from a copyright infringement suit.)

CLASSROOM GUIDELINES ARE A STRICT DEMARCATION, NOT A GENUINE GOOD FAITH ATTEMPT

Many of the guidelines and particularly the Classroom Guidelines demarcate a strict line, measured by counting words and instances of copying, in an effort to define fair use.

Their very existence destroys the congressional intent of the notion of "fair use." Good faith may intrinsically require an understanding and application of the law. Guidelines can be a method for establishing good faith. Guidelines for employees, faculty, or anyone else in a position to make fair-use decisions may demonstrate the good faith of the organization, and the application of the guidelines by the individual can manifest that person's good faith as well.

A set of guidelines may be a valuable tool for establishing good faith. In specific instances the existing guidelines may not be appropriate. In these instances, documentation of the efforts expended in producing fact-specific guidelines should be documented. For example, discussion with attorneys, law professors, with colleagues, and any other experts should be footnoted in the guidelines. If the objective of an educator making policy is to avoid litigation, adopting and following the guidelines offers the prospect of discouraging a lawsuit.

SUMMARY OF PRINCIPLES OF EDUCATIONAL FAIR USE

In summary, the U.S. Copyright Act now codifies broad principles underlying fair use, but ultimately offers few details for understanding its meaning in specific applications.[17] The court makes these decisions on a case-by-case basis or an individual-specific basis. Each case must be evaluated independently and decided upon the specific facts presented. It was the intention of Congress that the law governing the fair use of copyrighted materials in an education not-for-profit setting be an adaptable law that is flexible and useable, applicable to changing needs and circumstances. The law itself provides no clear and direct answers about the scope of fair use and its meaning in specific situations. These insights are gained by reviewing the various courts' interpretations of the law of Congress. No court has referred to the guidelines to evaluate, case by case, what is and what is not a fair use of a material subject to copyright. The significance of this important fact is that the guidelines are not the law. They are clearly not included in any statute, nor has any court ever relied on them for decisions they have reached regarding issues of copyright infringement. In sum, they are neither statutory law nor are they common law. They are no more and no less than their title implies; they are *guidelines.*

WHAT CAN WE COPY PURSUANT TO THE LAW?

Not all material is copyrighted. If the copyright has expired you are free to include any or all of the data in a class presentation or student paper. This material is considered to be in the "public domain." For example, ninety percent of the math taught K–12 was discovered by A.D. 1400 and the most significant development in mathematics took place in ancient Greece. A leading mathematician of the turn of the twentieth century addressed the International Congress of Mathematicians in 1900 in Paris, and in his address he described twenty-three important mathematical problems. Clearly, his address is no longer copyrighted and covers problems that are relevant today. These twenty-three problems can be used by any math teacher today.

The ALA (American Library Association) Washington Office, a litigious group, is a good source to turn to when the right to copy a material is in doubt. They can be found online at http://www.ala.org/washoff/copyright.html (accessed January 31, 2003) and have an opinion and a lawsuit on almost every issue. You are not out there without a lifeline. You may not agree with their position on every issue, and it is not necessary that you do. No matter your opinion, you can benefit from this deep reservoir of copyright information. Remember, these are only guidelines and what works in New York City is not expected to work in Hot Coffee, Texas.

The best defense to copyright violations in your school is a good offense. How is that done? Provide your students with easy access to public domain information on the World Wide Web.

- First, understand what is and is not public domain information.
- Second, know where to locate it so the faculty can incorporate it into lesson plans.
- Third, students can locate public domain data and incorporate it into their projects and school databases. Many state library organizations have already composed extensive public domain lists and Public Domain Resource Guides highlight many public domain texts and data for student and faculty use. As a group project, a class can build an Internet bibliography on a specific topic that would benefit other classes.
- Fourth, teach students when to give credit to copyrighted material, where to place that credit on their project, and how to search to determine if the material is copyrighted, noting the subtle but very real difference between plagiarism and copyright infringement.

Public Domain

United States government information is for the most part public domain information. Our government is the largest collector of statistical data in the world and most of it is public record (although it is important to note that not all of this information is public domain). The Smithsonian is a government agency. The Library of Congress is a government agency. There are special government indexes and Web sites designed for every age for access to this government information and data.

Facts cannot be copyrighted and are public domain information. However, it is important to educate students on the distinction between opinion and fact. It is both the librarian's and the classroom teacher's responsibility to educate and supervise the student on the evaluation of the sources of facts. Material on which the copyright has expired is public domain material. The literary classics are public domain material and readily available on the Internet.

Copyright expiration occurs eventually on all information; no copyright lasts forever. The classic literature was never copyrighted and is public domain information. Material published before 1923 is considered to be in the public domain; material published after 1989 is not. For all years in between consult chapter 6, "Tracing Copyright." (See chapter 3 for examples of public domain works and more detail.)

Database Protection

United States copyright law does not protect database collections, as the U.S. Supreme Court held in 1991 in *Feist Publications, Inc. v. Rural Telephone Service Co.* The European Union (EU) and other nations, however, do protect databases, and Congress has been considering database protection for several years. Although several database protection bills have been introduced in Congress, they have not passed because of the differing interests of database owners—such as legal publishers and telephone companies—and database users—such as financial and media analysts and Internet services. The increased importance and value of electronic databases and the increased clout of the database industry may put pressure on Congress to enact database protection. In addition, the European Union's 1996 database directive contains a reciprocity clause, which means that database producers in the United States will not get protection under the EU database law unless Congress enacts protection similar to the EU directive.

Works out of Print

Courts have viewed works out of print in two diametrically opposed approaches. One court has held that the owner of a work that is out of print would have but one source of income from that work, and that would be those copying that work. For that reason the court found that copying works that are out of print would be a violation of copyright. Another court stated: "If the work is 'out of print' and unavailable for purchase through normal channels, the user may have more justification for reproducing it than in the ordinary case."[18]

Parody Is Allowed

One of the beloved domains of teens is parody. They love it! It reaches them, it speaks a language they innately grasp, and they in return speak the language of parody. Teens still see the world in black and white and apply this concept to an adult world that too often sees gray. They take this gray and repackage it with all its hypocrisies into satire and parody. This is why it is so important to understand the law of parody and to teach them what the limits of parody are while not taking this important form of expression away from them and to even encourage it. Some of the antismoking Web sites welcome teen input and encourage the use of their parodies of the tobacco industry.

Copyright law Section 107 provides that the fair use of a copyrighted work for purposes such as criticism or comment does not constitute an infringement. Further, trademarks can also be parodied. However, there is no hard-and-fast rule as to what is comment or parody; that is decided on a case-by-case analysis. (See chapter 2 for analysis of *The Wind Done Gone*, a parody of *Gone with the Wind*).

The U.S. Supreme Court decision in 1994 regarding 2 Live Crew's parody of Roy Orbison's song "Pretty Woman"[19] established parody as an acceptable freedom of expression by defining parody and permitting it the status of a defense against copyright infringement claims. In the case of trademarks, the law provides some statutory fair-use protection. The courts have added three categories for fair-use protection: (1) nominative (discussed above), (2) comparative advertising, and (3) parody.

The nominative use of trademarks and copyrighted material is allowed. A nominative use occurs when a reference is made to the trademarked or copyrighted material; for example, a student Web site might refer to Pepsi. However, if Pepsi were used as an identifier of the student Web site, this would not be allowed. The student could claim Pepsi as his drink of choice but could not call his Web site the Official Pepsi Web Site. However, Coca-Cola could refer to Pepsi in a comparative advertising campaign noting that four out of five people tested preferred Coke to Pepsi. *Saturday Night Live* could spoof both Pepsi and Coke in any way they saw fit.

The courts have held that parody requires ridicule or criticism of the prior work, but merely copying the work's best known elements "to get attention or maybe even to avoid the drudgery of working up something fresh" is not parody.[20] When an author copied Dr. Seuss' *Cat in the Hat* to reflect the murders associated with O.J. Simpson, the court found parody did not exist.

A contrary finding appeared in the U.S. Supreme Court's ruling pertaining to the film, *Naked Gun 33⅓: The Final Insult*. In order to promote the film, Leslie Nielsen's face was imposed over a picture similar to one on the cover of *Vanity Fair* with the caption, "Due This March." Previously, Annie Liebowitz had photographed a nude Demi Moore, eight months pregnant, in black and white with shadowy lighting for the actual magazine cover. The court found a "smirking, guilty looking" Mr. Nielsen to be a legitimate parody and the promotion to be a "joinder of reference and ridicule." The court held that the movie promotion "relies for its comic effect on the contrast between the original—a serious portrayal of a beautiful woman taking great pride in the majesty of her pregnant body—and the new work—a ridiculous image of a smirking, foolish-looking pregnant man." The *Naked Gun* film "was intentionally linked to the issues of childbearing and pregnancy that are central to the plot of *Naked Gun 33⅓*." The movie plot addresses the issue of a man being pressured by his wife to begin a family. The court found the parody took no more of the work than was necessary, although certainly all but the face of Demi Moore was taken, and clearly Demi Moore joined in the fun when the face of her then husband Bruce Willis appeared superimposed on her body.

The court found the promotion to be a transformative work of the original Annie Liebowitz photograph and held that the more transformative the parodying work is, "the less will be the significance of other factors, like commercialism, that may weigh against a finding of fair use." It found that as a transformative work it was not likely to become a market substitute for the original Liebowitz photograph or cause any other "cognizable" market harm.

The two courts carefully weighed the transformative purpose of the parodying work and evaluated the quality and quantity of the amount taken. Just as the U.S. Supreme Court made its evaluation of the *Naked Gun* case, school librarians, who are neither attorneys, nor judges, may be called upon to make a similar analysis. Some of the successful illustrations of parody that follow will be helpful in making those determinations.

Doctors Ought to Care, an effective group against the use of tobacco and alcohol, successfully uses parody. They have sponsored the Emphysema Slims Tennis Tournament featuring Martina Nosmokanova.

Miller Brewing Co. filed suit against Doctors Ought to Care alleging that DOC's parodies of the "Miller Lite" trademark and the "We're having a party" slogan that Miller had used in advertisements for Miller-sponsored parties and concerts constituted infringement. DOC's parodies appeared on T-shirts sold by DOC to raise money for the Texas Special Olympics. The T-shirts were sold outside the Houston Astrodome, where the first of the Miller parties and concerts took place. One side of the shirts referred to "Killer Lite" beer and added the statement, "We're pushing a drug." The other side of the shirts parodied the "We're having a party" slogan with the words "We're grabbing a potty" and depicted a person vomiting into a toilet.

The shirts also bore a list of alcohol-related diseases. Miller alleged trademark infringement as well as a variety of other legal theories, including trademark dilution, unfair competition, copyright infringement, and interference with contractual relations. The case was settled, however, with neither party conceding that the other's position was valid.

Adbusters Magazine[21] has produced several Joe Camel parodies showing Joe Camel[22] on chemotherapy after he gets lung cancer. He looks extremely "uncool." He is depicted pale and wan, in his coffin and in a hospital gown. The classic image of the Marlboro County ad with the Marlboro Man on his horse is shown minus the Marlboro Man; only the horse is grazing in a cemetery. One Adbusters satire of the short-lived Dakota cigarette brand put it: "Dakota. Dacough. Dacancer. Dacoffin." Badvertising.org[23] (accessed January 31, 2003) modifies existing commercials, including tobacco ads, to make them more truthful. The "Joy of Smoking Gallery" urges the viewers to "Use these images in your research papers, on report covers, or as greeting cards to your friends. Check out our BADvertising Gear to see how you can bring these provocative images to your school or community." Here Joe Camel is depicted as the grim reaper. Young people are major contributors to these sites.

As a part of the tobacco litigation settlement against the tobacco industry a $1.5 billion antismoking campaign is being financed with proceeds from the industry's 1998 settlement with the states over claims for reimbursement for treating sick smokers. The state settlement agreement specified that the fund wouldn't be used for personal attacks on an individual or company. Although tobacco settlement funds cannot be used to attack specific tobacco companies, private funds may be used for that purpose.

Two commercials created with these funds have been withdrawn. One showed young people stacking body bags on the sidewalk outside a tobacco company building, and the other showed teens equipped with a lie detector trying to get into a tobacco company's offices to quiz sales executives about whether smoking was addictive. These commercials may have exceeded the contractual agreement between the states and the tobacco industry, but they did not exceed the right to parody the tobacco industry.

California Health Department's antismoking media campaign uses parody because it believes direct satires of the tobacco industry are a way to persuade children that smoking isn't as rebellious as they may think. When children understand they're being manipulated by the industry, the desirability of smoking as an act of rebellion is removed. One California commercial shows a smoky boardroom full of tobacco executives, one of whom announces: "Gentlemen, gentlemen, the tobacco industry has a very serious multibillion-dollar problem—[e]very day 2,000 Americans stop smoking and another 1,100 also quit. Actually, technically, they die. That means this business needs 3,000 fresh volunteers every day. So forget about all that heart disease, cancer, emphysema, and stroke stuff. We're not in this business for our health." Another ad simply shows footage of tobacco industry executives testifying before Congress that they believe tobacco is not addictive. The words "under oath" flash on the screen during the testimony, and as the ad closes the announcer intones: "Now the tobacco industry is trying to tell us that second-hand smoke isn't dangerous."

The most effective antismoking commercials were created by students. One featured teenagers in a yellow Volkswagen Beetle driving to the gates of Philip Morris, looking for the Marlboro Man, who had died of lung cancer. These commercials were so effective that they motivated the tobacco industry to include in the settlement provision the clause that specified that the fund wouldn't be used for personal attacks on an individual or company. These parody commercials created by students were the commercials the tobacco industry most feared.

It is important to understand the legal authority that does in fact allow parody. The impact of parody can be more effective than the slickest negative marketing campaigns, although many marketers have in recent years turned to parody. Successful parody is enjoyed by virtually everyone who is not the object of the parody. It has made *Saturday Night Live* a persistent success. Parody is an important defense mechanism to which all teens relate. Therefore, parody should not be removed from the student's rich perspective but should be retained as a legitimate and effective form of creativity, expression, and communication.

An excellent resource for educating students on the manipulation of the media can be found at the New Mexico Media Literacy Program (NMMLP), which addresses the need to educate future citizens in skills that will allow them to better analyze, access, and produce media. Your library can obtain state-of-the-art multimedia, CD-ROMs, and video to illustrate major skills and issues in media literacy. This information is available both in English and Spanish. The American Academy of Pediatrics, the National Center for Substance Abuse Prevention, and many professional, state, and private organizations support the NMMLP (http://www.nmmlp.org).

WHAT CAN WE COPY PURSUANT TO THE GUIDELINES?

Books and Periodicals

Fair use of copyrightable books and periodicals allows material to be used for educational purposes if it meets the following criteria:

1. Brevity;

2. Spontaneity;

3. Does this use lessen the market for the work?

4. What is the character of the work: a song, lyrics, workbook, or a passage from a book?

The acronym is BSMC—Be Sure to Monitor Copyright—Brevity—Spontaneity—Market—Character.

Brevity requires the educator to be brief in the use of copyrighted material. The specific amounts are listed below.

Spontaneity occurs when the copying is at the instance and inspiration of the individual teacher. That is, the inspiration and decision to use the work and the moment of its use for maximum teaching effectiveness are so close in time that it would be unreasonable to expect a timely reply to a request for permission.

Market Effect pertains to the copying of the material for only one course in the school in which the copies are made. Nine instances of multiple copying for one course during one class term is guideline approved.

Character defines the nature of the work and guides the user in the application of the guideline-approved quantity for copying.

WHAT IS THE MATERIAL?

How do you analyze your proposed material in light of these four rules? Examine the medium. Do you want to copy one lesson from a workbook for your class? The sole purpose of the workbook is to provide workbook lessons. Even using one lesson from a workbook will diminish the market value of the whole workbook. If one workbook has been purchased and then copied for all of the students, the workbook's market has been seriously harmed.

Don't Copy Workbooks!

Don't Do It. This is the only rule to remember. But it is by far the most difficult concept experienced elementary school faculty face. Even when they understand they cannot copy the entire workbook, they still want to know how much is acceptable to copy. Most school districts have a policy on copying from workbooks. In some school districts the policy is no copying at all and in others 10 percent is permitted.

The law is found in shades of gray where workbooks are concerned: reproducing a "portion" of a workbook could arguably be a fair use, and it could arguably be an infringement upon a copyright if it is done routinely. In a significant Supreme Court case, *The Nation Magazine* obtained without permission the unpublished manuscript of *A Time to Heal: The Autobiography of Gerald R. Ford*. Working directly from the purloined manuscript, an editor of *The Nation* produced a short piece titled "The Ford Memoirs—Behind the Nixon Pardon." The piece was timed to "scoop" an article scheduled shortly to appear in *Time* magazine. *Time* had agreed to purchase the exclusive right to print prepublication excerpts from the copyright holders, Harper & Row Publishers and Reader's Digest Association. As a result of *The Nation* article,

Time canceled its agreement. Justice Sandra Day O'Connor, delivering the opinion of the Supreme Court in *Harper & Row v. Nation Enterprises*, 471 U.S. 539 (1985) noted the following:

[T]he question of economic harm is properly considered under the fourth statutory factor—the effect on the value of or market for the copyrighted work, 17 U.S.C. § 107(4). . .

The Effect on the Market. The Court correctly notes that the effect on the market "*is undoubtedly the single most important element of fair use.*" *Ante* at 566, citing 3 Nimmer § 13.05[A], at 13–76, and the Court properly focuses on whether *The Nation*'s use adversely affected Harper & Row's serialization potential and not merely the market for sales of the Ford work itself. *Ante* at 566–567.

For purposes of fair use analysis, the Court holds, it is sufficient that the *entire article* containing the quotes eroded the serialization market potential of Mr. Ford's work. *Ante* at 567. On the basis of *Time*'s cancellation of its serialization agreement, the Court finds that "[r]arely will a case of copyright infringement present such clear-cut evidence of actual damage." *Ibid.* In essence, the Court finds that, by using some quotes in a story about the Nixon pardon, *The Nation* "competed for a share of the market of prepublication excerpts" *ante* at 568, because *Time* planned to excerpt from the chapters about the pardon.

The Nation's publication indisputably precipitated *Time*'s eventual cancellation. But that does not mean that *The Nation*'s use of the 300 quoted words caused this injury to Harper & Row. Wholly apart from these quoted words, *The Nation* published significant information and ideas from the Ford manuscript. If it was this publication of information, and not the publication of the few quotations, that caused *Time* to abrogate its serialization agreement, then whatever the negative effect on the serialization market, that effect was the product of wholly legitimate activity (emphasis added).

If the effect of the use of the workbook impacts the potential market of the workbook, then by Sandra Day O'Connor's analysis any copying is an infringement upon copyright. However, it should be noted that there were three dissents on the Supreme Court from the majority opinion.

Making a work sheet for the class from a math workbook instead of buying a workbook for each student would probably have a negative effect on profits for the author of the workbook. By the *Harper & Row* opinion, this would not likely be considered a fair use of a copyrighted material.

A use that is clearly a fair use based on three of the four factors may be found to be a fair use even if its use could have a somewhat negative effect on the market. A teacher who creates a work sheet with the workbook as inspiration violates no law. Then there is the question of making a teacher's own work sheet but using the graphics of the workbook. In this instance the guidelines should prevail and the taking of images could be governed solely by the Classroom Guidelines, which permit: "If images are used no more than 10% or 16 images from one work may be used."

Workbooks as Consumables

There is yet another wrinkle in the workbook dilemma. It is a technical argument, but then the law is a technical business. In general, fair use does not apply to "consumable" materials. A consumable is something that is consumed. Texts are used again and again, and are not consumables. Students use their workbooks or they "use them up" by writing in the workbook. The nature of the publication is, therefore, arguably a consumable. This is a weak argument, untested in the courts, and should be reviewed by the school district's attorney before any faculty member relies upon it for the purpose of routinely copying workbooks for students' use. It is included here because it is occasionally mentioned by faculty members, and the librarian should be prepared to address this position with the school's policy based on a legal decision made by the school administration.

The standard "four factors"—brevity, spontaneity, market, and character—should be the guide applied to an educational workbook, noting that the courts have generally found the third and fourth factors to be the most significant factors in a copyright infringement evaluation and they are:

3. the amount and substantiality of the portion used in relation to the copyrighted work as a whole; and

4. the effect of the use upon the potential market for or value of the copyrighted work.

Generally, it is stated that there is no bright line that distinguishes fair use from unfair use of copyrighted material. However, with workbooks, the line is brighter than in almost any other educational fair use territory. It blinks in neon red:

"NO. Don't Do It . . . DO NOT COPY WORKBOOKS!"

If a teacher intends to routinely teach from a workbook and provide portions of that workbook to the students, then one workbook for each student should be purchased. This position most closely follows the law of copyright.

QUANTITY OF WORK GUIDELINES

"The Guidelines Conforming to Fair Use for Educational Purposes Agreement on Guidelines for Classroom Copying" was authored by representatives of the educational community and publishers in 1976 and made part of the Congressional Record.[24] These guidelines delineate specific quantities that may be copied and apply to both the student and the teacher on a per year basis for K–12 and a per term basis for post–K–12 basis. Following these guidelines generally demonstrates that a good faith effort has been made to comply with the copyright law.

Single Copies

For teaching, including preparation, and for scholarly research, a faculty member may make, or have made, a single copy of:

a. a chapter from a book;

b. an article from a journal, periodical, or newspaper;

c. a short story, essay, or poem;

d. a diagram or picture in any of those works.

Multiple Copies

For one-time distribution in class to students, a teacher may make, or have made, multiple copies if he or she:

a. makes no more than one for each student;

b. includes the notice of copyright (writes it on the first sheet or includes copies of the page on which it appears); and

c. makes no charge to the student beyond the actual cost of the photocopying.

The right to make multiple copies is strengthened if the copying will not have a significant effect upon the potential market for the work.

Quantity and Types of Material

Library May Place Material on Reserve

At the request of a faculty member, a library may place on reserve excerpts furnished by a faculty member from copyrighted works in its collection in accordance with guidelines similar to those governing formal classroom distribution discussed above. When the excerpts are removed from the reserve shelf, such material is to be returned to the faculty member. The American Library Association (ALA) developed a model policy concerning college and university photocopying for classroom, research, and library reserve use in 1982. However, this policy has not been endorsed, or at least considered currently recognized, by the ALA because it has not recently been reviewed. These guidelines serve simply as models of good practices and are helpful in developing reserve practices for educational institutions. They are reprinted here with the permission of the American Library Association.

a. If the request calls for only one copy to be placed on reserve, the library may photocopy an entire article, or an entire chapter from a book, or an entire poem. However, requests for multiple copies on reserve should meet the following guidelines.

(1) The amount of materials should be reasonable in relation to the total amount of material assigned for one term of a course taking into account the nature of the course, its subject matter, and level;

(2) The number of copies should be reasonable in light of the number of students enrolled, the difficultly and timing of assignments, and the number of other courses that may assign the same material;

(3) The material should contain a notice of copyright;

(4) The effect of photocopying the material should not be detrimental to the market for the work.

b. A reasonable number of copies will in most instances be less than six, but factors such as the length or difficulty of the assignment, the number of enrolled students and the length of time allowed for completion of the assignment may permit more in unusual circumstances. If there is doubt as to whether a particular instance of photocopying is fair use in the reserve reading room, the permission of the publisher should be sought.

Television, Video, Film

Both the student and the teacher may use 10 percent of the entire work or three minutes, whichever is less.

Text and Prose

The student or the teacher may use 10 percent of the entire work or 1,000 words, of a novel, story, play or long poem, whichever is less.

Short Poem

When selecting poems from an anthology, five poems from different poets may be used or three poems by one poet. If the poem is obtained from the public domain and there is no copyright on the poem or the work, the student and the teacher are free to use the work in its entirety.

Music, Lyrics, and Music Video

A student or teacher may use up to 10 percent but not more than 30 seconds from a single work.

Images

If images are used no more than 10% or 16 images from one work may be used.

Numerical Data Sets, Computer Databases, and Spreadsheets

Up to 10% or 2,500 fields or cells, whichever is less, may be used from a copyrighted database.

STUDENT'S WORK

It is essential to respect the work of students! Art, poetry, school papers, diaries, memos, personal correspondence—are all protected by copyright. This protection is automatic from the moment a student creates something, whether on paper or electronically. Copyright applies to both published and unpublished works.

Often teachers will treat a students' work as if they had complete control over it. THEY DO NOT. Examples of exemplary work will be saved for years by the teacher and used as demonstrations for future classes. This is a violation of copyright guidelines and laws as they currently exist, and an invasion of the student's right to privacy.

A student's permission must be obtained to display that work outside the class in which the student is enrolled and in some cases to display the work in the class in which the student is enrolled. For example, if the student has not been advised prior to the delivery of the assignment that it will be shared with the public (e.g., posted for Open House) it cannot be posted without the student's permission. This could be an invasion of privacy. For example, in sharing the "family tree" of one student it could be revealed that parents or grandparents were unmarried. Be sensitive; be careful; it's the law.

This is not to be confused with the recent Supreme Court opinion[25] that did believe the privacy protections of the Family Educational Rights and Privacy Act were violated in allowing a student to grade the paper of another or one student to hear the grade of another when called out for the teacher as a result of grading. The Supreme Court stated,

[We do] not think FERPA prohibits such educational techniques. Moreover, saying that students are acting for the teacher in grading an assignment is different from saying they are acting for an educational institution in maintaining it. Other FERPA sections—e.g., §1232g(b)(4)(A), which requires educational institutions to maintain a record of access kept with the student's education records—support this Court's interpretation. The instant holding is limited to the narrow point that, assuming a teacher's grade book is an education record, grades on students' papers are not covered by the Act at least until the teacher has recorded them.

Some disclosure of certain less-private information is also permitted. Specifically, schools may release "directory information" although schools must give parents the opportunity to object to release of some or all directory information about their child. Second, schools are able to continue practices of peer grading, student group work, and display of student work if they identify legitimate educational interests in such activities.[26]

A professor who puts online students' work from previous years could be in violation of the copyright law. Further, the professor violated the student's right to privacy if the student's work was published with his or her name.

COPYING FOR WHICH PERMISSION SHOULD BE OBTAINED

Repetitive Copying

Photocopying on a repetitive basis will not be considered a fair use for educational purposes. If a faculty member copies the same materials each year for a class, consideration should be given to purchasing those materials for the class. Otherwise, permission must be obtained from the copyright owner to carry over copies made for library reserve from one semester to another.

Copying for Profit

Fair use for educational purposes extends only to nonprofit copying. Faculty may not charge students more than the actual cost of photocopying, and should not make copies for students who are not in their own classes, without obtaining permission.

Creation of Anthologies of Texts

Creation of collective work or anthology by photocopying a number of copyrighted articles and excerpts to be purchased and used together as the basic text for a course will in most instances require the permission of the copyright owners. Such photocopying is more likely to be considered as a substitute for the purchase of a book and thus is less likely to be deemed fair use.

Obtaining Permission for the Use of Copyrighted Materials

When a use of photocopied material requires permission, complete and accurate information should be sent to the copyright owner. The American Association of Publishers suggests that the following information be included in a permission request letter in order to expedite the process: title, author and/or editor, and edition of materials to be duplicated; the exact material to be used, giving amount, page numbers, chapters and, if possible, a photocopy of the material; number of copies to be made; use to be made of duplicated materials; form of distribution (classroom, newsletter, etc.); whether the material is to be sold; and type of reprint (ditto, photography, offset, typeset).

When providing guidelines to students and faculty requesting permission, advise them to include the following information in their request:

1. The request should be sent, together with a self-addressed return envelope, to the permissions department of the publisher in question. If the address of the publisher does not appear at the front of the materials, it may be readily obtained from the library.

2. The process of granting permission requires time for the publisher to check the status of the copyright and to evaluate the nature of the request. It is advisable, therefore, to allow enough lead time to obtain permission before the materials are needed.

3. The Copyright Clearance Center also has the right to grant permission and collect fees for photocopying rights for certain publications. Libraries may copy from any journal that is registered with the CCC. They must report any copying beyond fair use to the CCC and pay the set fee.

MULTIMEDIA

Employing multimedia in the classroom improves the quality of instruction offered while acknowledging and accepting of students' various learning styles. Computers make digital materials available to students and serve as a research tool for locating Internet resources. These nontraditional and nonprint materials, when combined with the use of multimedia software, allow an instructor to create a seamless educational program that uses portions of copyrighted text, photographs and other graphic works, music, and film clips to create a stimulating educational experience, which appeals to the various learning styles (i.e., aural, visual, and tactile) of the students.[27]

Multimedia Guidelines

A multimedia work is an assemblage of text, sound, visual images, and other materials "cut and pasted" in digital form onto a single disk or other storage unit. The Multimedia Guidelines are applicable only to nonprofit educational and curriculum-based uses at institutions that have education as a primary mission.

Clips of text are limited to the lesser of either one thousand words or 10 percent of the original work. Sound clips are limited to the lesser of either thirty seconds or 10 percent. A multimedia project may utilize only thirty seconds of a lengthy symphony or only eighteen seconds of a three-minute popular song. The project may be retained and used for only two years, although it may be retained in the individual's portfolio for employment purposes.

These guidelines are a part of CONFU and were developed in conjunction with Consortium of College and University Media Centers (CCUMC) and are a product of negotiation and collaboration between representatives from industries in the fields of print publication, music, video, and motion pictures. They are an attempt to balance the interests of Consortium of College and University Media Centers (CCUMC). To a great extent the CCUMC follows the model of the Classroom Guidelines.

Multimedia Work—Students and Faculty

Student projects and teacher presentations may contain multimedia work and not be in violation of the copyright laws or guidelines if specific steps are taken with regard to that copyrighted material. Multimedia work is governed by CONFU Guidelines, which are similar to the Educational Fair Use Guidelines.

Unpublished Works

Unpublished works may be subject to fair use. For example, portions of a teacher's video presentation may be fairly used by a student. Unpublished works may be subject to more stringent protection, the theory being that the author might still have the opportunity to modify the work. Unpublished work can be registered for copyright protection just as published work.

Copyright Symbol

To copyright your work, the correct form for a copyright notice is "Copyright 200? (year of creation) by Your Name." You may also use the C-in-a-circle symbol instead of the word "Copyright." Copyright notices stopped being mandatory in this country in 1989 when the United States joined the Berne Convention. But using a notice is still a good idea. That way, you put others on notice that you consider a work to be your property—and that nobody should use it without your permission.

Students' Multimedia Work

Students' multimedia work may be used in the class for which they were created. The works may be retained indefinitely by the students in portfolios maintained for job interviews or college applications.

Teacher's Multimedia Work

Teachers may keep the multimedia presentations they create for a class for a period of two years. Should they obtain a release from a student to display his or her work, it should contain a time limit. Student projects and teacher presentations may contain multimedia work and not be in violation of the copyright laws or guidelines if specific steps are taken with regard to that copyrighted material:

The opening screen of the multimedia work and any accompanying printed materials must contain a notice that the work contains copyrighted materials that have been used under the fair-use exemption of the U.S. copyright law. Notice of the use of copyrighted material must be made. In a Power Point presentation notice should be given in the initial slide.

OFF-AIR TAPING

Librarians are typically not involved in off-air taping, however, it is important to understand these guidelines for several reasons. Faculty members often tape television programs for classroom use. However, they may not understand the legal copyright limitations involved in their classroom use.

In 1979, Congress appointed a negotiating committee to define fair use to recording, retention, and use of television broadcast programs for educational purposes. The guidelines reflect the negotiating committee's consensus as to the application of "fair-use" for these purposesand were entered into the Congressional Record on October 14, 1984. Because these are simply guidelines, the law is not automatically violated if the use exceeds the limits of the guidelines. As with all guidelines, use must be evaluated in accordance with the fair use consideration factors provided in Section 107 of the Copyright Act.

Guidelines for Off-Air Taping for Educational Purposes

The guidelines were developed to apply only to off-air recording by nonprofit educational institutions.

A broadcast program (including cable programs) may be recorded off-air and retained by a nonprofit educational institution for a period not to exceed the first forty-five consecutive calendar days after the date of recording.

Off-air recording may be used once by individual teachers in the course of relevant teaching activities, and repeated once only when instructional reinforcement is necessary in classrooms and similar places devoted to instruction within a single building, cluster, or campus, as well as in the homes of students receiving formalized home instruction, during the first ten consecutive school days in the forty-five-calendar-day retention period. "School days" are school session days—not counting weekends, holidays, vacations, examination periods, or other scheduled interruptions—within the forty-five-calendar-day retention period.

Off-air recordings may be made only at the request of and used by individual teachers, and may not be regularly recorded in anticipation of requests. No broadcast program may be recorded off-air more than once at the request of the same teacher, regardless of the number of times the program may be broadcast.

A limited number of copies may be reproduced from each off-air recording to meet the legitimate needs of teachers under these guidelines. Each additional copy shall be subject to all provisions governing the original recording.

After the first ten consecutive school days, off-air recordings may be used up to the end of the forty-five-calendar-day retention period only for teacher evaluation purposes, that is, to determine whether to include the broadcast program in the teaching curriculum. They may not be used in the recording institution for student exhibition or any other nonevaluative purpose without authorization.

Off-air recordings need not be used in their entirety, but the recorded programs may not be altered from their original content. Off-air recordings may not be physically or electronically combined or merged to constitute teaching anthologies or compilations.

All copies of off-air recordings must include the copyright notice on the broadcast program as recorded.

Some broadcasters have more extensive taping rights than are found in the guidelines. The Public Broadcasting System (PBS; http://www.pbs.org) provides extended videotaping rights intended to allow for a free preview of programming to give teachers adequate time to review videotapes, evaluate their appropriateness for classroom use, and either schedule that use or purchase program videotapes. But because these rights are negotiated on an individual basis with program producers and copyright owners, the effective length of the free preview may vary. In some cases, PBS has secured for teachers permission to use off-air recording for the life of the tape (in perpetuity). More commonly, however, the agreement covers a specified time period, sometimes three years but more frequently one year. The time period is usually defined from the date of the broadcast from which the recording was made, although sometimes it is defined from the date of the national, original broadcast on public television. On occasion there may be a fixed expiration date for the rights granted. It is important to review the rights of each individual PBS film.

Educational institutions are expected to establish appropriate control procedures to maintain the integrity of these guidelines.

CONCLUSION

The Classroom Guidelines articulate a negotiated, agreed measure of fair use between interested parties, generally publishers and educators. The guidelines are not the law. The negotiators developed the guidelines on a relatively rigorous schedule and at the behest of members of Congress, who sought to avoid detailed legislation. The guidelines, while not directly related to the law of fair use and the four statutory factors (which are the law), are intended to be a starting point for each institution to determine and implement an appropriate theory of fair use. It is not unreasonable for a librarian to have the authority to make exceptions on a case-by-case basis if the decisions are founded upon an understanding of and respect for the law.

Even though the legislators have given vague legal guidelines concerning fair use, they have left the interpretations to those on the front lines and in the trenches. It can be the librarian who determines what is and is not an educational fair use of a copyrighted work. Reviewing the statute itself and cases interpreting it, as well as speaking with the school district's attorney, is a good start in understanding the educational fair use of a copyrighted material. Educating the faculty and students is an essential element in the fair use for educational purposes of copyrighted material.

NOTES

1. The beginning of fair use under American law is generally traced to *Folsom v. Marsh*, 9 F. Cas. 342 (C.C.D. Mass. 1841) (No. 4901). See, for example, Pierre N. Leval, "Toward a Fair Use Standard," *Harvard Law Review* 103 (1990): 1105–25.

2. Copyright Act of 1976, 107, 90 Stat. at 2546. Since its original enactment in 1976, the fair-use provision has been amended by the Judicial Improvements Act of 1990, Pub. L. No. 101–650, 104 Stat. 5089 (1990), and further amended in 1992 to address the fair use of unpublished works.

3. See Black's Law Dictionary 415 (6th ed. 1991).

4. 758 F. Supp. 1522 (S.D.N.Y. 1991). A Federal District Court in New York ruled that Kinko's Graphic Corporation infringed when it photocopied "course-packs" designated by professors that included book chapters. Kinko's then sold the coursepacks at a profit to students for classroom work. The court found that most of the fair use factors worked against Kinko's in this case, especially given Kinko's profit motive in making the copies. The court found that the Classroom Guidelines did not apply to Kinko's. The court did not rule that coursepacks cannot constitute fair use in other circumstances.

5. The principle that the fourth factor is the most important factor was underscored in a decision from the U.S. Supreme Court. *See Harper & Row, Publishers, Inc. v. Nation Enters.*, 471 U.S. 539, 566 (1985). At least one district court judge has been highly critical of that principle, asserting that the Supreme Court and lower courts actually have not held that the fourth factor is of greater importance, even though they make such a statement in the decisions. See *American Geophysical Union v. Texaco Inc.*, 802 F. Supp. 1, 20–21 (S.D.N.Y. 1992), aff'd on other grounds, 60 F.3d 913 (2d Cir. 1995), cert. dismissed, 516 U.S. 1005 (1995).

6. The reversals of many leading fair-use cases also reflect an incongruity among the various federal courts and evidence a failure of a uniform and cohesive direction in the law with regard to the fair use of copyrighted materials. See, e.g., *Harper & Row, Publishers, Inc. v. Nation Enters.*, 557 F. Supp. 1067 (S.D.N.Y.), aff'd in part, rev'd in part, 723 F.2d 195 (2d Cir. 1983), rev'd, 471 U.S. 539 (1985) (granting damages award, which was reversed by the court of appeals, that was in turn reversed by the Supreme Court); see also *Salinger v. Random House, Inc.*, 650 F. Supp. 413 (S.D.N.Y.), rev'd, 811 F.2d 90 (2d Cir. 1986) (denying plaintiff's motion to enjoin defendant's publication of a biography about the plaintiff; decision reversed by court of appeals based on differing interpretation of fair-use standard).

7. See 17 U.S.C. 107 (stating the first factor). *Princeton Univ. Press v. Michigan Document Servs., Inc.*, 99 F.3d 1381, 1400 (6th Cir. 1996); *Basic Books, Inc. v. Kinko's Graphics Corp.*, 758 F. Supp. 1522, 1532 (S.D.N.Y. 1991).

8. See *Kinko's Graphics Corp.*, 758 F. Supp. at 1532–33 (emphasizing that factual works are given less protection). See *New Era Publications, Int'l v. Carol Publ'g Group*, 904 F.2d 152, 158 (2d Cir. 1990) (holding that use of a small percentage of

a published work is fair use). See also *Michigan Document Servs., Inc.*, 99 F.3d at 1389 (stating that the greater the volume or signficance of the portion copied, the less likely the copy will be considered fair use).

See Kinko's Graphics Corp., 758 F. Supp. at 1534 (finding infringement occurred where "in almost every case, defendant copied at least an entire chapter of a plaintiff's book" for classroom use). See id. at 1533 (noting that out-of-print material may be particularly problematic because fees for copying and use of such material may be the only source of income for such material); infra notes 102–03 and accompanying text (discussing the importance of the fact that the copied materials in the Kinko's case were out of print). But see *Maxtone-Graham v. Burtchaell*, 803 F.2d 1253, 1264 n.8 (2d Cir. 1986) ("If the work is 'out of print' and unavailable for purchase through normal channels, the user may have more justification for reproducing it than in the ordinary case." [citation omitted]).

9. Nimmer on Copyright, Section 1.10(d) and *Sony Corp. v. Universal Studios, Inc.*, 464 U.S. 417, 449–50 (1984).

10. See Harper & Row, Publishers, Inc., 471 U.S. at 568 (noting that "to negate fair use one need only show that if the challenged use 'should become widespread, it would adversely affect the potential market for the copyrighted work'" [citation omitted]); see also Leval, supra note 15, at 1124–25 (asserting that the doctrine of fair use should be negated when impairment to the copyright holder's potential market is substantial).

11. To prove prima facie infringement, the author must have a valid copyright, be in compliance with statutory requirements if any exist, show copying, which can be established by showing that the infringer had access to the work, and show that the two works were substantially similar. See *Narell v. Freeman*, 872 F.2d 907, 910 (9th Cir. 1989).

12. See 17 U.S.C. § 411 (1994 & Supp. IV 1998).

13. See 17 U.S.C. § 504(c) (1994 & Supp. IV 1998).

14. § 504(c)(1).

15. § 504(c)(2).

16. U.S. Copyright Act of 1976, 17 U.S.C. §§101 and 107, et seq. passim.

17. 17 U.S.C. § 107 (1994).

18. *Maxtone-Graham v. Burtchaell*, 803 F.2d 1253, 1264 n.8 (2d Cir. 1986). The court noted that the plaintiff's work was out of print and not likely to appeal to the same readers. This case affirms that quotations in a subsequent work are permissible, sometimes even when they are lengthy. Implicit throughout the case is the fact that the plaintiff was unwilling to allow limited quotations in a book that argued an opposing view of abortion; thus, fair use became the only effective means for the second author to meaningfully build on the scholarly works of others.

19. *Campbell v. Acuff-Rose Music, Inc.*, 114 S.Ct. 1164, 127 L.Ed.2d 500 (1994).

20. *Dr. Seuss*, 1997 U.S. App. LEXIS 5822 at *21, quoting *Campbell* (internal quotation marks omitted).

21. Adbusters.org. This is a nonprofit global network of "artists, activists, writers, pranksters, students, educators and entrepreneurs." Available: http://adbusters.org. (Accessed May 28, 2002).

22. Adbusters.org. Joe Camel Ads. Available: http://adbusters.org/spoofads /tobacco/. (Accessed May 28, 2002.)

23. See, Bonnie Vierthaler, Badadvertising.org. Available: http://www. badvertising.org/gallery.html. (Accessed May 28, 2002.)

24. 3 3 House Report No. 1476, 94th Cong., 2d Sess. 47 (1976). Reprinted in 1976 U.S.C.C.A.N. 5681–88. 3 House Report No. 1476, 94th Cong., 2d Sess. 47 (1976). Reprinted in 1976 U.S.C.C.A.N. at pages 5681–88.

25. *Owasso Independent School District v. Falvo*, 233 F.3d 1203 (10th Cir. 2000). Reversed and remanded on February 21, 2002. No case number assigned at this writing. Available: http://supct.law.cornell.edu/supct/html/00-1073.ZS.html. (Accessed on April 21, 2002.)

26. See 20 U.S.C. 1232g(b)(1)(A) (requiring that "legitimate educational interests" include "the educational interests of the child for whom consent would otherwise be required").

27. See Pierre N. Leval, Commentary, "Toward a Fair Use Standard," *Harvard Law Review* 103 (1990): 1105, 1105–07 (noting the confusion surrounding the Fair Use Doctrine).

REFERENCES

CONFU—The Conference on Fair Use. "Final Report of the United States Patent and Trade Office." Available: http://www.uspto.gov/web/offices/dcom /olia/confu/. (Accessed January 31, 2003.)

Legal Information Institute of Cornell Law School. 17 U.S.C. 107, "Limitations on exclusive rights—Fair use." Available: http://www4.law.cornell.edu/uscode /17/107.html. (Accessed January 31, 2003.)

5

LIBRARY ARCHIVING
AND SECTION 108
OF THE COPYRIGHT ACT

One thing is clear, no one, except speakers on ceremonial occasions, any longer
believes the comforting eighteenth-century myth about the inevitability of
progress.

—Grant Gilmore, *The Ages of
American Law*, 1977

In this chapter the following topics will be covered:

Specific affirmative steps in order to be afforded the Section 108 privileges
Section 108 privileges
Responsibility associated with Section 108 status
Ambiguities of Section 108 privileges and responsibilities

Section 108(h) of Title 17 U.S.C. (Copyright Act) provides an exemption
for librarians and archivists to have access to a limited group of works within
the last twenty years of a work's copyright protection term. Libraries may
digitize works in the last twenty years of copyright if the work is not subject
to normal exploitation. A library may digitize works of any year for preservation or replacement if the works are not in print and the copy is not circulated
but remains in the library. However, use of the exemption requires compliance with various conditions. Without compliance with Section 108(h)
requirements, Section 108 does not protect the activities of a library that is
not a qualifying institution or whose activities are not covered by its limited
scope. Section 108 of the Copyright Act was modified by both the Sonny

Bono Copyright Term Extension Act and by The Digital Millennium Copyright Act (DMCA). It was the DMCA that increased the number of archival copies permitted from one to three.

The rights to copy material that has been copyrighted provided to libraries pursuant to Section 108 of the Copyright Act are greater than those rights provided to educators pursuant to Section 107 of the Copyright Act for the fair use of copyrighted materials. These rights, found in Section 108 of the Copyright Act, are in addition to the "fair use rights" found in Section 107 for educators. Section 108 does not rely on "guidelines." This law provides a determined outcome, under specified circumstances, for libraries and archives when copies are made for the purposes of preservation and inter-library loan, and for immunity of the library from liability for the unsupervised use of on-site reproduction equipment.

In order for 108 to apply the following conditions must be met:

1. The reproduction or distribution is made without any purpose of direct or indirect commercial advantage;

2. The collections of the library or archives are (i) open to the public, or (ii) available not only to researchers affiliated with the library or archives or with the institution of which it is a part, but also to other persons doing research in a specialized field; and

3. The reproduction or distribution of the work includes a notice of copyright that appears on the copy or phonorecord that is reproduced under the provisions of this section, or includes a legend stating that the work may be protected by copyright if no such notice can be found.

The first question that must be asked is: Does your library make its collections or archives available to "other persons (not affiliated with your school or school district) doing research in a specialized field"? Many private schools and high schools with extensive collections do in fact make their collections available to those outside their schools and school districts. If your library does not do so, the second question is: Would it be worthwhile to make your library open in this manner?

Secondly, in order to qualify, all materials upon which the copyright has not expired must reflect notice of copyright on the work. If it is not there automatically, the library should stamp such a notice on the work with a legend that notes that a work may be protected by copyright law.

The benefits of complying with the prerequisites are that it is not deemed to be an infringement of copyright for a library or archives, or any of its employees acting within the scope of their employment, to reproduce more than one copy or phonorecord of a work, except as provided in subsections (b) and (c) of Section 106, or to distribute such copy or phonorecord under the conditions specified by this section. These copies, however, must be made for archival purposes. Archival copies are not circulating copies.

Okay, we have jumped those hurdles. The school library is open to the public for scholarly research (which does not necessarily mean books may be checked out) and we bought a little copyright stamp and we've stamped everything that doesn't move and some things that do. Now are we ready to archive? But what exactly is archiving?

ARCHIVE COPIES

Archive copies, which are not circulating copies, can be made of unpublished materials and published materials. An example of an unpublished material would be a faculty member's multimedia presentation. The faculty member would want to retain an original and one copy, but also they might want to place a copy on reserve in the library If that copy were damaged during use, an archival copy would be important for the library to have in order to continue providing the faculty member's work to the students. In order to copy an unpublished work, a library's purpose must be preservation or security and it must have a copy of the work in its collection. These are all logical, natural instincts for a librarian's sense of survival and self-preservation when sixty students are clamoring to check out the faculty member's assigned multimedia work.

For a published work, an archival copy can be made only if the work is out of print (not out of copyright). The library's purpose for making the archival copy can only be to replace a copy it has, or used to have in its collection, that has been damaged, that is deteriorating, that has been lost or stolen, or whose format has become obsolete.

Title IV of the Digital Millennium Copyright Act, Section 404, amends Section 108 of the copyright law to permit libraries to digitize analog materials for archival purposes without permission. So we can make just one "archival" copy? Section 108 has been expanded to permit libraries to make up to three copies. Although a digital copy can be made for preservation purposes, it cannot be made available off the library premises. It is important to remember that archival copies are not circulating copies.

Although libraries may make replacement copies for works they own, these may not be placed on the Web. However, there is precedent to allow works in their last twenty years of copyright to be placed on a library's Web site if the work meets limitations of not being subject to commercial exploitation (which has generally been interpreted to mean currently in print) and is available at a reasonable price or if notice has been filed with the copyright office of a limitation upon the use of the work in question.

PATRON COPIES MADE BY THE LIBRARY

Section 108 authorizes libraries to provide patrons with copies. For a patron the copy may be a photocopy, an electronic copy, or a copy sent by facsimile machine. In order for the library to make the patron copy without liability for copyright infringement:

- The copy must become the property of the patron;
- The library should have no knowledge that the copy will be used for a purpose other than private study, scholarship or research;
- The library should have both a display and order form titled "Warning of Copyright Violation."

The first requirement is very simple: the copy to be made will belong to the patron. The second requirement means that if the patron indicates openly to the library or its staff that the copy will be used for commercial gain, the library will be deemed to have infringed upon the copyright of the material, should infringement of a copyright be claimed. The library is not required to inquire of the patron their intended use or demand that the patron acknowledge only legal use. The library should deny requests for uses that it believes would violate the law should that potential use be made known to the library.

The third requirement refers to a warning sign that should be posted near all library copy machines,[1] printers, and possibly at the computer stations that indicates the following:

Notice: Warning Concerning Copyright Restrictions:

The copyright law of the United States (Title 17, United States Code) governs the making of photocopies or other reproductions of copyrighted material.

Under certain conditions specified in the law, libraries and archives are authorized to furnish a photocopy or other reproduction. One of these specified conditions is that the photocopy or reproduction is not to be "used for any purpose other than private study, scholarship, or research." If a user makes a request for, or later uses, a photocopy or reproduction for purposes in excess of "fair use," that user may be liable for copyright infringement.

This institution reserves the right to refuse to accept a copying order if, in its judgment, fulfillment of the order would involve violation of copyright law.

For fax requests of other requests not made in person, a copy of the "Copyright Warning" should accompany the transfer of the actual copyright document.

A different warning is required for the lending of computer software:[2]

Notice: Warning Concerning Copyright Restrictions:

The copyright law of the United States (Title 17, United States Code) governs the making of photocopies or other reproductions of copyrighted material.

Under certain conditions specified in the law, nonprofit libraries are authorized to lend, lease, or rent copies of computer programs to patrons on a nonprofit basis and for nonprofit purposes. Any person who makes an unauthorized copy or adaptation of the computer program or redistributes the loan copy, or publicly performs or displays the computer program, except as permitted by Title 17 of the United States Code, may be liable for copyright infringement. This institution reserves the right to refuse to fulfill a loan request if, in its judgment, fulfillment of the request would lead to violation of the copyright law.

PATRON COPIES MADE BY THE PATRON

Section 108(f)(1) relieves the library of responsibility for unsupervised patron use of copying equipment located in the library so long as the library displays the notice that making copies may be subject to copyright law. This should be displayed both at the photocopying area and at the computer printing area. Some libraries display this notice at all computer terminals because of downloads to floppy disks.

COPY THE NEWS?

Libraries may copy and retain in their collection audiovisual news programs pursuant to Section 108(f) (3). These are not simply archival copies but are allowed to become part of the circulation of the library. This allows not only local news but also regional and national network newscasts to be copied and retained. Interviews concerning current events can be retained. This does not include news-magazines and documentaries.

LICENSE AGREEMENTS THAT CONFLICT WITH SECTION 108

It is fundamental that parties can enter into any legal contract they so desire. Chapter 11, "License Agreements in the Library," points out that often companies and libraries agree to restrictions for the use of the licensed material that are more restrictive than Fair Use (Section 107) or Section 108 would allow.

Section 108 is not without ambiguity. The gray area occurs when libraries negotiate with vendors, typically for databases. It is common for the license agreement to place the obligation on the library to prevent patrons from copying images. Generally, license agreements require that the library meet the restriction on copying images by posting a notice that copying of images from the database is prohibited. This notice typically appears on an opening page to the database. Notice may also be posted in the computer areas.

Although the Copyright Act does allow archival copies, this statutory provision can be overridden by a contracted license agreement between the parties. Vendors can, with their license agreement, circumvent Section 108 by prohibiting the library's creation of an archival or reserve copy of the database.

Are these restrictions binding and can they in fact eliminate the libraries' and the patrons' fair-use rights and Section 108 rights? Technically, and the law is a technical business, the patron is not a party to the contract. The patron did not enter into any agreements with the vendor. The patron has a privilege pursuant to Sections 107 and 108 of the copyright law. Does the library have the right to contract away those statutory rights?

These issues have not yet been addressed in the context of educational fair use and library copying in a not-for-profit environment. However, it is important to note the distinction between a negotiated contract and a non-negotiated contract.

The general rule is that a negotiated contract is not preempted by federal copyright law. This means a library can negotiate away its federal copyright privileges while contracting with a vendor. The preemption of copyright law over contract terms is not so clear when it comes to a non-negotiated contract, such as a shrink wrap or "click-on" license to which a user has "agreed" to the terms by opening and using the product or clicking "OK." In cases involving terms in mass-market licenses that attempted to vary the provisions of the Copyright Act, some courts refused to enforce the contract, whereas other courts did enforce the contract.

INTERLIBRARY LOAN AND SECTION 108

Many libraries participate in interlibrary loan (ILL) agreements. Section 108 covers these agreements. A library has responsibilities as a requester and as a lender under interlibrary loan activities. In order to request a copy of a book a library must comply with Sections 108(e) and (g), which require the requesting library to take the following actions before a book is requested:

- Determine that a copy cannot be obtained at a fair price;
- The copy must become the property of the patron;
- The library should have no notice that the copy will be used for a purpose other than private study, scholarship, or research;
- The library should have both a display and order form "Warning of Copyright."
- The library must not be aware or have substantial reason to believe that it is engaging in related or concerted reproduction or distribution of multiple copies of the same material;
- The library must make its request with a representation that it has complied with copyright law and this is generally included in the standard form of request the library uses.

LENDING A COPY OF A BOOK THROUGH INTERLIBRARY LOAN

The lending library in an interlibrary loan transaction is not the library with the responsibility for compliance with copyright law; that responsibility belongs to the borrowing library. However, it is standard practice for the lending library to require a statement of compliance with copyright law from the requesting library.

The supplying library, in requesting this assurance, is attempting to protect itself from the potential resulting acts of copyright infringement, which may occur on the receiving end of the loan. Section 108(g) allows libraries to copy in accordance with the provisions of Section 108 so long as the library has no "awareness" or "substantial reason to believe" that it might be engaging in related or concerted reproduction or distribution of multiple copies of the same material.

Section 108 only applies if the library or archive offers the reproduction service without commercial advantage and is either open to the public or to nonaffiliated researchers. In the past, libraries have had to stamp all materials reproduced for patrons via ILL or other services with the ALA notice stating, "Notice this work may be protected by copyright."

108(a)(3) indicates libraries are now required to include the actual notice of copyright that appears in the front matter or label of the work along with the requested portion. Reproduction of the notice can be by any means, but often it will mean copying the title or verso page of a journal. This can be via photocopying or even handwriting the information onto the copy. In cases where the work does not include a copyright notice, the library should continue to use the ALA phrase.

SHOULD YOUR LIBRARY BECOME A SECTION 108 LIBRARY?

Here again, that term that guides the lives of all people, "balance," is applied. Are the benefits important to your library? You must balance the benefits to be gained by complying with the Section 108 requirements with the obligations placed upon a library to be eligible for the benefits. It is not likely that fourth graders will be making copies for commercial gain. However, high school students are a different matter.

Middle school libraries might consider Section 108 protection. Some high school libraries are supporting complex research already. Many bright and ambitious students are engaging in study and publication on a level with professionals and interlibrary loan supports their research. They require access to both extensive databases and print journals. Adopting Section 108 would be an aid to these serious and diligent students who often need inter-library loan materials and the right to copy materials for their work.

An example of a high school student who required extensive interlibrary loan facilities was Patrick Lashford as he set up Lashford.com, his own Web-serving company. Although he initiated the company in middle school, he has accessed many business journals and business models through his school library and through interlibrary loan.

Adopting Section 108 would be an aid to these serious and diligent students who often need interlibrary loan materials and the right to copy materials for their work.

Rarely will a stand-alone elementary school library consider eligibility for 108 protections. It is doubtful that outside researchers would desire to use this library or that the school's administration would allow such a use. This consideration in the K–12 environment is principally for large schools, generally private institutions, with rare-book collections and unique artifacts. In rural areas and in urban areas where the libraries are extensive, high school libraries may find themselves a candidate for this designation.

AMBIGUITIES IN SECTION 108 PRIVILEGES AND RESPONSIBILITIES

Section 108, as a result of the Sonny Bono Copyright Term Extension Act, now contains a limited exemption for libraries and archives to enable them to reproduce, distribute, display, and perform certain works in the final twenty years of their extended terms for research and preservation purposes.[3] Only published works are covered under this section and then they may be archived when the works are not subject to "normal commercial exploitation."

"Normal commercial exploitation" occurs when a copy cannot "be obtained at a reasonable price." However, defining that a work cannot be obtained can be a difficult matter. If a copy is available at a used-book store for a reasonable sum—even if it is available only in an obsolete format it can be "obtained at a reasonable price." Certainly an extensive Internet search of used-book stores' inventories is a simple matter and would be evidence of a good faith effort of compliance.

Notice can be filed with the Copyright Office with the copyright owner advising that the work is available. In December 1998, the Copyright Office issued interim regulations and requested comments on how a copyright owner or its agent may provide notice to libraries and archives that a published work in the final twenty years of its extended term of copyright is subject to normal commercial exploitation or that a copy can be obtained at a reasonable price. However, the Copyright Office has not, more than three years after issuing its notice, acted upon these comments or issued final rules.

Section 108(h) creates areas of legal gray in its conditions for archiving copyrighted works in the last twenty years of their copyright.

CONCLUSION

After reviewing "fair use" pursuant to Section 107 of the DMCA, any activity that can be undertaken without personal or school liability appears to be a gift. Section 108 provides specific immunity to a library. Typically only a library that serves a high school or a library that is a joint high school/middle school library would be an appropriate facility for adopting Section 108 privileges, but it is an important consideration for all librarians.

NOTES

1. *Federal Register,* on November 16, 1977, published the form that the warning signs to be posted in libraries must take. These must be posted near all library copy machines.

2. 17 U.S.C. §108(h).

3. 17 U.S.C. §108(n) includes nonprofit educational institutions.

6

---·•◦•·---

TRACING COPYRIGHT

"Okay, great, we gotcha on that one. We do not copyright things that have a copyright. That's easy enough. So what's got a copyright and what can we copy?" These are not just questions that students are willing to ask—they are, more significantly, questions that faculty are thinking but are often embarrassed to ask.

To answer the question, What has a copyright? you need to trace a copyright. This is not an easy task, but it is one that you must undertake to teach both students and faculty. In the olden days copyright symbols were placed on all works that had a copyright. That is no longer the case.

Step number one in tracing a copyright: Assume neither the faculty nor the students know how to trace a copyright. Step number two: Maintain good relations with the faculty. Do not insult their dignity. Never opine aloud that they may not know how to trace a copyright. It is much more tactful to approach the situation from the perspective of one who serves to refresh their collective faculty memories. Teachers have one another; they share commonalities that librarians do not always share. Often librarians are alone in their professional endeavors within their schools. Librarians must be the ones to tell the faculty, no. "No" comes in many forms and fashions where the faculty is concerned. The more detailed your guidelines and policies to the faculty are, and the more extensive your education of the faculty of library policies and guidelines, the less often you will have to say no.

In a small school more issues can be resolved on a case-by-case basis. The larger the faculty, the more rules and policies you will need. If you have a sign-up chart for classes to visit the library, the librarian does not have to be the one to say "No, this day is taken." The chart speaks for you. If the librarian has a policy on sharing holiday resources, the librarian does not have to call one teacher who has subjugated all the Thanksgiving resources under her control so that others may use them also. The policy that permits any teacher to access any materials when needed, whether they are located in the library or in another teacher's room, will ultimately create less conflict. Education of the faculty and detailed policies and guidelines are good business, good customer service so to speak.

Librarians are media research teachers of not only the students but of the faculty. Teach the faculty and you will teach the students. Reach the faculty and you will reach the students. Library Web sites are one very effective method of reaching both the faculty and the students. The tracing of a copyright is principally for the faculty and college-bound students, who should not be introduced to it until their junior or senior years.

AREAS OF DANGER IN TRACING

Jeopardy Category Number One—Things That Must Be Done in the Library

What is one of the first lessons a librarian teaches in student research? Use your time constructively. Use your time in the library to do what cannot be done elsewhere. Tracing a copyright can be as simple as opening the first page of the book and looking at the date of the most recent copyright. If you prepare a chart explaining copyright dates it can be given to each student and placed on the library Web site. If the resource to be traced is clearly copyrighted pursuant to the chart, the job is done. However, should it fall into one of the gray areas, online research will be necessary. This can be pursued outside the library if the student has Internet access elsewhere. However, for the first several searches the student (not to mention the faculty) will probably need librarian assistance.

Preparing a Web page and a booklet that provide instructions on copyright tracing is a simple task that will support oral presentations given by the library media center teacher and serve to educate the faculty and students. It will reinforce the oral and visual presentations and serve as a permanent research resource for students and faculty. It will serve as a cohesive school policy on copyright and will simplify life for the students, the faculty, and the librarian.

Jeopardy Category Number Two—Dates That Make Copyright an Easy Matter

Copyright is a simple matter when the material is published after January 1, 1978.[1] The term of copy is life plus seventy years for a work created by an author and ninety-five years from publication or one hundred and twenty-five years from creation for works for hire.

Copyright is also a simple matter if the material was published before 1923: The copyright has expired and so the material resides in the public domain. Material published between 1923 and 1978 falls into a gray area; it is generally essential to consult the library's chart on this issue or the excellent Web page of Professor Gasaway of the University of North Carolina (http://www .unc.edu/~unclng/public-d.htm [accessed January 31, 2003]).

Jeopardy Category Number Three—What Must Be Done When It Cannot Be Determined If Copyright Has Expired—Fair Use Must Be Observed

No student should graduate from high school without the tools and the knowledge to participate in the trace of a copyright, with the complete understanding that in some instances only a cursory trace may be made and the result may be unsuccessful. The searcher cannot always find whether there is an existing copyright. There are gray areas, and it is quite possible there will be no definitive answer as to whether there is an active copyright. When that is the case, it is the duty of the librarian to define guidelines for the conduct a student (and faculty member). "No, do not use," is never the preferred answer, but sometimes this is the way it must be. Abandon the use of the copyrighted material or use only so much as would be classified by the school and library guidelines as a fair use of a copyright material.

A natural student response (and faculty thought) to this position is, "Gee, who will know, couldn't we just assume the risk and copy just this one time?" The firm, specific answer that is both given orally and clearly stated in the guidelines is no. Unless the student or the faculty member can absolutely determine that the copyright has expired, fair-use standards must be applied.

Searchers with years of experience and access to the physical files earn their living examining documents that identify sources of copyright, so it is unreasonable to believe that all copyright can always be traced from a student's computer or from the media center computer with a librarian's help. It is important to note, and for the student and the librarian to understand, that the best search that can be done through the Internet may simply be a cursory search that goes not further back than 1978. Searching copyright can be as difficult as understanding hieroglyphics, to which there was a key and to which logic and phonetics did ultimately apply.[2] There is no one location in which all copyright, even U.S. copyright, reposes but there someday will likely be such a repository, made possible by the Internet.

When there is no final resolution to a copyright search, a life lesson is taught by the librarian. Here is where the librarian draws the line in the sand and gives the student the tools to take with them to college and to life: If you cannot prove the copyright has expired, you cannot use the material outside the scope of fair use. It is just that simple and for many difficult to accept. The student response is often that no one will ever know, if no one can trace the copyright. The librarian has a wonderful opportunity to teach the final lesson in copyright: If you cannot determine that the copyright has expired, if you do not have a release and find it impossible to identify the owner of the copyright to obtain a release, you cannot use the material. This is a bitter pill for diligent students who have found the perfect resource. But if they are truly outstanding students they can adapt and apply the rules of fair use of copyrighted material and still produce a wonderful project.

Okay, So I *Have* to Assume This Material Is Copyrighted

When it is impossible to determine whether a copyright exists on a certain work, take the opportunity to educate the faculty and the students on just how much of the work they can use and help them identify the facts found in the work, because facts are not the subject of copyright. Bitter pills often provide wonderful learning experiences. Provide them with the school and library guidelines on the quantity that may be copied.

Out of Print Is Not Out of Copyright

A work that is out of print does not necessarily mean that it is no longer protected by copyright.[3] The Library of Congress (http://www.loc.gov /copyright/index.html [accessed January 31, 2003]) can help you trace the copyright holder, as can the Copyright Clearance Center (http://www .ccc.com [accessed January 31, 2003]).

The simplest method for searching the owner of a copyright, which is not always the author, is through the Library of Congress Copyright Search Web site. They have recently implemented a new and easier search system for copyright information. A search can be initiated by selecting one of the databases: "Books," "Music," and "Serials and Documents." Each of these three databases contains records of registrations and ownership documents since 1978. The information in the databases is searchable by author, claimant, title, and registration number. Students and faculty are generally disappointed that searching copyright by subject is not available at this time.

Works Registered for Copyright Since January 1978

Included are books, films, music, maps, sound recordings, software, multimedia kits, drawings, posters, sculpture, and so forth. Also included are renewals of previous registrations. Many items are not retained in the Library's permanent collections, and the system is updated weekly. Serials (periodicals, magazines, journals, newspapers, etc.) registered for copyright since 1978 are updated twice yearly.

METHODS OF APPROACHING A COPYRIGHT INVESTIGATION

There are several ways to investigate whether a work is under copyright protection and, if so, the facts of the copyright. Even though not all of these are options for students, they should be aware that these options exist. It helps them to understand why they cannot perform a complete copyright search. These are the type of directions that can be placed in a directive sheet and placed on a library Web page.

First and perhaps most simply, examine a copy of the work for such elements as a copyright notice, place and date of publication, author, and publisher. If the work is a sound recording, examine the disk, tape cartridge, or cassette in which the recorded sound is fixed, or the album cover, sleeve, or container in which the recording is sold. It is important for students to know that works are still subject to copyright even though they are not registered for copyright. For example, a student's work is copyright protected even though it is not registered. Look at the copyright chart provided to the student, and hopefully found on the library Web site should it be unavailable to a student working online from a remote location, and determine into which category the work falls.

Searchers can themselves make a search of the actual Copyright Office catalogs and other records from the date of registration, and the virtual copyright database from 1978; or for a fee, the Copyright Office will make the search for you. This is typically not an option for a student but is used by businesses and scholars. In some instances it may be necessary to consult with a copyright attorney before reaching any conclusions regarding the copyright status of a work; this too is not a student option, however, it is important for them to understand the mechanics by which a full copyright search may be accomplished.

FACTS OF COPYRIGHT A STUDENT SHOULD KNOW

The Copyright Office does not maintain any listings of works by subject or any lists of works that are in the public domain. Individual works such as stories, poems, articles, or musical compositions that were published as contributions to a copyrighted periodical or collection are usually not listed separately by title.

Before 1978, unpublished works were entitled to protection under common law without the need of registration. Works published with notice prior to 1978 may be registered at any time within the first twenty-eight-year term. Works copyrighted between January 1, 1964, and December 31, 1977, are affected by the Copyright Renewal Act of 1992, which automatically extends the copyright term and makes renewal registrations optional.

The 1909 Copyright Act and the 1976 Copyright Act as originally enacted required a notice of copyright on published works. For most works, a copyright notice consisted of the symbol ©, the word "Copyright," or the abbreviation "Copr.," together with the name of the owner of copyright and the year of first publication. For example: "© Joan Crane 1994" or "Copyright 1994 by Abraham Adams."

Prior to March 1, 1989, the requirement for the notice applied equally whether the work was published in the United States or elsewhere by authority of the copyright owner. Compliance with the statutory notice requirements was the responsibility of the copyright owner. Unauthorized publication without the copyright notice, or with a defective notice, does not affect the validity of the copyright in the work.

Advance permission from, or registration with, the Copyright Office is not required before placing a copyright notice on copies of the work or on phonorecords of a sound recording. Moreover, for works first published on or after January 1, 1978, through February 28, 1989, omission of the required notice, or use of a defective notice, did not result in forfeiture or outright loss of copyright protection. Certain omissions of, or defects in, the notice of copyright, however, could have led to loss of copyright protection if steps were not taken to correct or cure the omissions or defects.

There are many reasons why a search of the copyright records is not a conclusive search. First, the work may have never been registered, such as a student's work. All students understand this example when they are used as the subject of the example. Because searches are ordinarily limited to registrations that have already been cataloged, a search report may not cover recent registrations for which catalog records are not yet available. Also, the work may have been registered under a different title or as part of a larger work.

Even if you conclude that a work is in the public domain in the United States, this does not necessarily mean that you are free to use it in other countries. Every nation has its own laws governing the length and scope of copyright protection, and these are applicable to uses of the work within that nation's borders. Thus, the expiration or loss of copyright protection in the United States may still leave the work fully protected against unauthorized use in other countries.

Fundamental Information Needed to Search Copyright

The following information is necessary to complete a copyright search:

- The title of the work, with any possible variations;
- The names of the authors, including possible pseudonyms;
- The name of the probable copyright owner, which may be the publisher or producer;

- The approximate year when the work was published or registered;
- The type of work involved (book, play, musical composition, sound recording, photograph, etc.);
- For a work originally published as a part of a periodical or collection, the title of that publication and any other information, such as the volume or issue number, to help identify it;
- The registration number or any other copyright data.

Titles and Names Not Copyrightable

Students should understand copyright does not protect names and titles. This is easily demonstrated by the multitude of works that bear identical names. For example "The Mummy" is a very popular title for movies and books for teens and adults alike. These books, Web pages, short stories, and cartoons deal with everything from the curse of unearthing the tomb of King Tutankhamen to an English nanny. Titles belong to the public. The copyright records list many different works identified by the same or similar titles.

Titles May Be Protected as a Trademark

Although not all titles are protectable under copyright law, some brand names, trade names, slogans, and phrases may be entitled to trademark protection or under the general rules of law relating to unfair competition. Registered trademarks can be easily checked online through the Trademark Electronic Search System, http://tess.uspto.gov (accessed January 31, 2003), which allows a search of trademark names.

Works Not Already in the Public Domain

Neither the 1976 Copyright Act, the Berne Convention Implementation Act of 1988, the Copyright Renewal Act of 1992, nor the Sonny Bono Copyright Term Extension Act of 1998 will restore protection to works that fell into the public domain before the passage of the laws.

Under the copyright law in effect prior to January 1, 1978, copyright could be lost in several situations. The most common were publication without the required notice of copyright, expiration of the first twenty-eight-year term without renewal, or final expiration of the second copyright term. The Copyright Renewal Act of 1992 automatically renews first-term copyrights secured between January 1, 1964, and December 31, 1977.

Works Originally Copyrighted on or After January 1, 1978

A work that is created and fixed in tangible form for the first time on or after January 1, 1978, is automatically protected from the moment of its creation and is ordinarily given a term enduring for the author's life plus an additional seventy years after the author's death. In the case of "a joint work prepared by two or more authors who did not work for hire," the term lasts for seventy years after the last surviving author's death. For works made for hire and for anonymous and pseudonymous works (unless the author's identity is revealed in the Copyright Office records), the duration of copyright will be ninety-five years from publication or 120 years from creation, whichever is less.

Works created before the 1976 law came into effect but were neither published nor registered for copyright before January 1, 1978, have been automatically brought under the statute and are now given federal copyright protection. The duration of copyright in these works will generally be computed in the same way as for new works: the life-plus-70 or 95/120-year terms will apply. However, all works in this category are guaranteed at least twenty-five years of statutory protection.

Works Copyrighted Before 1978

Under the law in effect before 1978, copyright was secured either on the date a work was published with notice of copyright or on the date of registration if the work was registered in unpublished form. In either case, copyright endured for a first term of twenty-eight years from the date on which it was secured. During the last year of the first term, the copyright was eligible for renewal. The copyright law extends the renewal term from twenty-eight to sixty-seven years for copyrights in existence prior to January 1, 1978.

However, for works copyrighted prior to January 1, 1964, the copyright still must have been renewed in the twenty-eighth calendar year to receive the sixty-seven-year period of added protection. The amending legislation enacted June 26, 1992, automatically extends this second term for works first copyrighted between January 1, 1964, and December 31, 1977. For more detailed information on the copyright term, write or call the Copyright Office and request Circular 15a, "Duration of Copyright," and Circular 15t, "Extension of Copyright Terms."

Works Published Before 1978

In investigating the copyright status of works first published before January 1, 1978, the most important thing to look for is the notice of copyright. As a general rule under the previous law, copyright protection was lost permanently if the notice was omitted from the first authorized published edition of a work or if it appeared in the wrong form or position. The form and position of the copyright notice for various types of works were specified in the copyright statute. Some courts liberally overlooked relatively minor departures from the statutory requirements, but a basic failure to comply with the notice provisions forfeited copyright protection and put the work into the public domain in this country.

Absence of Copyright Notice

For works first published before 1978, the complete absence of a copyright notice from a published copy generally indicates that the work is not protected by copyright. For works first published between 1978 and March 1, 1989, the copyright notice is mandatory, but omission could have been cured by registration before or within five years of publication and by adding the notice to copies published in the United States after discovery of the omission. Some works may contain a notice; others may not. The absence of a notice in works published on or after March 1, 1989, does not necessarily indicate that the work is in the public domain.

Unpublished Works

No notice of copyright is now required on the copies of any unpublished work. The concept of "publication" is very technical, and it was possible for a number of copies lacking a copyright notice to be reproduced and distributed without affecting copyright protection.

Sound Recordings

Reproductions of sound recordings usually contain two different types of creative works: the underlying musical, dramatic, or literary work that is being performed or read and the fixation of the actual sounds embodying the performance or reading. For protection of the underlying musical or literary work embodied in a recording, it is not necessary that a copyright notice covering this material appear on the phonograph records or tapes on which the recording is reproduced. As noted above, a special notice is required for protection of the recording of a series of musical, spoken, or other sounds that were fixed on or after February 15, 1972. Sound recordings fixed before February 15, 1972, are not eligible for federal copyright protection.

The Sound Recording Act of 1971, the present copyright law, and the Berne Convention Implementation Act of 1988 cannot provide any retroactive protection for sound recordings fixed before February 15, 1972. Such works, however, may be protected by various state laws or doctrines of common law.

Derivative Works

An example of a derivative work would be the movie, *Gone with the Wind*. It was derived from the book, *Gone with the Wind*. In examining a copy (or a record, disk, or tape) for copyright information, it is important to determine whether that particular version of the work is an original edition of the work or a "new version." New versions include musical arrangements, adaptations, revised or newly edited editions, translations, dramatizations, abridgments, compilations, and works republished with new matter added. *The Producers* has been both a movie and a Broadway play. The play is a derivative work.

The law provides that derivative works, published or unpublished, are independently copyrightable, which means a new date of copyright is begun for the derivative work, and that the copyright in such a work does not affect or extend the protection, if any, in the underlying work.

Under the 1909 law, courts have also held that the notice of copyright on a derivative work ordinarily need not include the dates or other information pertaining to the earlier works incorporated in it. This principle is specifically preserved in the present copyright law. Thus, if the copy (or the record, disk, or tape) constitutes a derivative version of the work there could be a new copyright date.

Copyright Clearance Center

Copyright Clearance Center (CCC) is a for-profit center that indexes and catalogs works and has obtained permission to copy a significant number of these works from the publisher already. Where the permissions have already been obtained they provide a listed fee for their use.[4] Where the permissions have not been obtained, they will contact the owner of the copyright for permission and a royalty fee. This is an option used to benefit the faculty more than the student. However, the college-bound student should be aware of this option.

CCC's Electronic Course Content Service (ECCS) provides a method for obtaining permission to use copyrighted material in a digitized format for academic use. Permissable material through ECCS can be accessed by students and professors as electronic coursepacks, distance learning, or electronic reserves. Through the ECCS title catalog their collection of titles and copyright holders is identified. Many of these titles are pre-authorized which allows instant permission to use the work(s). There is a fee per page for this service in addition to the royalty fee.

Through copyright.com (http://www.ccc.com [accessed January 31, 2003]), permissions may be viewed online as CCC updates them. The ECCS fee is not charged here. Permissions for all pre-authorized titles (i.e., copyright holders have given immediate authorization) are granted right away. It is recommended to apply four to six weeks prior to the date in which the material is needed. Although many permissions are pre-authorized and granted instantly, in other cases, CCC may have to contact the copyright holder; a reply is not always immediate nor is it always granted. An alternative request is a good idea.

Academic Permission Service allows one to obtain permission to make photocopies of copyrighted material for academic use. Both students and their instructors will have lawful access to these materials via coursepacks and classroom handouts. The Transactional Reporting Service (TRS) allows instant permission to photocopy copyrighted materials for library reserves or inter-library loans.

Licensing Associations

The use of certain copyrighted materials—for example, film clips—by students and faculty may exceed the scope of fair use and thus require permission to comply with U.S. copyright law. A potential user of copyrighted information can secure licenses or permission from organizations for its legal use. Obtaining a license or permission from the licensing organization ensures the user of complying with the copyright law.

Authors of dramatic works typically negotiate with the theaters and producers themselves and entrust a collective management organization only for the collection of remuneration. The use of such works takes place in a relatively small range of locations; thus, direct licensing by authors is feasible both practically and economically.

The National Writer's Union (http://www.nwu.org) is the union for freelance writers working in U.S. markets and can license their work.

The WATCH File (Writers, Artists, and Their Copyright Holders) is a database containing primarily the names and addresses of copyright holders or contact persons for authors and artists whose archives are housed, in whole or in part, in libraries and archives in North America and the United Kingdom. This is in part sponsored by the Ransom Center at the University of Texas at Austin. The objective in making the database available is to provide information to scholars about whom to contact for permission to publish text and images that still enjoy copyright protection. WATCH is a joint project of the Harry Ransom Humanities Research Center at The University of Texas at Austin (http://www.hrc.utexas.edu/home.html) and the University of Reading Library, Reading, England.

Ebscohost (http://www.ebsco.com) offers the complete texts of 1,000 periodicals with one license to clients.

The Copyright Clearance Center (http://www.ccc.com) is a nonprofit organization that licenses works for both publishers and authors.

The Association of American Publishers (AAP; http://www.aap.org) has 310 members located throughout the United States and is the principal trade association of the book publishing industry. Its represents publishers of hardcover and paperback books, audio- and videotapes, computer software, looseleaf services, electronic products, and services including online databases, CD-ROMs, and a range of educational materials including classroom periodicals, maps, globes, filmstrips, and testing materials.

Cartoonbank.com (http://www.cartoonbank.com) is the online home of The Cartoon Bank, a New Yorker Magazine company. It provides a searchable database of cartoon humor and contains 85,000 records in its central archive—including all the cartoons ever published in *The New Yorker.*

United Media (http://www.unitedmedia.com) represents many cartoonists and media personalities including Snoopy, Dilbert, and a number of editorial cartoonists. To use a comic strip for a presentation, newsletter, book, memo, or any other type of distribution, United Media may grant permission on a case-by-case basis. Send a letter with a brief explanation on how you intend to use the strip and include the date (located on the strip) and a description of the strip.

The Harry Fox Agency (HFA; http://www.harryfox.com), established in 1927 by the National Music Publisher's Association, licenses the uses of music in the United States on CDs, digital services, records, tapes, and imported phonorecords.

The Motion Picture Association and the Motion Picture Association of America (MPA and MPAA; http://www.mpaa.org) were formed in 1945 and license the use of films.

The Motion Picture Licensing Corporation (MPLC; http://www.mplc .com) provides licenses on an annual basis for home-use videotapes or videodisks of public performances.

Movie Licensing USA (http://www.movlic.com) is a licensing agent for authorized studios such as Walt Disney Pictures, Touchstone Pictures, Hollywood Pictures, Warner Bros., Columbia Pictures, TriStar Pictures, Paramount Pictures, DreamWorks Pictures, Metro-Goldwyn-Mayer, Universal Pictures, Sony Pictures, and United Artists; it provides movie public performance site licensing to schools for the use of entertainment videos. This licenses the showing of copyrighted movies produced by the studios represented and used by schools for numerous extracurricular activities.

Music Publisher Association (http://www.mpa.org) is a trade organization that operates as a nonprofit association and addresses issues pertaining to every area of music publishing, with an emphasis on concerns relevant to the publishers of print music for concert and educational purposes.

The American Society of Composers, Authors and Publishers (ASCAP; http://www.ascap.com) is an association with over 140,000 members. ASCAP has a board of directors elected by and from its membership. It licenses and distributes royalties for the nondramatic public performances of members' copyrighted works.

Broadcast Music, Incorporated (BMI; http://www.bmi.com) is a U.S. performing rights organization that represents approximately 300,000 songwriters, composers, and music publishers. This nonprofit company, founded in 1940, collects license fees on behalf of those U.S. creators it represents.

The Society of European Stage Authors and Composers (SESAC; http://www.sesac.com) is a U.S. performing rights organization that represents songwriters, composers and music publishers. This company collects license fees on behalf of those U.S. creators it represents and is located in Nashville. By securing a license from SESAC, for example, music users (i.e., television and radio stations, auditoriums, hotels, theme parks, malls, funeral homes, etc.) can legally play any song in the SESAC repertory. SESAC recently notified all dance schools that they required a license to use music for their students.

The Recording Industry Association of America (RIAA) is a trade group that represents the U.S. recording industry. Its members are recording companies, and it licenses the use of its members' music for digital distribution. There are two types of performance licenses you'll need for any given song: one for the musical work (the song as it's written on paper) and one for the sound recording (the song as it's recorded). You can get the musical work license from ASCAP, BMI, or SESAC, depending on where the song you want is registered. If you're going to program a noninteractive station (and there are guidelines for what this means), you can get the sound recording license by registering with the Copyright Office. If you want to program an interactive station, you need to get the license directly from the copyright owner. The RIAA manages webcasting, for which it issues licensing and collects royalties.

Catalog of Copyright Entries Through the Copyright Office of the Library of Congress

The Copyright Office of the Library of Congress is a government entity. Although this office does charge to perform a copyright search, it provides some free online access for a copyright search.[5] The Copyright Office published the Catalog of Copyright Entries (CCE) in printed format from 1891 through 1978. From 1979 through 1982 the CCE was issued in microfiche format. The catalog was divided into parts according to the classes of works registered. Each CCE segment covered all registrations made during a particular period of time. Renewal registrations made from 1979 through 1982 are found in Section 8 of the catalog. Renewals prior to that time were generally listed at the end of the volume containing the class of work to which they pertained. CCE, like the CCC, is a source used principally by the faculty. However, it is not unreasonable to familiarize the advanced college-bound student of its existence.

A number of libraries throughout the United States maintain copies of the CCE, which may be a good starting point for a search. There are some cases, however, in which a search of the catalog alone will not be sufficient to provide the needed information. The catalog does not include entries for assignments or other recorded documents; it cannot be used for searches involving the ownership of rights. The catalog does contain the essential facts concerning a registration, but it is not a verbatim transcript of the registration record.

It does not contain the address of the copyright claimant. Effective with registrations made since 1982 when the CCE was discontinued, the only method of searching outside the Library of Congress is by using the Internet to access the automated catalog. The automated catalog contains entries from 1978 to the present.

The various records freely available to the public include an extensive card catalog, an automated catalog containing records from 1978 forward, record books, and microfilm records of assignments and related documents. Other records, including correspondence files and deposit copies, are not open to the public for searching. However, they may be inspected upon request and payment of a $65 per hour search fee. Fee increases have been proposed.

The Copyright Office files may be accessed on the Internet via the World Wide Web at http://www.loc.gov/copyright (accessed January 31, 2003) or via Telnet at locis.loc.gov (accessed January 31, 2003).

CONCLUSION

Teaching a student to first examine the copyright information, and then follow a specific approach from that point, teaches them not only the law of copyright but to follow the law, even when no one will ever know and no one is looking. It is a good foundation for life. This is yet another example of the value of the library and the librarian. Every student should perform the trace of both a difficult copyright that involves a derivative work published prior to 1949 and has been renewed and a simple copyright of their favorite recent novelist.

Setting a standard for research and bibliography through the library that includes the ability to research and trace a copyright is a reachable goal for the librarian, the faculty, and the college-bound student. These are not just research skills; these are life skills.

NOTES

1. On October 19, 1976, the president signed into law a complete revision of the copyright law of the United States (Title 17 of the United States Code). Most provisions of this statute came into force on January 1, 1978, superseding the copyright act of 1909. These provisions made significant changes in the copyright law. Further important changes resulted from the Berne Convention Implementation Act of 1988, which took effect March 1, 1989; the Copyright Renewal Act of 1992 (P.L. 102–307) enacted June 26, 1992, which amended the renewal provisions of the copyright law; and the Sonny Bono Copyright Term Extension Act of 1998 (P.L. 105–298) enacted October 27, 1998, which extended the term of copyrights for an additional twenty years.

2. Egyptians had been using hieroglyphics for thousands of years. However, it ultimately became a dead language. There had been no person who understood hieroglyphics since the days of Anthony and Cleopatra. The Egyptian hieroglyphics

within a hundred years of the demise of the Ptolemaic dynasty were no longer used or understood.

The Rosetta Stone was carved in 196 B.C. by priests to honor the events of the time. In 1799, while extending a fortress near Rosetta, a small city near Alexandria, a young French officer found a block of black basalt stone, three feet nine inches long, two feet four-and-a-half inches wide, and eleven inches thick, which contained three distinct bands of writing. The most incomplete was the top band containing hieroglyphics; the middle band was an Egyptian script called demotic (he did not know that), and the bottom was ancient Greek (he did recognize the bottom band). This stone was called the Rosetta Stone. The Rosetta Stone was written in the three scripts of its time so that the priests, government officials, and rulers of Egypt could read what it said.

In deciphering hieroglyphics, Champollion identified the names of Cleopatra and Alexandrus and verified Ptolemeus. He then deciphered "Ramses." Utilizing his knowledge of Coptic, he continued to successfully translate the hieroglyphics opening up an understanding of the ancient Egyptians. We as librarians must be like Champollion. We must use what we know of copyright in specific situations to apply it in different applications.

3. See chapter 4, section titled "Works Out of Print," for two differing court views. One allows copying favoring the use, whereas one does not favor copying, because the only source of income may be income from the use and copy of the out-of-print material.

4. Information courtesy of Copyright Clearance Center (http://www.ccc.com) 222 Rosewood Drive, Danvers, MA 01923. Phone: (978) 750-8400. Fax: (978) 750-1470.

5. Information courtesy of U.S. Copyright Office, a part of the Library of Congress, 101 Independence Ave. S.E., Washington, D.C. 20559–6000. Phone (202)-707-3000.

7

LIBRARY BIBLIOGRAPHIES: CRITERIA FOR SELECTION AND THE LEGAL IMPLICATIONS AND LIMITATIONS OF LINKING

> The whole spread of the Web happened not because of a decision and a mandate from any authority, but because a whole bunch of people across the 'Net picked it up and brought up Web clients and servers, it actually happened. The actual explosion of creativity, and the coming into being of the Web was the result of thousands of individuals playing a small part.
>
> —Tim Berners Lee

In this chapter the following topics will be covered:

The Web Is Linking—Linking Is the Web

Library Web Bibliographies Do's and Don'ts

Purpose of Library Bibliography

Criteria in Building Web Bibliographies

Detailed Criteria for Multiple Web Bibliography Creators

Linking Do's and Don'ts in the Bibliography

Web Linking Is Legal Generally

Getting Sued for Not Linking

Trademark Infringement and Linking in Bibliographies

Trademark Dilution and Linking in Bibliographies

False Advertising and Students

INTRODUCTION

If you link, you can be sued, and people have been. If you do not link, you can be sued, and libraries have been. Although refusing a link is primarily a public library issue, the lessons can be transferred to the school library. This chapter is divided into two parts: how to avoid getting sued for linking, and how to avoid getting sued for not linking. This will guide school librarians to tactfully relate their position to the faculty when a request has to be denied, for example, by stating, "We cannot link to your site because it is contrary to our established guidelines."

The purpose of this chapter is to educate librarians not only for the benefit of their own libraries but also for the benefit of their students. The building of Web pages by student for school projects is becoming a standard element of computer and media center education. Students must be responsible in their Web page building and observe legal limitations. Library bibliography Web pages must also respect the law. Establishing guidelines that govern this activity is the first step in following the law. Applying and enforcing those guidelines is the ongoing responsibility of the school librarian. The Child Online Protection Act is a tool intended to help librarians which had some promise and little or no effect and seems to have been permanently derailed by the U.S. Supreme Court.

Library Web sites serve their users: the faculty and the students. They can also unify a school's learning and research process, putting both the faculty and the students on the same page and making research a straightforward, unified process. This is done by adopting one standard bibliographic format, or one standard word list, that is published at the library Web site. This word list is generally promulgated by the English department, although the sciences have terminology that should be included. Students can refer to this list, which includes vocabulary typically required for their homework. The library Web site is often the logical venue for this word list and the standard school bibliographic format. Bibliographies, while first supporting the research process, can then support the subject matter of the curriculum of the faculty and all this can be accomplished well within the confines of the law.

The library Web site reinforces the potential legal importance of respecting another's Web site; it educates the students and the faculty on the concept of intellectual property. It teaches that a Web site actually belongs to someone else and that right of ownership should be respected just as any other right of ownership. There is a line of demarcation one simply does not cross. You do not take that which belongs to another in the physical world or in the cyber world. Students can understand this concept, but must simply be introduced to it and it must be reinforced throughout their education. Senator Mike DeWine points out, "People who would never even consider shoplifting a CD or a videocassette from a store sometimes think the same rules about respecting private property should not apply in cyberspace."[1] Often, the library offers students their first concrete information on a concept to which they can relate: "cyberlaw."

THE WEB IS LINKING—LINKING IS THE WEB

The extensive use of links or interconnections between Web pages is the reason the medium is termed the "Web." The power of the Web stems from the ability to link to a point in any document, regardless of its status or physical location. Hyperlinks are points embedded in Web documents through which users may branch or link outward to other bodies of information at a different location. A hyperlink can be compared to a library card catalog in that it simply directs the user to a new site, or it can be viewed as a way of enhancing the value of one site by incorporating someone else's work into it.

A Web surfer may connect to other Web pages and retrieve information within seconds, without having to perform new searches or other complex tasks. All Internet users browse, link, and surf. That is the attraction and the bane of the Internet. Browsing, linking, and surfing an almost infinite Internet can expend tremendous amounts of time and energy. That is why librarians pre-sift these sites and build bibliographies or pathfinders.

LIBRARY WEB BIBLIOGRAPHIES DO'S AND DON'TS

The role of the librarian in inviting the World Wide Web (WWW) into the library is to make order out of the chaos of the Internet. Librarians have historically made order from chaos in their selection of print media and the building and weeding of a print collection. This collection building and weeding process has now expanded to the creation of Web bibliographies or Web reading lists. This is an activity and process for which librarians are particularly well suited and well trained. Our Web bibliographies link to Web sites that we as librarians, by our accepted criteria, have determined to be appropriate for our patrons.

PURPOSE OF LIBRARY BIBLIOGRAPHY

What is a librarian's purpose in building a Web bibliography? The foremost purpose is to educate students and faculty about the library and its services. Many school librarians are called upon to teach information literacy and research skills that are considered by many to be life skills. The American Library Association has developed *Information Literacy Standard(s)*[2] to guide school librarians in teaching a student to (find, analyze, use, and evaluate) use information sources, literature, and technology. Pathfinders and directions prepared by the school librarian are the tools with which to accomplish these goals.

Developing a library Web page and adopting a specific bibliography style simplifies the learning process for the student and the teaching process for the faculty. Including Internet links to bibliographic sources and using one bibliographic style school- or district-wide is an important service of the library.[3] Pathfinders or Web bibliographies and examples and directions are a natural format for education and school standardization of a bibliography format linked directly from the library's Web site.

The same Web site can link to directions and pathfinders for the laws of copyright as they apply to a student's research and Web pages.

This uniform bibliography Web page serves not only to educate the students, but also allows the teachers to collaborate with research as taught by the library media center. The faculty can coordinate their lesson plans around those available from the library without redundancy but as a reinforcement. Ideally, they will be able to pencil in on the library calendar their visit to the school library at a time that coordinates with their schedule and both the teacher's and the student's progress in the research project.

Some departments have descriptive word lists that are similar to the SAT and ACT word lists and require students to use a specific number of these words in their papers. These word lists may also be published at the library's Web site. This allows not only students to access these words but faculty may add words by simply e-mailing the library.

CRITERIA IN BUILDING WEB BIBLIOGRAPHIES

What are a librarian's criteria in building Web bibliographies? Generally, these criteria are compatible with a collection development policy, which is presumably in place and already supported by guidelines. The Web policy follows these existing guidelines in addition to Web site guidelines that are used to evaluate both the content and the quality of the Web site. A major distinction between a collection development policy and bibliography development policy is investment. In print and electronic resource development purchase and maintenance costs are relevant. These do not exist in Web bibliography development. Here the major cost is staff time both in the creation of the bibliography and maintenance to determine whether the links are still active and whether new sites should be added or old sites replaced. This is not an insignificant investment and the return on investment should be analyzed as an element of the technical facilities offered by the library.

Librarians must periodically determine whether the bibliography is used sufficiently by its patrons to warrant the annual input of time and effort involved in maintaining the site. The bibliography development policy should reflect the student's needs, which in turn reflect the curriculum as presented by the faculty. Specific subject areas can be prioritized.

The school policy on bibliographies should indicate who selects the Web sites and state the criteria to employ in that selection. Web sites could be selected by the head of each academic department of the school (i.e., math, humanities, fine arts, science, etc.) or it could be selected by the librarian after conference with each department. The policy should indicate the method by which the library staff and the faculty evaluate the Web sites and the process for handling modifications to the bibliographies, which is ideally done on an annual basis.

- A policy based on information categories is an important element of the process. Viewpoint-neutral sites are preferred and the library's policy may dictate that only viewpoint-neutral sites be included. United States government, academic, and cultural resources will generally be viewpoint neutral. The Web site inclusion policy should specifically exclude commercial sites, illegal sites, hate sites, or sites violating school policies.
- The Web bibliography chosen content should be consistent with the library collection development policy; if it varies, the explanation for the variance and guidelines for this variance should be included in the Web selection policy.
- The policy for the Web bibliography form and format should be current, from a recognized authority, organized for easy access and easy use; the design should be inviting; content should be accurate and appropriate; and the scope of the chosen Web site should be appropriate for the users.
- ADA Web site accessibility should be evaluated and considered. Software for this evaluation should be adopted and that software should be evaluated annually.
- The Web selection policy should reflect the mission of the library, the curricula and research interests of the faculty and students, and be relevant to the collection for content and educational value.
- The Web selections should be checked periodically; the period of review, as well as updating procedures, should be specified in the policy.
- Extensive guidelines are not necessary and may overregulate choices. However, the greater the number of faculty and staff that are involved, the more detailed the guidelines should be for Web bibliographies. It is important to remember that in creating order from chaos excessive links do little to tame the Internet. It is better to have a manageable number of well-chosen links than an excessive number of links that overwhelm the user.

DETAILED CRITERIA FOR MULTIPLE WEB BIBLIOGRAPHY CREATORS

If Web links will be selected by staff outside the library, links should be supported by guidelines for their inclusion. These criteria join the policy for Web site inclusion with the procedure to be employed by the faculty in the Web site selection. The larger the number of persons selecting Web sites, the more detailed the criteria should be.

The introduction section of your Web site selection policy should identify the goal of the bibliography. Web sites should be produced and sponsored by "credible organizations" to be included in your electronic collection management.

The category of Web page is relevant in application guidelines. An informational Web page is one whose purpose is to present factual information. The URL address frequently ends in .edu or .gov. Information Web pages are often sponsored by educational institutions or government agencies.

When evaluating the authority of a Web site for bibliography inclusion consider the following:

- Is it clear who is responsible for the contents of the page? If it is not clear, the Web site should not be used.
- Is there a link to a page describing the purpose of the sponsoring organization? If this does not exist, the Web page should not be used.
- Is there a way of verifying the legitimacy of the page's sponsor? Is there a contact link readily visible, or is the contact information itself readily visible? Contact information should include an address and telephone number. This means a physical address, and not just a post office box. If the legitimacy of the sponsor is in question in any way, the site should not be included. Remember, sites are subject to modification by the sponsor and if the sponsor is not a reliable authority and its site will not be consistent, it should not be used. Librarians cannot check sites each month to reevaluate their content.
- The author of the material is often not evident on government and institutional Web sites. However, some Web sites, such as Ludwig van Beethoven— The Magnificent Master, available at http://www.geocities.com/raptus/ (accessed January 31, 2003), will have an author. Review their qualifications before accepting the Web site.
- If the material is protected by copyright, is the name of the copyright holder given? This element of the evaluation process can be waived. Although it is not essential that the identity of the copyright holder be given, that identity does support the legitimacy of the Web site. Remember, U.S. government information is generally not subject to copyright.

When evaluating accuracy consider the following:

- Are the sources for any factual information clearly listed so they can be verified in another source? This criterion is less important if linking to a major or local newspaper or a government Web site and criteria designed more for the faculty than the librarian. Often the faculty will choose a site that is less mainstream and more nontraditional. This is an important basis from which to reject a faculty-chosen Web site.
- Is the information free of grammatical, spelling, and typographical errors? These kinds of errors indicate a lack of quality control, and students can be confused by them. Such Web sites should never be used.

• Is it clear who has the ultimate responsibility for the accuracy of the content of the material? This authority must be just that, an authority.

• If there are charts and/or graphs containing statistical data, are the charts and/or graphs clearly labeled and easy to read? Sometimes increasing the font is all that is needed to make the charts more readable.

When evaluating objectivity consider the following:

• The first element to be considered with regard to objectivity is also the first point of evaluation. Consider the source. Does the source have a bias or a polarized position, or is the source neutral, giving both sides of the information? Students do not have the world experience necessary to differentiate between biased and unbiased viewpoints. Advertising on Web sites is inappropriate for a school environment. However, advertising can be hidden in the content; consequently, the content should be reviewed for advertising.

• You may want to go one step further and advise your faculty of the library's method of identification of an advocacy Web page and the policy of avoiding all advocacy Web pages. An advocacy Web page is one sponsored by an organization attempting to influence public opinion. A Web page that tries to commit persons to a point of view is an advocacy Web page. The URL address of an advocacy Web page frequently ends in .org (organization).

• When evaluating currency consider whether there are dates that indicate when the page was last updated and first published. These detailed criteria will serve as an aid when multiple faculty members are involved in Web site inclusion.

LINKING DO'S AND DON'TS IN THE BIBLIOGRAPHY

Linking is a fundamental function of the Web bibliography. This familiar link from one Web page to another is known as an outline link. The library's bibliography simply links to another Web page or Web site. Each Web site has a "home page." Linking to the home page of a Web site may not be the first choice; rather the Web page builder may prefer to go straight to the more relevant page. This is known as deep linking. Technology may be resolving the conflicts involved in "deep linking."

A popular site for science teachers is Bill Nye the Science Guy (available at http://www.billnye.com [accessed January 31, 2003]). In this site, it is possible to link only to the home page. Flash technology delivers all the Web pages to a single URL. Cells Alive (http://www.cellsalive.com [accessed January 31, 2003]) uses frames to deliver the same technology, creating one URL and only one possible link to the Web site.

The Houston Museum of Natural History (http://www.hmns.org [accessed January 31, 2003]) does not use this technology. Here it is possible to bypass the home page and go straight to an exhibit page. By linking to a specific page that may more specifically address the subject of the Web bibliography, the Web page maker is engaging in "deep linking." Although it is very possible that Web masters will begin to employ flash technology to prohibit deep linking, it is for now an issue of potential legal consequence and respecting another's Web site. Avoiding deep linking is good library policy, good school policy, and an important issue to teach students. It helps students understand the concept of intellectual property.

The legal theory presented in several cases is that deep linking could potentially infringe upon the rights of the copyright of the owner of the Web site to which the link is made by allowing the linker to bypass advertisements. Further deep linking could give the impression that a deep linked site is a part of the Web site that created the link rather than the Web site that created the Web page. Several U.S. lawsuits have been brought, but none have been litigated.

Seattle Sidewalk (owned by Microsoft) is an online city guide to entertainment, events, restaurants, and hotels. This guide linked directly to Ticketmaster's Seattle Web page, bypassing the introductory information found on Ticketmaster's home page. Ticketmaster sued Seattle Sidewalk for copyright infringement and trademark violation. Seattle Sidewalk settled.

There are no laws that prohibit deep linking in the United States. There are no litigated cases that define deep linking as a violation of copyright or trademark infringement. However, it is important to educate students on the proprieties of Web pages and explain that there is potential liability in that area.

WEB LINKING IS LEGAL GENERALLY

One of the shining stars of hypertext markup language (HTML) is the ability to link. HTML was developed by the same man who "invented" the World Wide Web, Tim Berners-Lee.[4] Berners-Lee believes linking is a fundamental facet of the Web. One of the purposes in his creation of HTML was for "an intuitive interface" that would permit "the computers, networks, operating systems and commands . . . to become invisible." This permits the "surfing" phenomena of the Web that is so inviting and intriguing. It is linking that takes a "surfer" from one link to another, not quite certain of what is around that next cyber-corner.

Universality is essential to the Web: It loses its power if there are certain types of things to which you can't link. Linking can take the surfer from the greatest museums in the world to the complete works of Shakespeare to the greatest abominations of man and beast.

The director of the World Wide Web Consortium, Tim Berners-Lee argues for the freedom of a Web publisher "to . . . link to absolutely any piece of information that can be accessed using networks" as a natural-law proposition of the computer age.[5] This type of linking is not appropriate in a school environment, and as is often the case, science and the world of business do not agree. Science and the world of education of children may not always be of one mind either. In business, proprietary information is now placed on the Web. This information has in some instances cost the developing corporation millions of dollars. They object to the notion that simply placing information on the Web causes it to lose its right of copy.

Educational institutions are mandated to both educate and protect children. Full access to the Web has been deemed to be excessive access for students. For this reason, schools are mandated by law to filter student access to the Internet.

1. Hypertext Reference ("HREF"). These convenient links permit a viewer to jump from one Web page to another; clicking on the link instructs the viewer's Web browser software to go to the linked location, which is often another Web site and which is specified in the markup written in the HTML language. This form of linking is the most common and is generally determined to be non-problematic as long as it does not involve one of the linking methods mentioned below.

2. Framing creates links or associations between Web pages; it is a method, which Web browsers introduced to Internet users in 1996, of arranging and viewing Web pages. Framing allows the operator of a Web site to divide a browser window into multiple, independently scrollable frames with different layouts, and to place separate documents, from different Internet sources, into each window. Framing is the linking method subject to the greatest abuse. When the HTML instructions called "Frame Tags" allow the Web page designer to display a window within a window, the contents of two or more Web sites, often located on different servers, are displayed on the same Web page. These frames may or may not have visible borders, and the user may reasonably believe that all the information displayed is from the same Web site.

Framing may infringe the derivative rights of copyright holders. A derivative work is a work based upon one or more preexisting works, such as a translation, musical arrangement, dramatization, fictionalization, motion picture version, sound recording, art reproduction, abridgment, condensation, or any other form in which a work may be recast, transformed, or adapted. A work consisting of editorial revisions, annotations, elaborations, or other modifications that, as a whole, represent an original work of authorship, is a derivative work.

In framing, the copyrighted documents are displayed under circumstances different than those intended by the creator. The frame is often accompanied by work created by the referrer, other works accessed and framed together by the referrer, or a combination thereof. In such cases, the portion accessed and displayed using framing may appear to be an integral portion of the referring page.

Framing could be considered to "recast, transform, or adapt" the referred Web page, thus constituting a derivative work. Framing is performed at the express direction of the Web site author in order to give the appearance that the display is one integrated Web site. Framing occurs when the Web site to which the surfer has linked retains its frame or its titled format while the surfer links to other sites found in the frame. As a result the frame actually "frames" the Web site of a totally unrelated entity. Some Web surfers are confused by this technology and are uncertain as to who is sponsoring the site to which they have surfed. In some instances this is an intended consequence and in others it is an unintended consequence. When a framer attempts to fool the surfer into believing the area to which there has been a link is a part of the framer's work product or Web site, lawsuits can result. The legal theory is that the Web site to which there was a link created a misappropriation of that Web site.

In *International News Service v. Associated Press,* 214 U.S. 215 (1918), frames were used by one news agency to link to the articles of another news agency. The inference was that the linking news agency actually reported the news to the agency to which it linked. This cause of action essentially prohibits the unauthorized interference by one party with another party's valuable and time-sensitive information. This is an activity easily accomplished by student Web site builders. This activity should be specifically prohibited in student Web page design. Information misappropriation is a tort theory and not protected by current trademark law per se.

3. Inlined images linking enables graphics to be visible on-screen as part of a Web document's main body even though they originate outside the document's HTML code—that is, somewhere else on the Web site publisher's server, or even at a different Web site.[6] The copyrighted inlined linked image is displayed under circumstances different than those intended by the creator. When the inlined image link causes a Web image to be displayed and integrated into the referring Web page, this represents an adaptation and could be considered an infringement of the derivative rights of the copyright holder. Image inline linking also infringes upon other rights of copy such as display rights.

4. Deep-links are links that take the viewer to portions of a Web site below the home page and its identifying information and advertising. Such interior links, as opposed to surface links (which send browsers to another site's home page), are problematic because they present the site's content out of context. Hence, once the jump is made (via the out-link) to the linked-to site from the original linking site, the user sees no frame or further trace of the original site.[7]

Linking can be misused and abused. Linking can potentially infringe upon the trademark of a business or violate a copyright. Linking can tarnish a trademark or logo or actually be a misappropriation of the property of another. Linking can create unfair competition. The same violations that can occur with metatag abuse can occur with linking.

GETTING SUED FOR NOT LINKING

School libraries are not legitimate candidates for lawsuits based in their failure to provide a link. However, school librarians can maintain better faculty relationships if they have clear guidelines regarding sites to which faculty may request a link. It is much easier for a librarian to say, "No, I cannot link to that site because it is contrary to our guidelines. Do you have a copy of our guidelines? May I send you one?" than to say, "No, because I said so." A friendship or at least a professional working relationship may be saved by specific, detailed guidelines. Many of the guidelines mentioned above will provide a librarian with a legitimate basis from which to reject inappropriate Web sites and will serve to gently educate the faculty in their own Web site selection. They are students in this area as much as the students themselves.

Public libraries have been sued for not linking to requested sites. In the case of *Putnam Pit, Inc. v. City of Cookeville*, 221 F. 3d 834 (6th Cir. 2000), suit was brought against the city suggesting the city violated the First Amendment rights when it denied a request for placing a hypertext link to the Putnam Pit Web site on the city's Web page. Putnam Pit alleges the city created a nonpublic forum by allowing links to other Web sites, and its denial of the plaintiff's request pursuant to its policy may have been based on impermissible viewpoint discrimination.

The significant issue that was appealed was that the policy permitting links on the city's Web site was vague, overbroad, and violated First Amendment rights by giving local officials unfettered discretion to deny a link to the publication based on its content. The important element in this case, and lesson for libraries, is that the policy employed by the library must not be overly broad and vague, but specific to a sufficient degree so as not to give unfettered discretion to deny a link. Although K–12 education facilities do not have the same responsibilities that public libraries have, it is still important to have specific detailed guidelines for the evaluation of Web site inclusion for bibliographies. There are several Internet reference sites that provide guides in developing Web site bibliographies.[8]

TRADEMARK INFRINGEMENT AND LINKING IN BIBLIOGRAPHIES

Linking can infringe upon the trademark of another entity. This occurs when one party uses a mark that is so similar to that of another that consumers are likely to be confused.[9] Likelihood of confusion depends on many factors, including: (1) the strength of the owner's mark; (2) the similarity between the owner's mark and the alleged infringer's mark; (3) the degree to which the products compete with each other; (4) the alleged infringer's intent to "pass off" its goods as those of the trademark owner; (5) incidents of actual confusion; and (6) the type of product, its cost, and conditions of purchase.[10] Reverse trademark confusion may occur when a trademark infringer so saturates the market with promotion of his mark that consumers come to believe that the infringer, rather that the plaintiff, is the source of the trademarked product.

A domain name may infringe upon a preexisting trademark. The Trademark Electronic Search System, available at http://tess.uspto.gov (accessed January 31, 2003), allows a search of trademark names prior to registering a domain name. By researching the trademark regulations and knowing whether there is a conflict with an existing trademark or domain name, heartbreak down the road may be avoided. Students do not want to be the recipients of cease and desist letters, and at all costs desire to avoid the possibility of litigation.

The United States Patent and Trademark Office, available at http://www.uspto.gov (accessed January 31, 2003), indicates, "A mark composed of a domain name is able to be registered as a trademark or service mark only if it functions as a source identifier. The mark as depicted on the specimens must be presented in a manner that will be perceived by potential purchasers as indicating source and not as merely an informational indication of the domain name address used to access a Web site." In other words, the use of a domain name must not be used simply as an address to direct customers to a Web site, but must be used to identify the products or services of the business claiming the trademark, which provides products or services via the Internet.

TRADEMARK DILUTION AND LINKING IN BIBLIOGRAPHIES

Tarnishing a trademark occurs when the trademark is associated with some entity other than its original trademark association. Students cannot use trademarks on their Web sites. Confusion occurs when consumers think there is a connection with the trademark owner and product with which it is confused. Federal law prohibits dilution of "famous" marks and state laws, in addition to the federal law, prohibit trademark dilution. Businesses often assert dilution in Internet cases to stop the use of their trademarks by other parties who are not their direct competitors.

In determining whether a trademark dilution has occurred it is important to determine whether a trademark exists. If a student's mother gave the student a photograph of Elvis Presley and that photo became the chief logo of the student's Web site, is that image of a famous person a trademark? The answer is no, and the image can go on the Web site.

Elvis Presley's image was involved in an attempt by a not-for-profit foundation in Elvis's hometown of Memphis, Tennessee, to sell pewter replicas of a planned Elvis statue in Memphis as a fund-raising technique. In refusing to issue an injunction requested by a company that had been assigned Elvis' rights of publicity, a U.S. appeals court explained that "fame is often fortuitous and fleeting. It always depends on the participation of the public in the creation of the image. It usually depends on the communication of information about the famous person by the media. . . . The memory, name and pictures of famous individuals should be regarded as a common asset to be shared."[11]

The Diana, Princess of Wales Memorial Fund, established quickly after Diana died as a charitable conduit to disperse the millions of pounds that flowed in from the public, commemorative recordings, and worldwide donations, is having similar difficulties in finding support in the area of intellectual property for her identity, symbol of a rose, and signature as trademarks.

These famous individuals cannot completely retain their image for their own (or their estate's) personal gain. There is a standard question often posed in the world of intellectual property: Just because something has value does that mean it must be owned? The clear answer is a simple, no. Clearly the images of Princess Diana and Elvis Presley do have value and that value has many levels and tiers, but it is not always a value that can be owned on all levels and on all tiers.

FALSE ADVERTISING AND STUDENTS

Students are often the victims of false advertising on the Internet. A library Web page educating students on the latest scams could be helpful to both the students and their parents. Children are enticed to join a club or register for a "free" toy or trip. In the act of registering, they deliver directly to the false advertiser personal information, including name, address, phone number, favorite product information, and facts about parents and siblings. Marketers then sell the child's and the family's personal information to send mailings, make phone calls, or develop targeted computerized advertisements. Interactive advertising entices children to participate further in the marketer's scheme.[12] Computer technology makes it possible for companies to track every move your children make while they are using commercial online computer services or the World Wide Web.

One of the largest Internet fraud scams perpetrated on students is for student scholarships.[13] The National Consumer League cautions students and their parents that a search company that offers to locate scholarships for a fee is probably a scam company. At best, they note, a search service should be willing to give you a detailed explanation of exactly how it works and how much it costs. They recommend College Parents of America, 703–761–6702 or http://www.collegeparents.org (accessed January 31, 2003) as a source of information.

Section 43(a) of the Lanham Act contains a broad prohibition against the making of false statements in connection with commercial advertising or marketing and has been characterized as creating a federal law of "false advertising," "deceptive marketing," or "unfair competition."[14] Whatever its name, the sweep of the claim created by this section is wide: it covers any "false or misleading description of fact" made in commercial advertising or marketing activities, that relate to one's own, or a competitor's, goods, services, or commercial activities. A violator may be liable in a damages action for the harmed party's lost profits, the violator's own profits due to its misconduct, and, in exceptional cases, for treble damages and an award of attorney's fees. There are very few occasions when students might participate in false advertising. However, there are many instances in which they may be the victims of false advertising.

False advertising is also covered by Section 5 of the Federal Trade Commission Act (15 USC 45[a]). The FTC should be contacted if a Web site is suspected of false advertising to either children or adults. They can be reached by phone at 877-FTC-HELP (1-877-382-4357); by TTY at 866-653-4261; or via the Internet at http:// www.ftc.gov (accessed January 31, 2003). Children should be educated about completing forms that require personal information. Web site operators collect a child's email address and ask many other questions about the child and their family. This information is often required for many popular online activities for kids, including contests, online newsletters, homework help, and electronic postcards. Children can be advised not to fill out the data or to enter the letter and the number 1 for this data, if they insist on access and this policy can be incorporated into the library policy and placed on the library's Web site. The COPA Commission on Internet policies is an excellent resource for information about children and the Internet, available at http://www.copacommission.org/commission/ (accessed January 31, 2003). Here the amended statute may be reviewed and there is an excellent collection of papers submitted to the legislative committee for review.

CONCLUSION

Library Web sites are an important resource for the students and the faculty. They serve to unify methods of research and research skills for the entire school, and this in return can make life much simpler for the librarian and the faculty. They allow students to become proficient at a single annotation method and therefore, they are not confused by varying bibliography formats and varying expectations from one faculty member to the next.

Students are capable of learning cyberspace law just as they are capable of learning that you do not take something that is not yours. This is something to which they must simply be exposed, and this exposure should be reinforced repeatedly. Educating a student in where the line is drawn between what belongs to someone else and what does not is an attainable goal. Once students know what can and cannot be "taken," they begin to understand that it is possible to cross that line. There are no cyber police running radar on the Web, but it is a matter of character, just as plagiarism is a matter of character, or not taking the money out of the wallet found on the school steps. The duties of the librarian have expanded, yet again.

NOTES

1. 144 Cong. Res. S12972–01 (daily ed. Oct. 21, 1998) (statement of Sen. Dewine).

2. Excerpted from chapter 2, "Information Literacy Standards for Student Learning," of *Information Power: Building Partnerships for Learning.* Copyright © 1998 American Library Association and Association for Educational Communications and Technology. ISBN 0–8389–3470–6.

3. MLA (Modern Language Association) and APA (American Psychological Association) are both featured in many online guidelines published by many educational organizations.

4. Tim Berners-Lee, *Weaving the Web: The Original Design and Ultimate Destiny of the World Wide Web by its Inventor* 3 (HarperCollins, 1999). Berners-Lee traces his interest back to a conversation with his father, a mathematician, when his father sought ways "to make a computer intuitive, able to complete connections as the brain did."

5. Ibid.

6. See Richard Raysman and Peter Brown, "Dangerous Liaisons: The Legal Risks of Linking Web Sites," *New York Law Journal*, 8 April 1997, Computer Law; Wassom, supra note 16, at 193.

7. See Beverly M. Wolff, "Electronic Media: Recent Litigation Relating to Jurisdiction, Copyright and Other Legal Issues," SC40 ALI-ABA 549, 567 (1998).

8. The Best Free Reference Web Sites from the American Library Association's Reference and User Services Association (RUSA), Internet Scout Report, and Librarians Index to the Internet. It also lists various resources from which links have, euphemistically, been "borrowed," such as Digital Librarian: Reference Sites; Louisiana State: Ready Reference Sources; and Martindale's—the Reference Desk.

9. 15 U.S.C. 1114 (Supp. V 1999).

10. *Co-Rect Prods., Inc. v. Marvy! Adver. Photography, Inc.*, 780 F.2d 1324, 1330 (8th Cir. 1985); see also *Squirt Co. v. Seven-Up Co.*, 628 F.2d 1086, 1091 (8th Cir. 1980) (holding that an alleged mark had not acquired secondary meaning due to insufficient time in the marketplace and insufficient evidence establishing the effectiveness of the company's advertising linking the mark to the mark's source in consumers' minds); *C. Blore & D. Richman, Inc. v. 20/20 Adver.*, 674 F. Supp. 671, 681 (D. Minn. 1987) (quoting Co-Rect Prods., 780 F.2d at 1330).

11. *Memphis Development Foundation v. Factors Etc., Inc.* 616 F.2d 956, 958, 960 (6th Cir., 1980) *cert denied* 449 US 453 (1980).

12. The Child Online Protection Act of 1998 (COPA) was intended by Congress to address these issues, specifically, to "identify technological or other methods that will help reduce access by minors to material that is harmful on the Internet." COPA was immediately subjected to a First Amendment challenge by the American Civil Liberties Union and a group of other plaintiffs. A federal judge in Philadelphia prevented the law from being enforced while the case was underway by issuing a preliminary injunction. The Justice Department appealed the injunction to the U.S. Court of Appeals for the Third Circuit, which upheld the preliminary injunction.

13. National Consumer's League Internet Fraud Watch. "Internet Fraud Scam: Scholarships." Available: http://www.fraud.org/tips/internet/scholarship.htm. (Accessed May 29, 2002.)

14. 15 U.S.C. 1125(a) (Supp. V 1999); see also S. Res. No. 100–515, at 40 (1988), reprinted in U.S.C.C.A.N. 5577, 5603 (stating that 43(a) "has been widely interpreted as creating, in essence, a federal law of unfair competition"); Restatement (Third) of Unfair Competition 2 (1995).

8

——◆·◆——

LIBRARY WEB SITES

Consider first the critical problem that university libraries are now confronting—the increasing costs of serials and other forms of scholarly publication. Faculty members sign over their rights to their articles to journal publishers, who then require university libraries to pay high prices for the hard copies they would rather not have in order to gain access to the digital versions they prefer. Many academic publishers reap large profits while university libraries struggle to cover their increasing costs. Faculty in their role as producers benefit little, and faculty in their role as consumers suffer much, along with their colleagues, students and their institutions.

—Dennis F. Thomson, "Intellectual Property Meets
Information Technology," *Educom Review*

In this chapter the topics that will be covered are:

When does a faculty member own the copyright to faculty-created web sites?

How the work-for-hire doctrine applies to Internet resources created for classroom course.

The danger of believing in the teacher exception to the work-for-hire doctrine in all instances.

You have spent years developing your library bibliographies and Web pages, and suddenly you find you will be relocating. You want to take your Web pages and bibliographies with you. Can you? You have put yourself into them; they are a part of what you have to offer as a librarian; they are a part of you. Who owns them? Do you have a joint interest in them with your educational institution? Internet-based content for courses is becoming more and more common as faculties, and particularly librarians, use technology to enhance traditional library services and classroom courses. Who owns these materials?

THE FAIRY TALE OF MELINDA'S BEAUTIFUL WEB PAGES

Once upon a time there was a naïve, beautiful, young librarian named Melinda. She found herself all alone in her library and had no way to communicate with the faculty and students except for memos, which she found all too often in the trash. So she began to send beautifully colored memos, and they too ended their short and often unread lives in the trash, lost forever, and never to be used as the reference for which they had been so lovingly created and intended.

Melinda looked into her computer and said, "Computer, computer, on the wall, who's the loneliest one of all?" For she was the only librarian in her entire school. The computer answered with a Web page. Yes, that was what she needed, a library Web site. Everyone in her school approached footnotes and bibliographies from a different perspective. Mrs. Johnson's students used MLA, Mr. Reeve's students used APA, and she was afraid Coach Reeve's students were using some unknown format. Students spent hours searching the Web and were quoting from "Billy Bob's History of the American Revolution" which dated the revolution as "sometime around 1750" and re-created the spelling of History to "Histry."

Melinda began to order her projects, and she would call them Melinda's Magical Web Pages. Project number one: "Melinda's Uniform Library Citation System for Jungle Gym High School." She would place on the library Web site a format to be used for bibliographies and then invite comments from the faculty. They could e-mail the suggestions to her. Coach Reeve called her a genius and from that day forward sent his students to the library for a lesson on footnotes and bibliographies. Soon other teachers did the same. Melinda was less lonely, students used the same format for footnotes and bibliographies in all their classes, and Melinda was ready for project number two!

Melinda began bibliographies of approved sources for different periods of history. There were no more Billy Bob Web page citations in bibliographies thanks to "Melinda's Links to History," which consisted of twelve different Web pages that she had lovingly composed and meticulously updated.

After three years of Web page building and sixty Web pages, Melinda's prince came along and Melinda began to plan her wedding. Sadly, she sighed, she must leave her library kingdom for a new school in a new kingdom. She looked around at all she had accomplished in her library kingdom and the years she had put into it. No problem she thought. Her Web pages would fit neatly on one small CD and she would continue "Melinda's Magical Web Pages" in her new library kingdom. Oh, her new kingdom would be so glad to have her Magical Web Pages, and she could simply expand on the base she had so lovingly constructed whenever she had a free moment. The hours she had labored on her Web pages during the holidays and summer vacation seemed nothing more than a small memory and had been well worth her time.

Melinda looked at her little golden CD containing her Web pages and labeled it, "Melinda's Magical Web Pages—Melinda's Good Thing." This would be the CD for the new kingdom. But wait, she might need several copies for job applications so she could demonstrate her great accomplishments to potential employers.

Melinda traveled to her new kingdom and began her job interviews. Her first interview was at Darkly High School. She took her CD out of her purse and handed it to a potential new employer during a job interview. He took the golden CD and placed it in the D drive of his computer. Suddenly, as if by magic, Melinda's Magical Web Pages began to glitter and sparkle from what had only been a dark little screen.

These are so beautiful my dear, he said hungrily as he licked his greasy moustache. No, we do not have an opening for a librarian, but I think I shall just keep your resume and your golden CD, so that I may remember you and call you if we have an opening. Melinda was very, very sad. But soon, all was well. Brightly High School hired Melinda and the first thing she did was install her Magical Web Pages. Yes, it was a fair kingdom, once again.

Until one day, Melinda found, while expanding her Magical Web Pages that Darkly High's library also was using her very own Magical Web Pages, and on that very same day, a call came from the attorney for Jungle Gym High School. The message had been delivered by one of her favorite student aides, and it read: "Call Mr. White Shark, attorney for Jungle Gym High, regarding the use of Jungle Gym High School's Web pages at other institutions." Melinda's mind began to swirl. Yes, Darkly High had indeed stolen her Web pages, but why was Mr. White Shark calling? They weren't his Web pages, were they?

TEACHERS' EXCEPTION TO WORK-FOR-HIRE DOCTRINE

Teachers are employees. They are hired to teach and they work for or are employed by a school district. They create lesson plans; they create stories; they dress up like characters from history or characters from books. They even write plays for their class, and sometimes their students write plays for the class. Their students own their works, and it is copyright protected. So surely the teachers owns their own work too, right? Surely Melinda owned her own Web pages too, right? Sadly, no, not exactly.

Normally, copyright belongs to the author or creator of a work. Copyright covers not only the right to reproduce a work, but also the rights to distribute it, make derivative works, and perform or display the work. Historically universities have tended to claim an interest in patents but not in lecture materials, textbooks, books, or articles.

However, copyrights belong to an employer if the work is created pursuant to employment, unless there is a contractual agreement to the contrary. Until 1976, the statutory term "work made for hire" was not defined, and some courts had adopted a "teacher exception" whereby academic writing was presumed not to be work made for hire. The authority for this conclusion was in fact scanty, because virtually no one questioned that academic authors were entitled to own and copyright their writings.

College and university teachers do academic writing as part of their employment responsibilities and use their employer's library, computer, Internet access, electronic library access, paper, copier, and secretarial staff in that writing. It was simply always assumed, and it was the common practice that the right to copyright such writing belonged to the teacher rather than to the college or university. This was an assumption no one challenged for a very long time.

There does exist a theory that supports a "teachers' exception" to the work-for-hire doctrine. This theory of law (which is vastly different from the actual law) serves to vest ownership of the work produced by the teacher in the teacher rather than the employer. In other words, faculty own the property they have created. However, this is an unsettled area of the law.

Although the legal issue is not settled, an analysis of the work-for-hire doctrine indicates that courts will probably find faculty to be employees of educational institutions and their course materials to be prepared in the scope of employment. This means the educational institution owns their bibliographies and Web pages.

The best course of action with regard to Internet and Web materials that are faculty created is a written contractual agreement that addresses the allocation of Web rights between the faculty and the school. Without such an agreement educators do not necessarily own their works of scholarship and course preparation. Under the current state of the law, which is unsettled in this area, educational institutions should negotiate written agreements that meet the needs of all the parties with an interest in copyright and licensing of the intellectual work product. No reported case has addressed directly the copyright ownership of such materials; however, such cases are likely to emerge in the coming years.

Arthur Miller and Harvard Law—Harvard Law Wins

Professor Arthur Miller is a law professor at Harvard, a legal editor for ABC's "Good Morning America" and host of "Miller's Court," a television program in which a panel of experts examines a wide variety of public policy issues. Professor Miller has gained a celebrity status. In the summer of 1999, Miller entered into a contract with Concord University School of Law, the online distance-education law school owned by Kaplan Educational Centers. Miller is a member of Concord's Board of Advisors. When Harvard Law School learned of this arrangement, it objected, citing its policies that prohibit its faculty from teaching for another educational institution during the academic year without the dean's permission.

Miller did not agree that he "taught" at another university, rather he adopted the position that he created educational material to be used by another institution, because he never "meets, interacts, or exchanges e-mail with any of the Concord students." Miller gave up his Concord course. A Harvard committee advanced a proposal forbidding faculty to teach, conduct research, or offer consulting outside of Harvard, either in person or online, without permission from the appropriate dean.

WORK FOR HIRE

Work for Hire is the legal doctrine that applies to the ownership of faculty-created Web sites and work. The legal issue is whether or not the material can be considered a work for hire. However, the Work for Hire legal doctrine is strongly influenced by the law of agency. Section 101 of the 1976 Copyright Act determines that work for hire must fall under one of two categories. It must be either:

- material created by an employee in the scope of his employment, or
- a specially commissioned work subject to a written contract between the two parties and agreed to as a work for hire, and which falls within certain categories listed in the statute.

Historically (prior to the Internet) educational institutions have operated under the policy that educators own the copyright to academic work they have authored or created. Publishing has been an important facet of academic life and professors have always been encouraged to publish. But once a work is published, the copyright belongs to the publisher. This means that universities, which have financially subsidized the academic work with their resources and facilities, must now repurchase the work they have subsidized in the form of expensive journals, that in many instances they cannot afford. The academic freedom associated with publishing by faculties is being reviewed, and the fundamental basis of that review is money.

Educational institutions have an interest in the work of their faculty because of the faculty's use of their resources in its creation. Producing the published work is part of the educators' employment obligation by their "salaried employee." Harvard was quite upset that Arthur Miller provided his product to another institution (in which he had a financial interest). Although Kaplan online is not a direct threat to Harvard Law, in other instances these materials could compete directly with the institution for which they were produced.

Materials Produced by Faculty

Materials produced in conjunction with education are not clearly defined in the Copyright Act. The most relevant factor of the law of agency seems to be the extent to which the manner and means of employment are controlled. Other factors are also taken into consideration, for example:

- the method of payment and employer responsibility for the payment of benefits and taxes;
- whether or not the employer provides the materials and equipment;
- where the work occurs, for example in a location provided by the employer or elsewhere;
- the length of the relationship between employee and employer;
- the right of the employer to assign duties to the employee; and
- the employee's discretion in deciding when and for how long to work.

These factors are elements viewed in total to determine whether a contract for hire exists. They are used as a balancing test. Not all of them need to be present in order for the courts to decide that an employer-employee relationship exists.

Are Faculty Members Employees? Almost Always

Faculty members of a K–12 environment are more likely to be considered employees than university faculty. However, generally speaking it is likely both K–12 faculty and university faculty will be determined to be employees for the institution for which they work.

Faculty members of universities are required not only to teach but also to conduct significant research and publish findings in order to obtain tenure. The K–12 faculty is required to simply teach (and serve on committees, and participate in extra-curricular activities, and pursue higher education, and act as sponsors for school organizations).

Skill to Perform Task

In determining whether a faculty member is an employee, the faculty skill levels and the skills required to perform the task will be considered. Generally, university faculty members are more educated and more topic specific than the K–12 educator. Many faculty members do not have the skills to publish their own works electronically and depend on their school's information technology personnel or librarians to convert their intellectual output into Internet-published works.

Employee Benefits

The provision of employee benefits will also be considered in determining whether a faculty member is an employee. Employee benefits in the form of health-care insurance, retirement, and a number of other benefits exist in both the university and K–12 environments. The tax treatment of faculties in both cases favors finding faculty to be employees. Both K–12 schools and universities withhold federal and state income taxes and withhold the faculty member's portion and pay the employer's share of F.I.C.A. taxes.

Employer's Right to Assign Work

The fourth factor of the test is the hiring party's right to assign additional projects to the hired party. The K–12 environment does pass this test. There are mixed results with regard to the university environment. Universities do assign the courses taught to the professors.

Unique Web Page Considerations

Most faculty members who place their work product on a Web site use their institution's Web site or at a minimum link to their personal Web site from the institution's Web site. These Web sites are generally constructed by using the institution's software, hardware, server pace, and Web resource personnel. These factors all make the ownership of the Web site by the institution more likely. However, were a faculty member to use his or her own personal computer and software to research and create the material and acquire and pay for "publication" space from a commercial Internet service provider (ISP), then this factor would support a finding that the faculty member is not an employee.

Educators are not likely to leave behind the material they prepared for a course at one institution when they take a position at a different institution. Further, an educator may incorporate concepts and expressions in her course materials that she developed as a consultant or through other outside activities. Nonetheless, in many cases, a court could find that materials were prepared in the scope of the educator's employment at the university at which he or she is a faculty member.

Was Work Created in Scope of Employment?

Establishing that faculty are employees is only the first step in deciding if the work-for-hire doctrine applies. The second step is determining whether a specific work was prepared in the scope of the educator's employment.

Courts have developed a three-part test based on the Restatement (Second) of Agency for determining whether an employee acted within the scope of employment when preparing a copyrightable work. Those factors, all of which must be shown to establish that the employee was acting within the scope of her employment, are:

- whether the work is of the type that the employee is employed to perform;
- whether the work occurs substantially within authorized work hours; and
- whether its purpose, at least in part, is to serve the employer.

Faculty-Created Books, Articles, and Teaching Materials

Faculty-created scholarly articles, books and teaching materials are generally held to have been prepared outside the scope of employment. However, library Web pages are significantly different. Typically librarians do not "teach" specific courses. If a librarian does offer a specific course in research that is taught as a regular course, their materials could be considered to be "teaching materials" because it is clear these works are created to serve the institution.

Publishers are beginning to be concerned with regard to the copyright of some faculty-created works. Educators and their institutions should have policies that clearly spell out the respective rights of the parties so as to avoid litigation and lost opportunities for profit from educator-created works. Some institutions' policies sanction a joint ownership of the work. Whether an educator is willing to forgo the right to make future use of certain materials is an issue to be addressed. Ambiguity invites disputes and litigation. Policies, guidelines and other agreements naturally will vary from institution to institution.[1] Although your library policy cannot dictate the school district policy, it is important to clear these issues with your school district initially rather than have bad feelings and litigation later.

AND MELINDA LIVED HAPPILY EVER AFTER

Whatever happened to Melinda in her new library kingdom? Melinda, always being the sensible librarian, decided to call Mr. White Shark from her home, after school. She dialed the number and heard the receptionist respond, "Mr. White Shark's Office, you catch 'em, we clean 'em."

"This is Melinda, the former Jungle Gym librarian."

Because this is a fairy tale, Mr. White Shark's receptionist responded, "Ah, yes, Melinda, Mr. White Shark has been eagerly awaiting your call. I'll put you right through."

"Hello, Melinda, how is your new job?"

"Just great Mr. White Shark."

"About those Web pages you are using at Brightly High, Melinda."

"You know about those?" Melinda asked, beginning to worry.

"Certainly, all the kingdom knows about Melinda's Magical Web Pages. You know, Melinda, it is our position that those were made while you were an employee of Jungle Gym High. We do not accept the teacher exception to the Work for Hire doctrine, and besides you really weren't even a teacher. So we own them, lock, stock, and barrel."

Melinda saw her entire career flash before her eyes—more Web pages; embarrassment beyond belief as she told her principal she had stolen her own Web pages. She would be the dunce of the kingdom. But then, she could not believe her ears. Mr. White Shark's word began to calm her troubled mind.

"Well, at least that's what I told old Mr. Greasy Moustache over there at Darkly High. I told him to get those Web pages off his Web site or he'd be swimming with the sharks, not to mention sleeping with the fishes. Now about your Melinda's Magical Web Pages, I'll tell you what I aim to do. We're drawing up contracts with all our faculty members and telling them they own their Web creations. Thought we'd do the same for you, because you've done so much for our kingdom. How does that suit you?"

"Fine, Mr. White Shark, just fine."

"Just one more thing, Melinda. Once you own your Web pages, you'll have to deal with the next Mr. Greasy Moustache who steals your Magical Web Pages, and you'd better check your current school's position on who owns those pages."

And Melinda did, and Melinda lived happily ever after, thanks to the kindly Mr. White Shark.

NOTES

1. The American Association of University Professors ("AAUP") has prepared a Draft Statement on Copyright (Draft Statement), which advocates that faculty members should be the owners of "courseware" they develop for distance education programs. The AAUP notes that even though some institutions have policies that proclaim their ownership of such materials, the Copyright Act of 1976 requires a writ, signed by the author, to create a legally binding transfer of the copyright. Of course, this requirement is only relevant if in fact the educator who creates the material is its owner. Current copyright law leaves in doubt the issue of who owns such works. Even if current law recognizes faculty-creators as owners, colleges and universities could argue that employment contracts, which incorporate by reference such policies and which are signed by the educator, satisfy the signed written transfer requirement of the 1976 Act. Further, as in Arthur Miller's dispute with Harvard, universities may seek to prevent current faculty from selling their course materials to other institutions under outside employment restrictions contained in university policies or employment contracts.

The Draft Statement recognizes three categories of projects in which a college or university "may fairly claim ownership of, or an interest in, copyright in works created by faculty (or staff) members." Those three categories are "special works created in circumstances that may properly be regarded as 'made for hire,' negotiated contractual transfers, and 'joint works' as described in the Copyright Act." As to the first of these, the Draft Statement recognizes an institution's claim of ownership where the works were "created as a specific requirement of employment or as an assigned institutional duty." Examples given in the Draft Statement include "reports prepared by a dean or by the chair or members of a faculty committee, or college promotional brochures prepared by a director of admissions." Course examinations were specifically identified as materials that would be the exclusive property of the faculty member. As to the second category, contractual transfers, the Draft Statement identified as an example "a work prepared pursuant to a program of 'sponsored research' accompanied by a grant from a third party," noting in such circumstances that "a contract signed by the faculty member providing that copyright will be owned by the institution and will be enforceable." The Draft Statement continues:

> Similarly, the college or university may reasonably request that the faculty member—when entering into an agreement granting the copyright or publishing rights to a third party— make efforts to reserve to the institution the right to use the work in its internally administered programs of teaching, research, and public service on a perpetual, royalty-free, non-exclusive basis.

Finally, the Draft Statement provides: "In rare situations, it may be proper to treat a work as a product of the joint authorship of the faculty member and his or her institution, so that both have a shared interest in the copyright."

The Draft Statement expresses principles upon which a rational allocation of copyright could be based. Its first category proposes a logical analysis for whether a particular work created by an educator should be deemed a work-for-hire. It is not at all clear, however, that this is in fact the current state of the law. As to the second category, there appears to be no legal basis for the implication that, absent special circumstances, a signed writing purporting to transfer copyright from an educator to an institution at which she worked would not be enforceable. There is no language in the 1976 Act, or in case law interpreting it that indicates an educator lacks the capacity to transfer copyright of her work product to the institution that employed her.

When faculty members are considered authors of the works produced in conjunction with the employment at the institution there can be a contractual agreement regarding the assignment of ownership to the institution.

There are many contractual options for consideration with regard to faculty-created works. Below are some options, but in each option the contract should address who (the faculty member or the institution) will retain standing to sue for infringement.

1. The faculty member can contractually surrender management and control of the work to the institution. This can be surrendered as an incident to the employment agreement, or there can be an agreement for remuneration for the assignment of particular works consisting of either full or partial royalties.
2. The faculty member may retain control of the work and allow the institution the right to use the work under specific circumstances. Such circumstances could be for example, for as long as the faculty member remains with the institution, for a specific period of time, for as long as the course is taught, or for as long as the institution desires to use the material either modified or unmodified.

3. Faculty could be given the right to use the work they created in subsequent classes taught elsewhere, but the institution would retain control of the work and other faculty members would be allowed to use the work.
4. The faculty member could control and manage licensing of the work and subsequent royalties.
5. Faculty-created materials are owned wholly by the faculty. The faculty creator could be given exclusive rights, nonexclusive rights, or a royalty.
6. Faculty authorship with an assignment of all or partial rights or license to the institution.

A collection of university policies on copyright ownership is available at http://www.inform.umd.edu/CompRes/NEThics/copyown/policies/ (accessed January 31, 2003). Used with authority of AAUP.

9

PATRON PRIVACY AND FILTERING IN THE SCHOOL LIBRARY: GUARDING OUTGOING DATA— MONITORING INCOMING DATA

In this chapter the following topics will be covered:

Filtering Incoming Data
Patron Privacy
Impact of USA PATRIOT Act
Policy for Computer Access in the Library

PRACTICAL STUDENT PATRON PRIVACY CONSIDERATIONS FOR THE SCHOOL LIBRARIAN

The school librarian must understand both the laws that apply to educational institutions and the laws that apply to libraries. These laws monitor data that comes into a school library and school library patron data that is disseminated from the school library. These laws are both federal and state. The state laws are not identical; they vary from state to state. A school librarian must also distinguish student behavior and activity within the library from student library records because the laws governing these two categories may be quite different from one another.

At one end of the spectrum of the duties of the school librarian is the responsibility to safeguard information that is disseminated from the library regarding its student patrons. In order to accomplish this, it is important to understand the federal and state laws that apply to library patron privacy and student library patron privacy at an educational facility. Library policies addressing each facet of patron access to library facilities should be carefully drafted considering at each level the student library patron's rights of privacy. This policy should be communicated to all levels of employees within the library, the faculty, the administration, the students and their parents, and literary volunteers on an annual basis.

FILTERING INCOMING DATA

In addition to guarding the outflow of student patron information the librarian must also, at the other end of the spectrum of the duties, accept the responsibility of safeguarding information that is retrieved through the school library by its patrons. Which filtering system does your school library use?

Although the Children's Internet Protection Act[1] challenge did impact public libraries, it did not impact school libraries.[2] It is estimated that 74 percent of K–12 schools used filters prior to this act.[3] School districts chose not to join the litigation that pitted the ACLU (American Civil Liberties Union) and the ALA (American Library Association) against the United States government in defending the laws enacted by Congress.

The testimony during the CIPA litigation, which included some from the best experts in the country on the filtering systems, is insightful for school librarians. The four filtering systems that formed the basis of the litigation in the CIPA challenge[4] on behalf of public libraries (not school libraries) were: Surfcontrol Cyber Patrol 6; N2H2 Internet Filtering 2.0; Secure Computing SmartFilter 3.0; and Websense Enterprise 4.3. Experts with extensive Internet and software experience tested these systems and testified to the results of both over blocking and under blocking. The three-judge panel's factual finding with regard to these filters was that over blocking did occur:

We find that commercially available filtering programs erroneously block a huge amount of speech that is protected by the First Amendment. Any currently available filtering product that is reasonably effective in preventing users from accessing content within the filter's category definitions will necessarily block countless thousands of Web pages, the content of which does not match the filtering company's category definitions, much less the legal definitions of obscenity, child pornography, or harmful to minors. Even Finnell, an expert witness for the defendants, found that between 6% and 15% of the blocked Web sites in the public libraries that he analyzed did not contain content that meets even the filtering products' own definitions of sexually explicit content, let alone CIPA's definitions.

Filtering companies consider their "block lists" to be proprietary data and as such the precise method used for blocking is their stock in trade and is secret. The testimony, while not revealing proprietary information, provides expert insights into the effectiveness of the four filters. A detailed review of an expert's analysis of these blocking systems prepared for the benefit of the court can be found at Berkman Center for Internet & Society at Harvard

Law School.[5] This report provides insightful information on the winnowing process adopted by the various filtering companies.

Notwithstanding the CIPA decision with regard to public libraries, K–12 schools across the nation remain subject to the provisions of the Children's Internet Protection Act, which requires schools to install a "technology protection measure" to protect children from Internet pornography. Schools failing to comply will lose federal subsidies, which provide about $2.25 billion annually to schools and public libraries through its E-rate program of discounted technology and Internet access lines.

PATRON PRIVACY

A major education bill signed by President Bush on January 8, 2002, includes a new program providing funds for local schools to purchase library resources and technology, and to provide training for librarians. Grants under the program can also be used to provide students with library access during nonschool hours. Senator Jack Reed (D-RI), who originally introduced the school library measure, has stated that one of the reasons he favored the conference report was that it "helps school libraries." The bill, passed by the House on December 13, 2001, and the Senate on December 18, 2001, reauthorizes the Elementary and Secondary Education Act. It redirects federal aid for education to the poorest schools, mandates annual testing to measure student performance, and holds poorly performing schools responsible.

The education bill also addresses concern over the privacy of schoolchildren. Language added by the conference committee allows parents to bar for-profit firms from gathering data about their children at school. The amendment was offered by Senator Richard Shelby (R-AL) and Senator Christopher Dodd (D-CT), who cosponsored the Student Privacy Protection Act in 2000.

In drafting a Student Library Patron Privacy policy a distinction should be made between the privacy of student records and the privacy of student activities. The majority of state and federal laws apply to records. Student records have a higher degree of protection than consumer or business records. When evaluating the privacy of a student library patron, you should categorize the activities as activities of record and activities of behavior. Activities of student library patrons that generate records are governed at a minimum by federal law and at a maximum by state and federal law. They are governed by laws relating to records, laws relating to libraries, and laws relating to students and education. They are governed by statute and its case law interpretation.

There may be laws that govern student records as an educational institution, and there may be state laws that govern student library patron records as a library facility. But there is no federal law that governs library patron records, with the exception of video records for videos obtained through a library facility. Although the federal law does not govern print circulation of general public library records, it does govern video circulation library records. There are federal laws that govern student records created through the library whether they represent video recordings or any other recordings.

In most states there are no laws that govern the nonrecorded or nondocumented activities of students within the library. This information and its privacy are determined by the library's policy.

Recently, librarians and their patron's records have come under close scrutiny with regard to the actions of the September 11, 2001, terrorists. It is more important than ever to know where the line is drawn with regard to patron privacy. Some states have extensive patron privacy laws, but most have adopted the Uniform Model Open Records Act, which includes a provision that provides for the confidentiality of library records. Library patron privacy laws all have one thing in common: they protect the records of the patron. In most states, the fact that a student patron has visited a library is not protected by law. Federal and state laws are not the same as professional codes and guidelines. Statutes take precedence over professional codes and guidelines. In some instances the American Library Association Policies may not conform precisely to the state's law. It is important to understand both, and it is the librarian's duty to reconcile them for the benefit of the library and the patrons.

FERPA Governs the Privacy of Student Records

The Family Educational Rights and Privacy Act (FERPA) is a federal law designed to protect the privacy of a student's education records. All library records are just such records. Do you log your computer access? That is a record governed by FERPA. Do you retain your circulation records? That is a record governed by FERPA. FERPA provides access rights to school records to parents and adult students. FERPA is both an inclusive statute in that it defines who can access records and exclusive in that in defines who may not access school records, which includes library records. For school libraries there exist statutory rights to privacy pursuant to FERPA (also known as the Buckley Amendment), which provides generally that:

No funds shall be made available under any applicable program to any educational agency or institution which has a policy of denying, or which effectively prevents, the parents of students who are or have been in attendance at a school of such agency or at such institution, as the case may be, the right to inspect and review the education records of their children. If any material or document in the education record of a student includes information on more than one student, the parents of one of such students shall have the right to inspect and review only such part of such material or document as relates to such student or to be informed of the specific information contained in such part of such material. Each educational agency or institution shall establish appropriate procedures for the granting of a request by parents for access to the education records of their children within a reasonable period of time, but in no case more than forty-five days after the request has been made.[6]

Once the library is fully FERPA compliant, the rights of privacy of a student patron do not end. FERPA covers student records but does not govern student activities in a library. Here the librarian must be guided by standards and codes of ethics.

Policy Governs the Privacy of Student Behavior

In determining the student's right to privacy outside the area of student records, librarians are guided by professional codes or guidelines relevant to and promulgated by their own area of expertise. Not all of these guidelines address the issue of a patron's right to access information. However, the ALA Code of Ethics and Bill of Rights does address this issue. It states: "We protect each library user's right to privacy and confidentiality with respect to information sought or received, sources consulted, borrowed, acquired, or transmitted." When there is a conflict between the ethical guidelines of the American Library Association and the law, it is important for the librarian not only to be aware of the conflict, but also to observe the law.

Behavior can be categorized as suspicious, particularly because our country remains on various levels of alert for terrorist activities and because of the 1999 shootings at Columbine High School in Littleton, Colorado. The confidentiality of student behavior is not protected by law. Each school should consider a policy on "suspicious behavior" observed of a student in a library "which reflects participation in illegal activities through the library and its facilities." The policy directive could be as simple as notice to the students, faculty, and parents of the library policy that any "suspicious behavior which may indicate an intent to participate in illegal activity will be reported to the principal/superintendent for further review." Such a policy gives librarians a directive in this super sensitive era of privacy. Many librarians do not understand the distinction between the legal protection of records and the fact that there is, in most states, no legal protection of the confidentiality of behavior in a library. A policy that simply addresses "suspicious activity" without addressing the nature of that activity such as "illegal" would be overly broad. Policies must have some degree of specificity so that the staff may clearly understand and enforce the policy and the patrons may understand the behavior that is prohibited.

Right to Privacy—Constitutional Analysis

In arriving at your library policy that will govern the privacy of the behavior of the students, it is important to understand the constitutional basis on which this right is based. The basis for these formal ethically enunciated protections of privacy is found in the United States Constitution and its Amendments. Although an inference may be drawn that there is a constitutional right to library patron privacy, no court has addressed the issue of library patron records as constitutionally protected by the right of privacy.

Such an argument might some day be mounted, but there is no indication that it will be successful. The success of the argument will depend on the framework in which the argument is couched. The United States Supreme Court has addressed the right of privacy as a right to be free of unwarranted governmental intrusion. This is a constitutionally protected right. The right "to be let alone" has been defined as the "most comprehensive right of individuals, one that should not be penetrable by the government."[7]

The right to privacy is not specifically set forth in the Constitution but it is provided through the penumbras or "protective shadows" of the Bill of Rights. Specifically, the penumbras surrounding the First, Third, Fourth, Fifth, Ninth, and Fourteenth Amendments create zones of privacy recognized by the courts. There is no clear boundary or limit to the right of privacy; the issue for librarians is whether or not patrons' rights should be protected from unjustified governmental intrusion. Neither the United States Constitution nor the Bill of Rights specifically protects a citizen's privacy. This protection has been inferred by the courts. It is the position of the courts that the full protection intended by the United States Constitution and its Bill of Rights cannot be afforded to the citizens without this inference.

As consumers we are accustomed to waiving our right to privacy. We accept the necessity of waiving the confidentiality of our medical records to our insurance carrier in exchange for health insurance. waiver becomes a part of our contractual relationship between the health insurance carrier and those insured. Some employees contractually agree to participate in drug screening tests, and they waive their right to privacy in exchange for their employment. In some states our driver's license records and information are sold by the state for profit to the state.

However, where the government is concerned, we do not have a contractual relationship governing our rights to privacy. Here we must rely on statutes and the case law interpreting these statutes to protect our rights of privacy. As citizens, we intuitively understand that our tax records will be private and this personal information will not be made public, although we may not specifically understand why this information is private. Private schools that receive government funds are governed by these privacy laws. The United States Congress has considered the issue of library patron privacy and has rejected the statutory codification of this right.[8]

Right to Privacy—Statutory Analysis

There is no federal library patron privacy statute nor any case interpreting the United State's Constitution's right to privacy as applied to a library patron. There are but a handful of states with library patron confidentiality or privacy statutes that provide a patron confidentiality policy that exceeds that of the Model Uniform Open Records Act.

When the United States Congress was asked to create a legal right (a statute) for the purpose of protection of library patrons' records it refused. There is no federal court case protecting library patrons' right to privacy. The constitutional right to privacy has never been tested in terms of a library patron's right to privacy or confidentiality. Congress was specifically requested to provide the same confidentiality rights and protections to libraries that it applies to video rental stores in its creation of The Video Privacy Protection Act of 1983. Congress refused to enact the proposed bill.

In essence there exist rights to privacy in federal legislation regarding every topic imaginable—except library patron privacy. There are privacy rights for video rentals (which include library videos), cable records, consumer records, banking records, employment records, health records, and tax records. But there are no federal library patron privacy record statutes.

Representatives Al McCandless (R-CA) and Robert Kastenmeier (D-WI) as well as Senators Patrick Leahy (D-VT), Paul Simon (D-IL), Alan Simpson (R-WY), and Charles Grassley (R-IA), introduced legislation to protect not only video files, but library records as well. The Congress considered the inclusion of the protection of library records and refused. This act enables customers whose video records are disclosed without their consent to sue for damages of up to $4,000. In order to obtain video records under the statute, law enforcement officials must secure a court order by showing that there is "clear and convincing evidence that the subject of the information sought would be material evidence in the case."

Further, the law gives an individual an opportunity to challenge the court order before records are disclosed. The "clear and convincing standard," the strongest one regulating law enforcement access to privately held files, is patterned after the confidentiality provisions of the 1984 Cable Communication Policy Act.

This bill was the result of the Senate hearings on the nomination of Robert Bork to the Supreme Court. A reporter for Washington's *City Paper* asked an employee at a video store about Robert Bork's rental practices. The employee provided the reporter with Bork's history of video selections maintained by the store. The paper published an article that the reporter claimed to be a description of Bork's viewing habits.

State Laws and Patron Privacy—Weak Tea

Forty-eight states have some modicum of a law that pertains to library records.[9] Many states adopt model uniform standard laws promulgated by professional legal associations, the most notable being the Uniform Commercial Code.[10] States choose whether to adopt these standards in whole, in part, or with modifications. The Open Records Acts is a model uniform statute that has been adopted by most states. This is more commonly known as the state Freedom of Information Act. The actual Freedom of Information Act is a federal statute.

Student patron privacy and confidentiality, in the context of the Uniform Open Records Act adopted by thirty-five states, is protected as an exception to the open records act in addition to FERPA protections. Pursuant to the Uniform Open Records Act the librarian, in the capacity of guardian of patron information, must withhold patrons' records from the public. When a privacy provision is an exception to an open-records law, the keeper of patron records is not required to divulge the information to an inquiring member of the public, but the librarian retains the option of divulging this information under specific circumstances.

The portion of the Uniform Open Records Act cited below is the standard Library Confidentiality statute found in the majority of states. Essentially this uniform statute excepts or excludes library patron records from being accessed through the State Freedom of Information Act; or put in a different light, library patron records cannot be accessed through the states' freedom of information acts. The pertinent section states as follows: "A record of a library or library system that is excepted from required disclosure under this section is confidential."

A Freedom of Information Act guarantees to *citizens* the right to access federal government records. The Open Records Act guarantees to citizens the right to access state government records and has generally been interpreted more narrowly than the federal act. That means more records have historically been accessed through the state act than the federal act.

The word "citizens" is italicized because typically government entities are not citizens. Member of law enforcement seeking records are not considered legally to be "citizens" requesting access through the Open Records Act or the Freedom of Information Act. The Federal Freedom of Information Act[11] and the Open Records Act have been enacted to provide citizen access to federal records. Individual state freedom of information acts guarantee citizen access to state records. Under freedom of information acts, governments and their agencies are required to provide the fullest possible disclosure of information to the public.[12] The purpose of the freedom of information act is to permit citizens to know and understand the business of their government.[13] Accessing private patron information does not serve a legitimate purpose of understanding the business of government.

Iowa has a standard Model Open Records Act law. In this state, law enforcement to access of records was not protected.[14] The state was permitted to obtain public library circulation records. The library and its patrons claimed a First Amendment protection of the circulation records. They alleged that forced disclosure of the library circulation records would violate the First Amendment because such disclosure would chill the library patrons' right to read and acquire information.

The court discarded the privacy claims of the library patrons favoring disclosure pursuant to a criminal investigation on the basis of a "weighing of interests" standard of review. The law enforcement interests far outweighed the patron's claims of privacy.

President Nixon refused to produce his taped conversations and claimed that the government could not force the production of tape-recorded conversations between the President and his advisers, as well as various presidential documents, for use in a pending criminal conspiracy trial. A generalized need for confidentiality of high-level communications and the doctrine of separation of powers were the theories advanced in support of the president's claimed privilege. But the government argued that its interest in the underlying criminal prosecution outweighed the president's generalized claim of confidentiality. The government's interest in obtaining the tapes and documents, in conjunction with claims that the confidentiality asserted by the president would violate Fifth Amendment due process protections and Sixth Amendment confrontation rights of the criminal defendants in the conspiracy trial, persuaded the Supreme Court to deny the president's claim of confidentiality.

These are arguments with which the librarian should be familiar when crafting a patron privacy policy.

Uniform Open Records Act Library Confidentiality

The Uniform Open Records Act is a model law promulgated by a national committee and recommended for adoption by state legislatures. This model law is designed to give the public the right to access government records. That is its whole purpose. It is a state law similar to the Federal Freedom of Information Act. Library records are in fact "government" records in many instances. For this reason, the Uniform Open Records Act protects these government records of the library from public access through the Open Records Act. This model law does not create an expectation of privacy regarding library records otherwise. It simply means that a patron's records may not be reached through the Uniform Open Records Act.

"Exception: Records of Library or Library System" states as follows:

(a) A record of a library or library system, supported in whole or in part by public funds, that identifies or serves to identify a person who requested, obtained, or used a library material or service is excepted from the requirements of the Open Records Act unless the record is disclosed:

   (1) because the library or library system determines that disclosure is reasonably necessary for the operation of the library or library system and the record is not confidential under other state or federal law;

   (2) under the Uniform Open Records Act; or

(3) to a law enforcement agency or a prosecutor under a court order or sub-poena obtained after a showing to a district court that:

(A) disclosure of the record is necessary to protect the public safety; or

(B) the record is evidence of an offense or constitutes evidence that a particular person committed an offense.

(b) A record of a library or library system that is excepted from required disclosure under this section is confidential.

A few states go a step further, and provide the option of civil damages for the disclosure of library user files without the user's consent. Some statutes require a subpoena to be obtained prior to obtaining the records; most do not. Some courts have interpreted open-records laws to apply only to citizen access to information. Thus, the laws have no power over government investigations. The more protective statutes are not attached to an open-records law and unequivocally prohibit disclosure of confidential patron information.

Most existing statutes provide for certain exceptions to the rule of patron confidentiality. Confidential information may be disclosed with the consent of the patron in question, for example, to compile statistical data on library use or to collect fines and penalties.

An important feature of this law is that it respects the rights of a law enforcement officer or a prosecutor to obtain patron information with a court order or subpoena. It does not deny the right to that information without a court order or subpoena. And notably it does not provide the same right to nonprosecutor members of the bar, criminal defense attorneys of a co-conspirator, or any civil attorneys. This law does not intrinsically protect a child's records from parental review or a cardholder's records from any actions on that particular cardholder's account, though a library may craft policies that address these issues.

Subpoenas and Court Orders

Subpoenas can be issued by attorneys, do not require a court hearing, and are not supported by a court's order. This statute does not address the obligation to respond affirmatively or negatively to subpoenas issued outside the domain of government investigators or prosecutors.

Court orders, unlike subpoenas, carry with them the direct possibility of contempt of the court for failure of compliance because court orders are just that, orders of the court. However, there are legal mechanisms by which court orders and subpoenas may be challenged for cause. Most states do have a criterion that the judge must apply in determining whether to issue the order for access to records. It is not always clear on the face of the order or the subpoena that these requirements have been observed, thus creating cause for review.

In the case of civil subpoenas the librarian may be caught in the middle and may face liability in either direction. A subpoena, issued by an attorney for a husband in a divorce matter, may be for records to which the husband is not entitled. The librarian may face liability to the wife for providing this information. Each and every employee of the library should be familiar with a library policy to contact the attorney for the library at any time a subpoena or court's order is delivered so that the attorney may review the legality of the subpoena.

Example of Effective State Patron Privacy Laws

The two best examples of patron privacy laws are found in Colorado and Arkansas.

Perhaps no state has a more effective patron privacy and confidentiality law than Arkansas. The law, enacted in 1989, applies to libraries that receive public funds of any nature. The irony here is that even though Arkansas may have the strongest library patron laws, it ranks among the lowest in pay to librarians and has one of the lowest librarian–patron ratios in the country.

In this statute, library records that contain names or other personally identifying details regarding the patrons of public, school, academic, and special libraries as well as library systems supported in whole or in part by public funds are prohibited from disclosure except as specifically permitted the statute. These exclusive circumstances allow a library to disclose personally identifiable information concerning any patron to:

- The student patron;
- Any person with the informed, written consent of the patron given at the time the disclosure is sought;
- A law enforcement agency or civil court, pursuant to a search warrant.

As a form of deterrence for information gained in violation of this statute, it additionally requires that personally identifiable information obtained in any other manner is not receivable in evidence in any trial, hearing, arbitration, or other proceeding before any court, grand jury, department, officer, agency, regulatory body, legislative committee, or other authority of the state or political subdivision of the state. This act also makes such disclosures of this information a crime subjecting the person disclosing such information to a $200 fine and not more than thirty days in jail. This would clearly deter any person from disclosing this information. This act notes that it does not create a case of civil liability for a disclosure, however, it does not prohibit one either.

Colorado has the most broad patron privacy law. Patron privacy is protected by Colorado Statute 24–90–119, titled simply enough: "Privacy of User Records." What is significant about this statute is that it protects the interaction between librarian and patron in addition to the records. This statute provides that:

A publicly supported library or library system shall not disclose any record or other information which identifies a person as having requested or obtained specific materials or service or as otherwise having used the library. Records may be disclosed in the following instances:

(a) When necessary for the reasonable operation of the library;

(b) Upon written consent of the user;

(c) Pursuant to subpoena, upon court order, or where otherwise required by law.

FERPA EXPLAINED

Who has FERPA "access" rights? The only groups given actual rights by the Family Educational Right to Privacy Act (Buckley Amendment) (FERPA) are parents and adult students.[15]

"Access"—Definition

Parents and adult students have the right, upon request, to access their own (or their child's) records within a "reasonable" time, and no later than forty-five days after the request. "Access" generally refers to in-person inspection of the original records, but in most cases does not entitle parents to obtain photocopies of the records.[16]

"Records"—Definition

Of significance to librarians is the definition of "records." In one extreme, we all know that grades are protected records. In the other extreme, school directory information is not protected. Where in this continuum do library records fall?

On one extreme FERPA has an emergency exception. Schools may release records to "appropriate persons" in a health or safety emergency, as necessary to protect the health or safety of the student or others.

Disclosures in connection with litigation and law enforcement are permitted. Schools may release records in response to subpoenas.

General data that does not personally identify the student can be released. However, the release of information without reference to a particular student's name may violate FERPA if the information is "easily traceable" to a student.

Information may be shared with other educators on a reasonable basis. It is the school's responsibility to set out a written standard for determining when there is a legitimate educational reason for inspecting student records.

Schools have obligations to keep a log of many of these disclosures, and persons who receive records have obligations not to redisclose them except as permitted by FERPA. Here again, the library needs a policy.

FERPA Definition of Records

FERPA defines records as "those records, files, documents and other materials which: contain information directly related to a student; and are maintained by an educational agency or institution or by a person acting for such agency or institution."

FERPA records are not limited to documents in the official "student file"—the material may be in a teacher's desk, nurse's office, or principal's file, among other places.

Regulations note that student information may be recorded in a variety of ways, "including, but not limited to, handwriting, print, computer media, video or audio tape, film, microfilm, and microfiche."

Regulations define "personally identifiable information" as not only that which includes a student's name, but also as records that include the student's parent's name, the family's address, an ID number such as a social security number, or information that makes the student's identity "easily traceable."

IMPACT OF USA PATRIOT ACT

While the USA PATRIOT Act (USAPA) was created as a result of the terrorist acts of September 11, 2001, it applies to school libraries. The bill is 342 pages long and makes changes, some large and some small, to over fifteen different statutes. Terrorists come in all forms, shapes, and sizes as we observed at Columbine High School. Within fifteen days of September 11, 2002, the USA PATRIOT Act became law. The acronym stands for: The Uniting and Strengthening America by Providing Appropriate Tools Required to Intercept and Obstruct Terrorism Act of 2001. The act recognized the advances in technology for law enforcement surveillance. Historically, wiretaps designated a particular technological device such as a telephone or specific computer. The USA PATRIOT Act permits law enforcement to apply to the judicial system for "roving wiretaps," which are "technology neutral" and cover a person located anywhere in the United States, rather than a particular technological device. E-mail headers and URLs visited by the designated person are also available for surveillance. The guidance for obtaining a "roving wiretap order" from a court as directed to federal agents by the Department of Justice is available online.[17]

Specifically the USA PATRIOT Act permits a law enforcement agency to apply to the court in a closed hearing for an order for: "production of any tangible things (including books, records, papers, documents and other items) for an investigation to protect against international terrorism or clandestine intelligence activities, provided that such investigation of a United States person is not conducted solely upon the basis of activities protected by the first amendment." Should the court determine that a reasonable basis to issue a search warrant has been made by the law enforcement agency, a court order will be signed by the magistrate or the judge hearing the matter. This means a search warrant has the authority of a court's order and failure to comply with this order will result in contempt. No one knows the extent to which this law will be applied by the courts, and because the hearing required to obtain the search warrant is closed, it will be hard to evaluate the standards used until these hearings are challenged through litigation. It is possible that the USA PATRIOT Act could extend to a school library.

For a school library this means that students using your computers may be tracked by law enforcement. You as librarian may or may not know that your computers are being tracked. The court's order may go directly to the superintendent and you will never be aware of the actions of law enforcement. However, library computers may be tracked without any physical intrusion to the computer system.

The existence of "Magic Lantern" has been confirmed by the FBI. Magic Lantern is reported to be a powerful version of a hacking tool known as a key-logging program. Such a program, when installed on a computer, monitors and stores copies of what is typed by the user, this could include a password that starts an encryption program.

Experts believe Magic Lantern may be able to secretly install itself on an unsuspecting user's computer in the same manner as a computer virus. The program could be disguised as a harmless computer file similar to a "Trojan horse" program, and sent as an attachment to a benign computer e-mail. The FBI states that Magic Lantern will only be used "pursuant to the appropriate legal process," which means as a result of and limited by a court-approved search warrant. However, lawyers in the field of privacy worry that the program could violate citizens' civil right to be free from unreasonable searches and seizures.

USAPA expands all four traditional tools of surveillance—wiretaps, search warrants, pen/trap orders, and subpoenas.[18] The government may now observe Web surfing of Americans, including terms entered into search engines, by merely presenting to a judge anywhere in the United States that the observation of Web surfing could lead to information that is "relevant" to an ongoing criminal investigation. The person being observed does not have to be the target of the investigation. This application to the court for observation, if granted, does not obligate the surveillance team to report their actions to the court.

Nationwide Roving Wiretaps

The FBI and CIA can now go from phone to phone and from computer to computer without demonstrating that the technology is being used by a suspect or target of an order. The government may now serve a single wiretap,

FISA wiretap,[19] or pen/trap order on any person or entity nationwide, regardless of whether that person or entity is named in the order. The government need not make a showing to a court that the particular information or communication to be acquired is relevant to a criminal investigation. In the pen/trap or FISA situations, they do not have to report where they served the order or what information they received. For pen/trap orders, ISPs or others who are not named do have authority under the law to request certification from the Attorney General's office that the order applies to them, but they do not have the authority to request such confirmation from a court.

Internet Service Providers (ISPs)

The law makes two changes to increase the quantity of information the government may obtain about users from their ISPs or others who handle or store their online communications. First, the law allows ISPs to voluntarily hand over all "non-content" information to law enforcement with no need for any court order or subpoena (Section 212). Second, it expands the records that the government may seek with a simple subpoena (no court review required) to include records of session times and durations; temporarily assigned network (I.P.) addresses; and means and source of payments, including credit card or bank account numbers (Sections 210, 211).

The government's scope of surveillance has increased significantly with the USA PATRIOT Act.

Government surveillance for suspected computer trespassers is now allowed with no need for a court order. Wiretaps to facilitate this surveillance are now allowed for suspected violations of the Computer Fraud and Abuse Act. This includes anyone suspected of "exceeding the authority" of a computer used in interstate commerce, causing over $5,000 worth of combined damage.

Significant increases to the scope and penalties of the Computer Fraud and Abuse Act have been added. This includes:

1. raising the maximum penalty for violations to ten years (from five) for a first offense and twenty years (from ten) for a second offense;

2. ensuring that violators only need to intend to cause damage generally, not intend to cause damage or other specified harm over the $5,000 statutory damage threshold;

3. allowing aggregation of damages to different computers over a year to reach the $5,000 threshold;

4. enhancing punishment for violations involving any (not just $5,000) damage to a government computer involved in criminal justice or the military;

5. including damage to foreign computers involved in U.S. interstate commerce;

6. including state law offenses as priors for sentencing;

7. expanding definition of loss to expressly include time spent investigating, responding, for damage assessment and for restoration.

The USA PATRIOT Act allows Americans to be more easily surveilled by U.S. foreign intelligence agencies. Just as the domestic law enforcement surveillance powers have expanded, the corollary powers under the Foreign Intelligence Surveillance Act have also been greatly expanded, including a general expansion of FISA authority. FISA authority for surveillance on Americans or foreign persons in the United States (and those who communicate with them) has increased from situations where the suspicion that the person is the agent of a foreign government is "the" purpose of the surveillance to anytime that this is "a significant purpose" of the surveillance. The provision adds collection of DNA for terrorists, and also adds collection for the broad, non-terrorist category of "any crime of violence."

The Act provides for increased information sharing between domestic law enforcement and intelligence. This is a partial repeal of the wall put up in the 1970s after the discovery that the FBI and CIA had been conducting investigations on over half a million Americans during the McCarthy era and afterward, including the pervasive surveillance of Martin Luther King in the 1960s. It allows wiretap results and grand jury information and other information collected in a criminal case to be disclosed to the intelligence agencies when the information constitutes foreign intelligence or foreign intelligence information, the latter being a broad new category created by this law.

Domestic surveillance limits can be skirted by the U.S. attorney general by obtaining a FISA wiretap against a U.S. person where "probable cause" does not exist, but when the person is suspected to be an agent of a foreign government. The information can then be shared with the FBI. The reverse is also true.

The USA PATRIOT Act was specifically designed for the legal and court-ordered acquisition of Internet service provider records of user billing information. An amendment to the act, which proposed for the purpose of a clarification that the Act would not preempt existing federal and state privacy laws, by maintaining existing criteria for records, such as library records, failed.[20]

It is also interesting to note that constitutional protections apply only in our country. The FBI can access matters abroad by means that exceed our Constititution. A good case in point would be the arrest of reputed Russian mobster Alimzhan Tokhtakhounov, arrested in Italy on a U.S. criminal complaint accusing him of fixing the results of the pairs and ice dancing competitions at the 2002 Winter Olympics in Salt Lake City, Utah. The complaint, filed in Manhattan federal court, was based on wiretaps made by the Italian government, which had been taping his telephone calls as part of an organized crime investigation. Poring through transcripts, FBI agents said they discovered conversations in which Tokhtakhounov appeared to be arranging a vote swap in which a French judge would support the Russian pairs team while the Russians would make sure the French team won in ice dancing.

POLICY FOR COMPUTER ACCESS IN THE LIBRARY

It is important for a school library to have and to follow clear policies and guidelines with regard to computer terminal use. Law enforcement has the authority to review all records relating to computer terminal use. Some libraries do not require students to register for computer use, whereas others, for reasons of accountability, do require registration for computer access. This accountability may include logging in and out as this allows for user identification.

A library's policy should determine whether Internet use records will be afforded the same privacy protections as other patron records and how long they should be kept.

ALA Policy Confidentiality of Records

The Council of the American Library Association strongly recommends that the responsible officers of each library, cooperative system, and consortium in the United States:

• Formally adopt a policy that specifically recognizes its circulation records and other records identifying the name of library users to be confidential in nature.
• Advise all librarians and library employees that such records shall not be made available to any agency of state, federal, or local government except pursuant to such process, order, or subpoena as may be authorized under the authority of, and pursuant to, federal, state, or local law relating to civil, criminal, or administrative discovery procedures or legislative investigative power.
• Resist the issuance or enforcement of any such process, order, or subpoena until such time as a proper showing of good cause has been made in a court of competent jurisdiction.

ALA Code of Ethics states: "We protect each library user's right to privacy and confidentiality with respect to information sought or received, and materials consulted, borrowed, acquired or transmitted."

Upon receipt of process, order, or subpoena, the library's officers should be required in all instances to consult with their legal counsel to determine if such process, order, or subpoena is in proper form and if there is a showing of good cause for its issuance; if the process, order, or subpoena is not in proper form or if good cause has not been shown, they should insist that such defects be cured.

Practical Student Patron Privacy Considerations for the School Librarian

In creating a library policy on student patron privacy, the librarian should first categorize each access point available in the library. If the library is also a media center, then the policy should govern each form of media. Second, the librarian should categorize each student activity that generates a record. Then the librarian should create a policy that governs both records and activities.

For recorded activities the librarian must determine how the records will be maintained and the period of time they will be maintained. Then the librarian must determine which category of individuals should have access to these records and the nature of the circumstances entitling that specific category of individuals to library record data regarding a specific student. This should be reflected in the library policy.

Student's Circulation Records

Book circulation records are the simplest form of student record. These records are generally maintained on computer databases although some libraries still record this circulation activity by hand. The librarian should consider how long this information is to be retained and the purposes for which it is retained. Most librarians like to retain computer circulation records to aid their weeding process. They do not, however, necessarily require the student identity for this process. The librarians should carefully weigh the student's right to privacy with the library's legitimate need for statistical data. It might be quite possible to retain this circulation information indefinitely by simply deleting the student identity. This contemplative process, which the librarian must undertake, balances the legitimate needs of the librarian, as applied to each transaction that identifies a student, with the student patron's right to privacy.

The librarian should consider whether a student's circulation record should be maintained for the period of time the student is enrolled at the educational facility served by the library. In some instances a student could benefit by documentation of their circulation records. For example, one student applying for a scholarship to a private institution requested her circulation records to identify her reading patterns while enrolled at the school. Each librarian is the best arbitrator of his or her student body's needs.

The librarian's policy should also address the administration and faculty access to student circulation records. In some schools this access may be open and in some schools it may be closed. Here the librarian will be in the best position to make that evaluation. However, keeping the restriction of FERPA in mind, a policy that opens student circulation records should be thoughtfully and carefully drafted with specific purposes and guidelines for faculty review of records. There is most likely no legitimate reason for a high school algebra teacher to review the circulation records of a fourth-grade student. There must be a nexus or a legitimate reason for the teacher to review the records of their own students, and the students and their parents should be advised of this policy. In some schools the faculty and the librarian may find it appropriate for the faculty member to review the circulation records of students in a specific class for a specific project. If the library policy allows for this and the students are notified of this option, then their records may be shared. Clear and specific guidelines are the key to sharing student circulation records with the faculty (elementary teachers often look at overdue notices on the computer screen as they are helping students check out, etc.).

Each librarian should decide whether or not signing a circulation card by a student, which can be viewed by future patrons, violates a student's right of privacy. An alternative is using a student identification number.

Policy Regarding Computer–Related Records

Access to computers often generates records. Some schools have sign-up sheets whereas others have access code identities that generate database records of student access. These are records. As long as these records exist and identify the student, a librarian's activities with regard to these records are governed by FERPA. When students log in to computers with access codes, there is a creation of a student library patron record. Developing a student privacy policy requires a working relationship with your IT (Information Technology) specialist. It is important to know what records of activities of identifiable students are retained and the period for which they are retained. Once you have a clear understanding of the identifiable student activities that are retained and the period for which they are retained you can begin to create a policy.

The policies regarding computer-generated records will be similar to the policies regarding circulation records in most instances and governed by the same balance between faculty access and student rights of privacy. Some schools have concerns regarding illegal activities of students from school computer terminals such as hacking or the viewing of illegal pornography. In these instances the librarian may want to retain the student computer access information for a specific period of time. However, an indefinite retention of these records would serve no valid purpose.

Some libraries find it important to advise students that their activities are being tracked while on a school computer. This notice serves as a deterrent to student access of inappropriate Web sites. Students should be given specific written guidelines and criteria regarding the Web sites they may access.

Some libraries randomly review sites visited by students through the school library facilities. If this is done, students should be advised of this tracking. If faculty members use your computer facilities, they should be notified that their Internet browsing will also be subject to random review.

You are not invading a student's privacy by simply observing their Internet activity for the purpose of enforcing the library's policies on Internet Web activity.

Students' Multimedia Projects

Student-generated multimedia projects are placed in the library for school-wide access. After you have evaluated the copyright compliance issues, you can then evaluate the student patron privacy issues. It is important to have a release signed by the student to place the project in either the reserve section of the library or in the open access section of the library.

Students' Activities Within the Library

A more difficult area with regard to student privacy is the sharing of behavioral information of students while in the library. Having a policy with regard to this issue is important in defining the limits of your obligations to faculty and in instructing library workers. For example, a casual conversation over lunch between the librarian and a faculty member might place a student in a false light. If a librarian indicates that a specific student had spent their library time reading their neighbor's composition rather than searching for resources, the faculty member could conclude that the student had relied on another student to perform the assigned task. A clear policy that all activities of students while in the library are private will serve to guide both the librarians and the faculty as to the limits of acceptable information on student activities.

In some schools when the students are assigned to the library for a specific class period, it might be appropriate to advise the faculty member of the student activities. If this is the case include this in your policy.

Library Policies of Privacy and Maintenance of Records

Access to various forms of media generally is governed by written or computer-generated sign-up sheets. These records should be subjected to the same forms of consideration as circulation records, balancing the library's right to govern and protect its equipment with the student's right of privacy.

The library privacy policy should advise students, parents, faculty, and administration of:

- The records that are generated with regard to identifiable students;
- How long these records will be maintained;
- Who has access to these records;
- Under what circumstances these records will be shared with persons other than students and parents;
- The library's position on sharing student behavior within the library.

The policy should adhere to your state's laws on library patron privacy, student's rights to privacy, and federal laws of privacy. This policy should be communicated to faculty, staff, administration, and students and be supported by guidelines to direct library staff.

CONCLUSION

There is a federal statute that protects student library patron records. There are some states that have statutes protecting student library patron records. There is a federal statute that protects the records of library patrons (including students) with regard to videotapes but there is no federal statute protecting the privacy and confidentiality of patrons' library records. It is important to know the laws of your state. It is also important to have and to communicate an explicit school library policy on every facet of the library's facilities and to educate all employees of the library on patron privacy. Each employee should be instructed to contact the designated library authority upon the presentation of a subpoena or court order of search warrant, and if such authority is absent, to contact the attorney for the library.

Clear library policy on patron privacy in every accessible facet of the library is more important than ever, as is the application of that policy to patron use of library facilities.

ONLINE APPENDIXES

- The American Library Association's (ALA) Code of Ethics: http://www.ala.org /alaorg/oif/ethics.html. (Accessed January 31, 2003.)

- American Library Association Bill of Rights: http://www.ala.org/work/freedom /lbr.html. (Accessed January 31, 2003.)

- Association of College and Research Librarians Standards and Guidelines: http:// www.ala.org/acrl. (Accessed January 31, 2003.)

- United States Freedom of Information Act, 5 U.S.C. §52: http://www.ala .org/acrl. (Accessed January 31, 2003.)

Used with authority of the American Library Association.

STATE LAWS (ONLINE)

- ALA link to individual state laws regarding confidentiality of library records: http://www.ala.org/alaorg/oif/pol_conf.html. (Accessed January 31, 2003.)

While the right to patron library privacy must be inferred from the Constitution some states have specific statutes protecting this right. Each library must consult its own state's laws to determine its legal responsibility with regard to patrons' privacy and confidentiality of library records.

- Pub. L. 100–618, Sec. 2 (a) (2), Nov. 5, 1988, 102 Stat. 3195

- Ark. Code 13–2-701 et seq. Confidentiality of Patrons' Records

NOTES

1. American Library Association. Children's Internet Protection Act. Available: http://www.ala.org/cipa/Law.PDF. (Accessed May 30, 2002.)

2. The Children's Internet Protection Act (47 U.S.C. § 254[h]) and 20 U.S.C. § 9134) (CIPA) limits access to visual depictions of "obscenity" and "child pornography," and access to materials "harmful to minors " (20 U.S.C. § 9134[f][1] and 47 U.S.C. § 254[h][6][B]-[C]). Congress used its spending power to require filtering to

accomplish this purpose. The Act continues to prohibit school libraries from obtaining funds for Internet service from the Federal Communications Commission or the Institute of Museum and Library Services unless the library certifies that it uses computer technology on all computers to block Internet access in the above described manner. A school library receiving federal funds for the provision of Internet service must certify that blocking software operates on "any of its computers with Internet access" during "any use of such computers" (20 U.S.C. § 9134[f][1][B] and 47 U.S.C. § 254[h][6][C]). This federal law was challenged by the ALA, national and state library associations, public libraries, library patron groups, and individual library patrons. The three-judge panel in Philadelphia convened to hear this case found no filtering software successfully differentiates constitutionally protected speech from illegal speech on the Internet.

3. Debra Lau, "CIPA Ruling No Effect on Schools," *School Library Journal*, 48, no.7 (July 2002):16.

4. *American Library Association et al. v. United States,* No. 01–1303 in the United States District Court for the Eastern District of Pennsylvania. ACLU challenge to the Children's Internet Protection Act, a federal law requiring the use of Internet filtering software in libraries and public schools that receive certain federal funding.

5. Ben Edelman, Edelman Expert Report for *Multnomah County Public Library et al. vs. United States of America et al.* The Berkman Center for Internet and Society at Harvard Law School. Available: http://cyber.law.harvard.edu/people/edelman /mul-v-us/. (Accessed May 30, 2002.)

John Zittrain and Mr. Edelman have also released a report on the effects of filtering in Saudi Arabia in which they found news sites, U.S. government sites, and Israeli government sites (excluding the Israel Defense Force) could all be viewed as usual. They found that the overwhelming majority of education sites remained accessible. The report is available at: http://cyber.law.harvard.edu/filtering/saudiarabia/. (Accessed May 30, 2002.)

6. 20 USC Section 1232(g), Buckley Amendment, Family Educational and Privacy Rights.

7. See *Olmstead v. United States,* 277 U.S. 438 (128), which addresses the issue of privacy and wiretapping of phone conversations. "The makers of our Constitution . . . sought to protect Americans in their beliefs, their thoughts, their emotions and their sensations. They conferred, as against the government, the right to be let alone."

8. Video and Library Privacy Protection Act of 1988 Senate Bill 2361 100th Congress 2d Session, not passed.

9. ALA State Privacy Laws Regarding Library Records. Available: http://www .ala.org/alaorg/oif/stateprivacylaws.html. (Accessed May 25, 2002.)

10. Uniform Laws are merely proposals made to states for standard laws. The state legislature has the option to adopt them, reject them, or adopt parts, reject parts, and modify parts.

11. 5 U.S.C. Sec. 552 Federal Freedom of Information Act.

12. House Report 100–199, Committee on Government Operations. 100th Congress. First Session.

13. House Report 100–199, Committee on Government Operations. No. 93–876, March 5, 1974 [To accompany H.R. 12471], p.3.

14. Brown v. Johnston the Iowa Supreme Court—28 N.W.2d 510 (Iowa 1983).

15. 20 U.S.C. Sec. 1232g.

16. Ibid.

17. See United States Department of Justice. Computer Crime and Intellectual Property Section. Field Guidance on New Authorities that Relate to Computer Crime and Electronic Evidence Enacted in the USA PATRIOT Act of 2001. Available: http://www.usdoj.gov/criminal/cybercrime/PatriotAct.htm. (Accessed March 3, 2002.)

18. Pen/trap orders allow law enforcement to access "routing, addressing and signaling" information included in any electronic communications. This information could include Web site addresses the target has visited, e-mail addresses or parties with whom the target has communicated, Internet protocol addresses, or port numbers of individual computer terminals. This does not include the body of the e-mail or the subject line information of the e-mail. Pen/trap orders may be issued nationwide and do not have to identify the Internet Service Provider (ISP). Some educational institutions are ISPs.

Carnivore may, with judicial authority, be installed by the FBI (http://www.fbi .gov/hq/lab/carnivore/carnivore2.html). This is a device that "watches" e-mail and other electronic communications on an ISP's servers, looking for communications initiated or received by the target of an investigation. The law appears to authorize a court to order the installation of Carnivore. By allowing Carnivore to be installed, ISPs can shift many of the legal and operational burdens of complying with a surveillance order to law enforcement. For educational institutions with ISP status, incentives to install Carnivore must be weighed against traditional commitments to ensure rights and practices of privacy and academic discourse for students, faculty and staff. Carnivore is described in great detail at the FBI's Web site, which describes its diagnostic tools.

19. The Foreign Intelligence Surveillance Act (FISA), Title 50 USC5, authorizes electronic surveillance for foreign intelligence. This act governs wire and electronic communications sent by or intended to be received by U.S. persons who are within the United States. (A U.S. person is defined to be a U.S. citizen, a permanent resident alien, or groups of such people.) FISA does not cover intercepts of U.S. persons who are overseas (unless the communications are with a U.S. person resident in the United States). Under FISA provisions, U.S. citizens could be subject to surveillance if they are aiding and abetting international terrorism.

A court order is normally required for a FISA wiretap, but there are two exceptions. Following a declaration of war, the president, through the attorney general, can authorize a wiretap for foreign intelligence purposes for up to fifteen days without a court order. The other exception can occur if the communications are exclusively between foreign powers or involve intelligence other than spoken communications from a location under the exclusive control of a foreign power.

FISA wiretap orders are granted by a special court, consisting of seven judges appointed by the chief justice of the United States. Applications for a court order are made by a federal officer and require approval by the attorney general. Semiannually, the attorney general must inform the House Permanent Select Committee on Intelligence and the Senate Select Committee on Intelligence of all wiretap activity. Although information on FISA wiretaps is classified, the attorney general is required to give the Administrative Office of the U.S. Courts an annual report on the number of FISA applications and orders. Since 1979, there have been an average of slightly over

500 FISA wiretap orders annually. As of 1988, over 4,000 requests had been made by the government for surveillance under FISA; none had been turned down.

20. USA PATRIOT Act H.R. 3162, Title II Section 215, amending the Foreign Intelligence Surveillance Act (FISA), Title V, Section 501(a)(1). Available: http://leahy.senate.gov/press/200110/USA.pdf. (Accessed March 3, 2002.)

10

◆◈◆

METATAGS IN WEB SITES
AND THE LAW: LIBRARY
BIBLIOGRAPHIES—
STUDENT WEB PAGES

The Internet and the Web have pulled us out of two-dimensional space.
—Tim Berners-Lee

This chapter covers the following topics on metatags:

- Metatag: What Is It? Where Is It? What Is It Used For?
- Metatags and the Law
- Metatags and Trademark Law
- Student Identity on Student and School-Created Web Sites

School librarians at one time were principally concerned with collection development and weeding collections. Suddenly the big "M"—Media centers—became an additional area of attention. Both physical space and time allotment were created for this new facet of the school librarian's attention. Media centers were expanded to include the World Wide Web (WWW). Students are not only passive participants of the WWW as surfers and browsers, they are active participants as Web page publishers, and in many instances these Web pages are made and published through the media center. Librarians must understand the laws that govern both the incoming data and the outgoing data. It has taken the U.S. Supreme Court to decide many of these issues, and those decisions were not unanimous. To make it more difficult, even the Supreme Court states these decisions must be made on a case-by-case basis. There are no hard-and-fast guidelines and rules. Librarians routinely face some of the same issues the Supreme Court faces. This chapter will help the school librarian recognize legal issues and create media center guidelines addressing these issues.

METATAG: WHAT IS IT? WHERE IS IT? WHAT IS IT USED FOR?

There is the visible Web and the invisible Web. Metatags are a part of that invisible Web world that creates visible results. They are a fundamental part of Web page development. If the librarian or a student is publishing Web pages, metatags are a part of that publication process. Metatags are HTML (Hyper-Text Markup Language) source codes created and embedded in the HTML text of Web pages. These specific identifiers, placed in Web pages by their creators for the sole purpose of attracting search engine "hits," allow search engines to classify and index Web sites. Some search engines index these terms by the use of a "spider" whereas others employ "editors" to forward Web sites to a directory. Web site creators want their metatags to cause the search engine to include their sites in its return list as prominently as possible.

Google—the latest development in natural language searching, or is it? This ubiquitous search engine has made the concept of so-called natural language searching the king of indexing and retrieval. Google, the product of a class paper by two students at Stanford, is an instant classic. Its hierarchical return represents an algorithmic calculation made for each Web page of the chosen search term. Search engines are optimized to give good answers to short queries. Being overly specific isn't more effective. Long queries do not result in better answers.

In essence, Google's hierarchical search returns a vocabulary that is weighted by the Google formula, which does not include metadata. Google now powers three of the four most used search engines and handles 75 percent of search traffic.

When Google ranks sites, it runs an algorithm on the Web pages with a spider. Google will search for any Web pages that mention your designated words at least once. Hierarchies return higher rankings for including all the searched-for words. The more times the words are mentioned in the site, the higher the score will be in terms of the hierarchies of return. However, if the phrase is mentioned over eight times, Google will begin to subtract points for the number of times it is mentioned. Google's search engine optimization looks at over 100 items.

The Google search engine assigns an emphasis to text that is found in the title tag. Most search results will show pages that have the searched words in the title tag. Here are some of the major items that Google analyzes on Web pages:

Words in title tag
Words in links

Words in headings

Words in bold

Words in the URL

Comment tags in HTML

Google gives more weight to Web pages that have between 250 and 450 words on a page, and more weight is given to the first 25 words. Phrases used to describe pictures are the methods by which images are returned. Google may also penalize for having too much repetition. It gives particular emphasis to words in heading tags such as H2 to H6.

Software exists to evaluate your Web page ranking. One is Web Position Gold (free download: http://www.webposition-gold-2.net/download.htm). This is not a true ranking because it does not consider all the variables that Google uses in creating its Web ranking such as back links, DMOZ listings, or alt tags.

The Google Search Engine Optimization site (http://www.internet-advertising-marketing-manual.com/google-optimization.htm) explains in detail the Google hierarchical system.

Metatags are not visible to a Web surfer while viewing the actual Web site. One way to view the metatags chosen by the Web page maker to attract search engines is to right click the mouse on the Web page. Select View Source (for Internet Explorer users; other browsers may differ) and the source code that supports the Web page and the meta data may be viewed. These metatags result in a link from the search engine to the Web page, which may ultimately result in a hit from the searcher.

Web site authors commonly use both keyword and descriptive metatags; however, a keyword is the most common form. Search engines give extra weight to certain keywords and phrases, which can bring significant traffic to a site when they are used. Keywords do not have to be invisible; they can be made invisible by making the text the same color as the Web page background color. Web site authors will often use keywords in their metatags that have no relation to the content of their sites. The most commonly included metatag is the word "sex."

However, Web designers typically insert keywords in the HTML code that relate to the content of the Web site. For example, a Web site devoted to the appreciation of ballet would presumably contain some of the following metatags arranged in HTML code:

<META NAME = "KEYWORDS" CONTENT = "ballet, petipa, bolshoi, mariinsky, russia, diagheliev, borkst ">

If a Web surfer is searching for Web sites devoted to the Bolshoi Ballet and enters several of the above-mentioned keywords in a search engine, the search engine would return the link to Russian ballet sites. The more keyword metatags there are that correspond to the Web surfer's search terms, the greater the likelihood is that a particular Web site will appear at or near the top of the results list. Additionally, some Web site developers insert the same word multiple times in the metatag list, so that a link to a Web site will appear higher on the search engine's results list.

Other keyword technologies work similarly to metatags. For example, search engines sell advertisements and featured placements based upon search words entered by their users. These are known as trigger ads. If a user uses a search engine to search for a particular product, the search engine operator may place on its search results screen a banner advertisement for a seller of that product, or may list that seller's Web page in a featured position. A Google search may result in trigger ads related to that search. Gambling ads are an issue of social well being currently being discussed. Visitors to gambling sites are subsequently bombarded with trigger ads for gambling. Almost half of the pathological gamblers that were part of a study that aimed to identify various characteristics of people with the gambling addiction say that advertisements—on television, radio, or billboards—can trigger their desire to gamble.[1] These gamblers are the targets of trigger ads.

Using the metatag that will provide the greatest access through the search engine is the most effective way to increase the exposure of the site to Web users. To this end Web page designers will use extensive numbers of terms, variations of a term, and repetitive uses of a term. Some businesses rely solely on search engine returns for their customer base. High search engine site recognition is directly related to their income and return on investment.

Metatags and the Law

There are legal limitations that govern the choice of metatags a library or a student can use to draw search engines to their Web sites. An understanding of what is and is not legal and legal trends in this area is important in making these choices and in understanding what your search has found and why it has been retrieved.

Like most laws related to the World Wide Web, metatag law is evolving. Initially attorneys and the courts attempted to apply print world laws to the cyber world. This has not always been effective or productive. Although this chapter cannot give you the ultimate law on metatags, because it has yet to be written, it can illuminate some of the issues with which the Congress, the courts, and Webmasters are currently grappling and show how technology and a free market are also addressing these issues. A path is emerging, and certainly ethical guidelines for the development of library Web page metatags and student Web page metatags can be created. Ten years ago the law of trademarks was a matter that impacted very few outside those marketing goods and services and their legal and advertising representatives. Trademark law now impacts everyone who publishes a Web page and to a lesser extent everyone who surfs the Web. The Internet has made complex and emerging laws relevant to faculties and students alike.

It is useful to keep the following points in mind:

• The World Wide Web is just that: worldwide—and in its worldwide scope it is inherently lawless. It is accessible by adults and children, and contributors to the Internet represent all ages, all points of view, for both the best of purposes and the worst of purposes. There are no metatag Web police or cyber-sniffing dogs that follow their noses to illegal metatag hijackers. No one has to cross through inspection prior to publishing a Web page.

• It is fundamental but important to keep in mind that the state law and federal law discussed in this publication refer to laws of the United States, not laws of the world; sometimes we forget, the United States is not the world. However, as librarians it is essential to be familiar with our laws and observe them with the understanding that many Web sites are created outside the United States and thus cannot be governed by our laws even though they are accessible in our country. The Internet and its "cybergeographic" reach extend to the deepest jungles and the highest mountains in every country on this planet. Consequently, copyright and trademark holders, those most at risk with metatags, must be aware that everyone who infringes upon their copyright ownership rights cannot be held accountable—many of the users remain untouchable, undetectable, and anonymous.

• There are currently no means of collecting damages for the use of copyrighted works on the Internet by persons in some third-world countries.[2] Some countries are much more restrictive than the United States in their laws pertaining to Web data, particularly China and Germany, whereas others are more liberal.

• Because the Internet is analyzed and classified by robots or spiders, some HTML and Internet metatag techniques may be viewed as de facto linking tools. The use of metatags to index Web pages, for example, is a kind of linking technology, and metatag disputes have emerged as linking law disputes.

TRADEMARK—DEFINITION

A trademark is "a symbol that allows a consumer to identify the source or sponsor of a particular good or service." Brand image and name recognition are important elements of a brand's success. Often, the most valuable asset a company owns is its name.[3] Trademark protection is "the law's recognition of the psychological function of symbols." Justice Felix Frankfurter observed that we live by symbols and thus spend significant money on goods and services bearing symbols.[4] Obvious examples are Coca-Cola, Pepsi, and Nike.

An exception arises with a word or phrase that has achieved "generic status"—that is, the name becomes so well known that it is used as a generic term for the underlying product. In the United States, "aspirin" was formerly a trademark of the Bayer company, but decades ago a U.S. court held that it had become a generic term and therefore was no longer protectable as a trademark. Generic terms are not subject to trademark status. Both Xerox and Kleenex launched extensive media campaigns to protect the trademark status of their products. Xerox was becoming interchangeable with the concept of reproduction of a document, and Kleenex was becoming interchangeable with the term "tissue." They were successful in the protection of their trademark identities. However, no one can trademark a generic term such as "auto" or "car."

Coca-Cola is a name that is subject to trademark status; its product has acquired a secondary meaning associated with its product. Coca-Cola is advertised in the most remote sections of the world and in Time Square in New York City. Although it is ubiquitous in its presence, it is still owned distinctly by the Coca-Cola Company. Marks that have been found to meet the "famous" requirement under the Lanham Act,[5] described below, are trademark protected. Examples include Budweiser for beer, Nailtiques for fingernail care products, and Candy Land as the name of a children's game.

When a competitor's trademark is used as a keyword in a metatag, the trademark owner is likely to find this to be an unacceptable use of a trademark in which they may have invested many millions of dollars. Competitors use trademarks as keyword metatags and trigger ads in several contexts.[6] Business entities use their competitors' trademarks as keyword metatags for the purpose of luring Web browsers to their Web sites and away from their competitors' Web sites. This is known as deceptive keyword metatagging. For example, if a clothing manufacturer chooses to use the term "Lands' End" in its metatag language, it would be deceptive metatagging. One business would be taking advantage of another business's trademark. Even though Lands' End has been purchased by Sears, the trademark still remains nationally and may not be used.

METATAGS AND TRADEMARK LAW

Trademarks are used in the creation of metatag data. This use can be a legal and fair use of a trademark under certain circumstances, and an illegal use under other circumstances. It is important in the supervision of students' Web sites to understand the legal use of a trademark. One of the most popular trademarks for student use is the Nike "swoosh" symbol. Other popular trademarks are the Playboy bunny and cartoon characters.

Their use is governed by trademark law, which is of both federal and state origin. Originally, the state common law provided the main source of protection for trademarks. In the late 1800s the U.S. Congress enacted the first federal trademark law. Federal trademark law has consistently expanded and become the dominant law in the area of trademark law. The federal statute on which the federal courts principally rely is the Lanham Act.[7] The Lanham Act defines the scope of a trademark, the process by which a federal registration for a trademark can be obtained from the Patent and Trademark Office, and penalties for trademark infringement. The federal courts are the chief and most important source of trademark rulings and provide the most extensive source of trademark protection, although state common law actions are still available.

Trademark Protection

Trademark owners have the right to protect their investment and this includes the right to prevent others from improperly using the same or similar mark. Therefore, trademark law protects a symbol, word, name, or device adopted and used by a merchant to identify his goods or services and distinguishes them from competitors.[8] One principle goal of trademark law is to protect consumers from confusion or deception. Trademark law provides that a party cannot use another's trademark if the use of that trademark will cause a "likelihood of confusion" among consumers, or "dilution," which is the potential diminution of the association between a trademark and the particular product or entity.

The basis of trademark rights in the United States comprises three important criteria: (1) the classification or type of goods or services offered, (2) the geographical area in which that mark is used,[9] and (3) the priority of trademark use in interstate commerce.[10] Identical trademarks may be used by multiple parties if the goods or services are offered in different geographic areas or through different market channels and the trademark has not reached national status.[11] For example there are many Merry Maids cleaning services across the country.

Similar products or services that compete in the national market, however, cannot use identical trademarks.[12] No one can go into the soft drink business and market their product as Coca-Cola because Coca-Cola has reached national status.

The Federal Trademark Dilution Act of 1995 (FTDA) provides for the protection of famous marks from dilution.[13] The definition of dilution under FTDA is "the lessening of the capacity of a famous mark to identify and distinguish goods or services regardless of the presence or absence of (a) competition between the owner of the famous mark and other parties, and (b) likelihood of confusion, mistake, or deception."

Trademark dilution can occur when a third-party Web site designer uses a competitor's trademarks as keyword metatags but the business or entity contracting with the third-party Web site designer does not authorize or have knowledge of the use of the competitor's metatags. Because no court has been confronted with this issue, it is unclear whether and to what extent this type of unintentional metatagging will result in liability.

Acceptable Uses of Trademark as a Metatag

In order to attract users to the Web site some Web site sponsors and creators have used trademarks in their metatags. This could include the word "Disney" or "McDonalds" or even "Playboy." When the search engine recognizes the trademark, it considers that site to be related to a search on the trademark, and returns that site in the search results.

A common phrase heard in both the entertainment world and the legal world is, "Don't mess with The Mouse." The mouse is Mickey Mouse of Disney, and messing with The Mouse means dealing with Mickey's legal counsel, whose sole function is to protect Disney images and characters. Mickey has appeared, however briefly, as an X-rated mouse. Disney attorneys were quick to remove Mickey from that dire fate. Disney protects Mickey's purity and association with Disney on all fronts. Further, Disney does not allow sites to exploit Mickey, or any of their characters, for any purpose other than those Disney deems appropriate and for which Disney has contracted and been compensated.

The same could be said of "the bunny." Playboy has taken its job of protecting its image seriously. Whereas the image of Mickey is for children and represents purity, the image of the Playboy Bunny represents sexuality. These images are diametrically opposed but they are clearly images that immediately connote an identity associated with a representation recognized over the entire world.

These images are protected by the law of copyright and by trademark law, which includes the Lanham Act. The bunny symbol is a trademark recognized worldwide as that of Playboy. Trademark owners whose marks have been used as a metatag feel that this use of their image and name is illegal.[14] Recently, trademark owners have objected to the use of their marks in metatags of unrelated Web sites and relied upon trademark law to block the use of their trademarks to attract viewers to Web sites.

The key to using another's trademark is how it is used. A nominative use occurs when use of a term is necessary for purposes of identifying another producer's product, not the user's own product. Nominative has a lengthy legal definition but in essence it is a manner of identifying a subject matter. If a student chose to use the Nike swoosh simply to identify their personal Web site, this would most likely not be an acceptable use of the trademarked symbol. However, if a student created a Web site that researched and compared various sports shoes and used individual company trademarks in the metatags to link to their various Web pages, then this trademark use could conceivably be a nominative use. Certainly, the term "Nike" can be used in the metatag to the student's Web site.

An example of a nominative use occurred when the newspaper *USA Today* ran a telephone poll, asking its readers to vote for their favorite member of the music group The New Kids on the Block. The New Kids on the Block sued *USA Today* for trademark infringement.

The court held that the use of the trademark "New Kids on the Block" was a privileged nominative use because: (1) the group was not readily identifiable without using the mark; (2) *USA Today* used only so much of the mark as reasonably necessary to identify it; and (3) there was no suggestion of endorsement or sponsorship by the group. The basic idea is that use of a trademark is sometimes necessary to identify and talk about another party's products and services. When the above conditions are met, such a use will be privileged.[15]

Another illustration of an acceptable use of a trademark is found in the 9th U.S. Circuit Court of Appeals ruling, which defined the boundaries of what is a "fair use" of another's intellectual property over the Internet. On February 1, 2002, in *Playboy v. Welles,* the court confirmed that the use of another's trademarks on Web pages and metatags, under certain circumstances, does not constitute trademark infringement.[16]

Terri Welles was chosen to be the Playboy Playmate of the year for 1981. Welles later registered and opened a Web site that offered information about herself, advertised photos for sale, and offered memberships in her Terri Welles club. Welles used the phrase "Playmate of the Year 1981" on the masthead of the Web site and in her banner ads that promoted her site. Welles included a biographical section on the Web site identifying herself as "Playmate of the Year" in 1981. The terms "Playboy" and "Playmate" also appeared in her metatags. These metatags drew searchers of these terms to her Web site, which diverted them from the true Playboy site.

Playboy Enterprises Inc. filed suit against Welles for trademark infringement. The district court granted Welles's motion for summary judgment and Playboy appealed. The 9th Circuit affirmed, holding that Welles's use of the Playboy trademarks was a permissible fair use of those trademarks. Because Welles was promoting herself and her history, the use of the words was held not to be an infringement of the Playboy name. Welles's use was found to be a "nominative fair use" of another's trademark.

The court adopted a three-part test for the nominative fair use of another's trademark in the context of the Internet. In order to meet this test, the party claiming fair use must demonstrate that the product or service in question is one not readily identifiable without the use of the plaintiff's trademark; that only so much of the mark or marks have been used as is reasonably necessary to identify the product or service; and that the user did nothing that would, in conjunction with the mark, suggest sponsorship or endorsement by the trademark holder.

The court held that Welles's use of Playboy's trademarks in headlines and banner advertisements was permissible because the trademark described "a person, a place or attribute of a product" and there was no descriptive substitute for the trademark. Agreeing with the district court's analysis, the 9th Circuit held that it would be impractical as well as ineffectual for Welles to describe herself as the "nude model selected by Mr. Hefner's magazine as its

No.-1 prototypical woman for the year 1981" instead of "Playmate of the Year 1981." Because Welles could only identify herself as Playmate of the Year 1981 by using Playboy's trademarks, the first part of the nominative fair-use test was met. The court indicated that a user must have a legitimate connection with Playboy in order to use the trademark. Being a subscriber to Playboy would not meet this test unless the Web site were about being a subscriber to Playboy. Can students use the Playboy trademarks for metatags? The answer almost certainly will be: no. Will Playboy in the future contract with individual Playmates to limit their use of the Playboy and Playmate name? Probably.

The court held that the second part of the nominative use test was met in that the use of the mark was reasonably necessary to identify Welles in the headlines and banner advertisements and the use was not found to be excessive. Nothing within the advertisements or headlines suggested sponsorship or endorsement of Welles's site by Playboy. Specifically, Welles's use of the terms "Playboy" and "Playmate" in metatags was examined. The court first defined metatags as keywords. Some search engines search metatags to identify relevant Web sites. For example, if a Web surfer entered the term "Playmate" into a search engine such as Google or Yahoo!, which was included in Welles's metatags, the results of that search would include Welles's site.

The court noted the terms were not used extensively in Welles's metatags, and that her site did not appear at the top of the list of search results. The use of the trademark terms was found to be nominative and not violative of trademark infringement. The Playboy court noted that "[p]recluding their use would have the unwanted effect of hindering the free flow of information on the Internet, something which is certainly not a goal of trademark law."

In a case that resulted in an opposite decision, where no link between the product and Playboy was found, the use of "Playboy" as a metatag was found to constitute federal trademark infringement, false designation of origin under the Lanham Act, federal trademark dilution, trademark counterfeiting, and common law trademark infringement. In one of the first cases involving metatags, Playboy filed suit against Calvin Designer Label (not associated with Calvin Klein) for using Playboy's trademarks within its Web site.[17] It can be easily inferred by the actions of Calvin Designer Label that it was their goal to exploit the Playboy image and name to attract customers to its Web site with their use of the terms "Playboy" and "Playmate."

Calvin Designer Label registered and used the domain name "playmate.com." On the Web site the words "Playboy" and "Playboy Magazine" were entered in black on a black background, making them invisible to the viewer but visible to the search engine. As a result of the defendant's use of these terms within its Web site, the Calvin Designer Label site was typically the first or second site returned in a search for these terms. Playboy's injunction against the use of its trademark was granted in this case. The court ordered the defendant to immediately stop using the "Playboy" and "Playmate" trademarks in connection with its Web site, and required the defendant to delete the marks from its Web site's metatags.

In supervising the building of students' Web sites, it is essential to view the source code and examine the metatags. In training students in Web site creation, they should be educated to be very careful when using the logos of others and understand clearly under what circumstances these logos may be used. Educating them on the limits of the "nominative use" of a trademark is important.

Trademark Infringement

Section 43 of the Lanham Act addresses and prohibits trademark infringement. To prevail on a trademark infringement claim, a plaintiff must show that the defendant's use of the plaintiff's mark is "likely to cause confusion, or to cause mistake, or to deceive" the relevant consumer base. This is an example of a legal doctrine applicable to print, which is not always effective in the world of the Web.

Trademark confusion is considered to be the "keystone of infringement." Each of the federal circuits has adopted different multifactorial, overlapping tests for determining if likelihood of confusion exists. The key factors can be summarized as:

1. the similarity of the two marks;
2. the similarity in channels of distribution;
3. the sophistication of the buyers and the care they are likely to use;
4. the alleged infringer's intent;
5. with noncompetitive goods, whether buyers would expect the mark owner to expand into the field occupied by the alleged infringer; and
6. evidence of actual confusion.[18]

It could easily be argued that Johnny's Web site, which sports the Nike swoosh and addresses his interest in desert reptiles could never be confused with a true Nike Web site or Nike product. However, Nike would object to the search engine returns in the thousands that included its name and trademark. If Johnny had not used the Nike name and the Nike trademark, and that use had been reserved solely to Nike, the search engine return would include only Nike.

A free market and technology are addressing this issue. Virtually any search engine will first return Nike.com, Playboy.com, and Disney.com for a search of any of these words. These companies may purchase their top location on the search engines, thus assuring their sites will be the first sites encountered in a search for their trademarked name.

Dilution of Trademark

Even in the absence of a likelihood of confusion, the Lanham Act protects well-recognized and famous marks from dilution, which is "the lessening of the capacity of a famous mark" by a subsequent user of the mark. Courts have recognized that dilution can occur through "blurring," "tarnishment," or "elimination."

Tarnishment arises when a defendant's use of a mark similar to a plaintiff's mark presents a danger that consumers will form unfavorable associations with the mark. This can occur when the unauthorized use of a famous mark is linked to products of poor quality or is portrayed in an unwholesome manner, such that the positive associations and the distinctive quality of a plaintiff's mark are degraded. In one of the first cases to apply the federal law of dilution to acts within cyberspace, the court held that Hasbro's famous Candy Land mark was tarnished by the defendant's use of "candyland.com" as a domain name for a sexually explicit Web site.[19]

A library may decide to build a Web site about the impact of divorce on children. This is perfectly acceptable. However, the library could not adopt Minnie and Mickey as their Web site mascots and title the Web site, "What Happens When Minnie and Mickey Divorce?" This not only exploits the Disney characters but it tarnishes their image. As Stanford Law School Professor Lawrence Lessig points out, the cordoning off of the Internet and other potentially public property may soon lead to a time when one can "quote Donald Duck" only with corporate permission.[20]

Anticybersquatting Consumer Protection Act of 1999

The Federal Trademark Dilution Act in January 1996 has been used to prevent cybersquatters from holding famous names hostage from trademark owners who want to use them on Web sites and to prevent others from using famous marks in metatags, which one court called "the essence of dilution." The application of dilution law to the Web is no accident. As Senator Patrick Leahy stated, "It is my hope that this anti-dilution statute can help stem the use of deceptive Internet addresses taken by those who are choosing marks that are associated with the products and reputations of others."[21] The continued growth of cybersquatting and increased sophistication of the cybersquatters motivated Congress to enact the Anticybersquatting Consumer Protection Act of 1999 (ACPA).[22]

This Act bans the bad faith registration or trafficking in domain names that are identical or confusingly similar to a "distinctive" trademark. This obviates the "fame" requirement and ties protection instead to the well-known trademark requirement of distinctiveness. Thus the legal bar is lowered when trademark protection demands it.

With the recent adoption of the ACPA, Congress attempted to support the value of trademarks. The effectiveness of the new act, however, is still uncertain. Only acts committed after the enactment of the ACPA will be covered by the new act and uncertainty remains as to what constitutes "bad faith" under the ACPA. The purposes of the ACPA include protecting consumers and business, encouraging e-commerce growth, clarifying the law, and allowing a cause of action against cybersquatters.[23] Cybersquatters move in and take a name that is identified with national entities. The bad faith and abusive practices of snatching away company names and registering them under a domain name is protected by this law.[24]

The Anticybersquatting Consumer Protection Act is the only federal law that specifically protects celebrity names. The Act therefore protects not only trademarks, but also "famous personal names" from exploitation by "unfair" domain name registrations, such as proposing to sell it to a celebrity or falsely suggesting celebrity endorsement of the site.[25] Although it is commonly thought that the government has taken a hands-off approach to the Internet, a number of laws affecting intellectual property have the effect of privatizing a great deal of what is available on the Internet and criminalizing any encroachment on the corporate interests protected there.

As students create Web sites it is important to advise them in the use of URL names they may and may not use. WWW.SylvesterStallone.com would not be an available name. Most common names have been registered and may be purchased, but many of these prices would clearly be outside the student's pocket book. Computer.com recently sold for $500,000 and wisdom.com sold for $475,000.00.[26] ACPA also targets its remedies to situations where domain names utilize another's trademark.[27]

Plaintiff Marianne Bihari was an interior designer and worked under the name Bihari Interiors, Inc. Defendant Craig Gross and his girlfriend hired Bihari Interiors to decorate Gross's condominium. Gross and Bihari's relationship soured, and Gross acquired the Internet domain names bihari.com and bihariinteriors.com, which he used to host Web sites that were highly critical of Bihari and her services. These sites also provided a means by which other disappointed clients of Bihari Interiors could post comments to voice their dissatisfaction. The Web sites used "Bihari Interiors" and "Bihari" in metatags embedded within the Web sites' HTML code. These metatags enable search engines to locate the Web sites with Bihari queries. Bihari served Gross with a complaint and motion for injunctive relief. Gross subsequently relinquished both domain names; however, he then acquired the domain names designscam.com and manhattaninteriordesign.com, which he used to house the same content.

Bihari sought to preliminarily enjoin defendants from using her name in the domain names or metatags of any of their Web sites, claiming violations of the ACPA and 43(a) of the Lanham Act. On the ACPA claim, the court stated that the plain language and legislative intent of the Act made clear that it did not apply to metatags nor was there any precedent for extending such protection. The court also denied the motion based on the Lanham Act trademark infringement claim. The court declined to find that the metatags created a likelihood of confusion, explaining that no reasonable viewer would believe that the disparaging comments regarding Bihari's business were endorsed by Bihari Interiors. Moreover, there was no "lengthy delay" between attempting to access the real Bihari Interiors Web site and learning that one has failed to do so by coming upon one of the disparaging Web sites. In addition, the court held that the defendants' use was fair, as the metatags were used in a descriptive context to identify the content of the Web sites and there was no intent to confuse customers as to Web site sponsorship. Because the defendants' use of plaintiff's mark in the metatags was not likely to cause confusion and was further protected as a fair use, the plaintiff failed to demonstrate likelihood of success on the Lanham Act claim.

In recognition of this line of legal reasoning, the George W. Bush Election Committee registered all possible offensive domain names for themselves. The owner of the www.Bushsucks.com is actually the George W. Bush Election Committee and Bushsucks.com will take you to that Web site.

Although Disney is generally the plaintiff in copyright cases, in the case of *Goto.com, Inc. v. Walt Disney Co.*, it found itself in the defendant's chair, and Disney lost. Here Disney and Goto both sponsored search engines. Goto's trademark was a green light with the words GOTO; Disney used a green light with the word GO. Goto.com and Disney were direct competitors because both sites offered search engines. The issue was "whether two remarkably similar logos used commercially on the World Wide Web are likely to confuse consumers under federal trademark law." The court found there was likelihood that Web users would be confused. The court emphasized "the overwhelming similarity of the marks." With regard to the second factor, the court noted "the potential for one company to provide a host of unrelated services" via the Web.[28]

Domain Names are Trademark Registered

Branding a product is an important marketing technique and having the right domain name—one that describes the products or services offered at the Web site—is an important element of the e-commerce branding technique. Having a memorable domain name that users relate to a product or online service is a valuable cyber asset and as such many e-commerce domain names are trademark protected. In 1995, Procter and Gamble registered hundreds of generic domain names and offered them for sale at auction Web sites five years later. Bank of America bought "loans.com" for $3 million from a California businessman who had no operating Web site but received 3,000 to 4,000 hits a day.

NEW THREAT: DOMAIN NAPPING

A librarian's well-researched links, which are safe, approved, and clearly meet the library's Web site criteria, could suddenly be hijacked and become X-rated sites overnight. A Uniform Resource Locator (URL) is the unique identifier of a Web site for the World Wide Web and that address is held on the server of an ISP. There are many Internet service providers but there are few domain registrars. There was one worldwide domain registrar, Network Solutions, which maintained the entire .com, .net and .org domain system, until the system was deregulated three years ago. The Internet Corporation for Assigned Names and Numbers (ICANN) governs the technical and policy functions of higher-level domains but registration is now in the hands of many approved registrars worldwide. A conscientious librarian should routinely check the library Web site links.

There are organizations that search for expired domains and install their own sites the moment the domain expires. Their goal is to find an active site that may have forgotten its renewal and move in while the legitimate owner is away. The Poetry Society, with 300,000 hits a month, was one such victim.[29] They did eventually recover their site. The domain nappers take one of two courses of action or sometimes both: They insert their own site, which often contains pornography, or they sell the site back to the original owner. Checking linked sites found routinely on a library's bibliography that are .com or .org is important.

The status of a particular domain may be checked by accessing http://www.whois.net (accessed February 1, 2003) and typing in the URL. You can also find advice on the Icann site (http://www.icann.org [accessed February 1, 2003]) and InterNIC (http://www.internic.net [accessed February 1, 2003]).

A domain-name registration secured in the United States is not necessarily secured worldwide, for each country has its own domain-name registry. Therefore, if a client or business has extensive business operations overseas, then it should also look into registering its name in those countries as well.

Some countries have profited greatly from registering domain names. For example, each country that hooks into the World Wide Web is given a two-letter country code that appears immediately after the second-level domain name, for example, www.xyz.us.com.[30] Two countries that experienced booms in domain-name registrations were Turkmenistan, whose country code is "tm," and American Samoa, whose code is "as."

Many common-law countries, such as the United States, use the letters "tm" to serve as notice of a common-law or unregistered trademark. Some companies and domain name profiteers have registered famous trademarks in Turkmenistan because its "tm" country code is the same as the "Trademark" abbreviation. New countries are granted new top-level domain name designations by the Internet Assigned Number Authority (IANA), a United States–based authority that assigns Internet addresses.

The Keeling Islands (Cocos), a group of small islands in the Indian Ocean that are an off-shore territory of Australia, have become the newest domain of choice. The islands were given "cc" as their two-letter country designation. As more top-level country domains are added to the Internet, it becomes increasingly likely that confusingly similar domain names will be registered elsewhere in the world. As for the people of the Cocos, they may never have to pay taxes again due to the money earned from registering top-level domain names. Cocos has a population of slightly more than 600 people.[31]

Idealab, which owns dotTV, paid the nation of Tuvalu $50 million in royalties for rights to e-mail and domain names ending in ".tv," which they plan to resell. Free.tv, china.tv, and net.tv were sold by dotTV for $100,000 each with an annual Initial Registrations Fee of $100,000.[32] Students may decide to register their names of choice in domains other than "dot com." The dotTV choice however, may be too pricey.

STUDENT IDENTITY ON STUDENT AND SCHOOL-CREATED WEB SITES

The dark side of life is reflected on the Internet. The profile of Internet pedophiles is understood and well documented. The Internet is not only a medium for distribution of child pornography, it also is a medium for initial contact between a child and pedophiles and pornographers.

A pedophile's first objective is to identify a child's age, sex, name, and location. If they can simply obtain a name and perhaps the name of a sports team or any activity in which they are involved, they can secure all other information from that source. They are extremely adept with Internet research. They then befriend the child online exploiting the information they have gathered. Suddenly the child's interests become the same interests as the pedophile. They encourage the child to see the world in which they live as hostile and uncaring. Parents are portrayed as indifferent and unloving, teachers as not caring and incapable of understanding the child's world, and friends as betrayers. The child is left to believe only the pedophile truly understands and cares for him or her. Pornography is sent softening the child to what will ultimately be expected, and then a meeting is set. Pedophiles will even send money or tickets to the child for transportation.

The media center's first objective is to protect the identity of all its students, particularly if they publish on the Web. Under no circumstance should the library or the media center in any way publish the identity of the students on the Web. The second objective is to educate the children as to the potential danger. The third objective is to have the students search their own name. Use all forms of their name and include any activities that might include the students name. Have each student evaluate how much information is available on the Web regarding that student. Many children's theaters publish their actors' names. Many Little League baseball teams publish the team's name, the players' names, and a group photo. It is not just mom-and-pop organizations that commit this blunder. Until May 2002, when the danger was brought to their attention, the Texas Parks and Wildlife Commission published children's Web sites with their full name, age, and hometown. This may not be in the child's best interest. These issues should be discussed. The Center for Missing and Exploited Children (http://www.missingkids.com [accessed February 3, 2003]) has rules for children in dealing with Internet stranger danger. These should be posted at all computers.

CONCLUSION

The media center is often the location of Web page and Web site creation for the student, the faculty, and the librarian. Often, the student is required to publish the Web pages created. It is important for the media center to produce guidelines for faculty and for students governing the creation and publishing of Web pages.

Trademark infringement is an important issue. The guidelines should define a nominative use and allow trademarks to be used nominatively. Metatags should be representative of the actual content of the Web page. No secret words should be encoded in the site, such as black type words on a black screen, and the source code should be accessible to the faculty. Students cannot adopt URL addresses that are the names of celebrities. They can, however, parody certain products and works of art. School librarians should not only understand nominative use but also educate their students on these laws and include them in their media center guidelines.

NOTES

1. Keith Mulvihill, "Many Problem Gamblers Say Ads Trigger Urge to Bet." Reuters Health. Available: http://ca.news.yahoo.com/020108/5/grw9.html. (Accessed May 25, 2002.)

2. Navin Katyal, "The Unauthorized Dissemination of Celebrity Images on the Internet . . . In the Flesh," *Cleveland State Law Review* 46 (1998): 739.

3. See Jamie J. Fitzgerald, "Remain.com: Don't Let Your Company Name Become Road Kill on the Information Highway," Metro. Corp. Couns. (Feruary. 1999): 21 (discussing the search process used by the ninety million people surfing the Internet, which involves use of company business names to search for their Web sites). Available in WL ALLNEWS Database.

4. *Mishawaka Rubber & Woolen Mfg. Co. v. S.S. Kresge Co.*, 316 U.S. 203, 205 (1942).

5. The Lanham Act is found in 15 U.S.C. §1051–1127 and is the federal law that covers trademark infringement.

6. 15 U.S.C. §1051–1127.

7. The Lanham Act is found in Title 15 of the U.S. Code and contains the federal statutes governing trademark law in the United States. However, this act is not

the exclusive law governing U.S. trademark law. Both common law and state statutes also control some aspects of trademark protection.

8. See 15 U.S.C. 1125(a) (1994) (protecting from infringement the use of regis-tered words, symbols, devices, and names); *Hasbro, Inc. v. Clue Computing, Inc.*, 66 F. Supp. 2d 117, 121 (D. Mass. 1999) (recognizing the scope of the trademark laws to include the protection of words, symbols, names, and devices); *University of Miami Law Review* 36 (1982): 297, 305. (A trademark includes any word, name, symbol, or device or any combination thereof adopted and used by a manufacturer or merchant to identify his goods and distinguish them from those manufactured or sold by others. It may be distinctive packaging or a character such as Spider-Man.)

9. See, for example, *Avery Dennison Corp. v. Sumpton*, 189 F.3d 868, 877–78 (9th Cir. 1999), which explains that the "fame in a localized trading area may meet the threshold element under the Act if plaintiff's trading area includes the trading area of the defendant"; *Hasbro, Inc. v. Clue Computing, Inc.*, 66 F. Supp. 2d 117, 123 (D. Mass. 1999), which concluded that Clue Computing does most of its advertising on the Internet, whereas Hasbro's Internet advertising represents a small percentage of the business in selling CLUE.

10. See, for example, *Interstellar Starship Serv., Ltd. v. Epix, Inc.*, 184 F.3d 1107, 1111 (9th Cir. 1999) (discussing that arbitrary words, such as "epix," make the strongest trademarks); *Data Concepts, Inc. v. Digital Consulting, Inc.*, 150 F.3d (6th Cir. 1998) at 625 (determining a question on the strength of the mark, "dci," because over ninety Web sites used the letters "dci" in their domain names); *Hasbro, Inc. v. Clue Computing, Inc.*, 66 F. Supp. 2d 117 (D. Mass. 1999) at 119 (declaring that "arbitrary and fanciful" trademarks are the strongest, whereas "generic" marks, such as "clue," are the weakest).

11. See *Minnesota Pet Breeders, Inc. v. Schell & Kampeter, Inc.*, 41 F.3d 1242, 1246 (8th Cir. 1994) (holding that a "geographically remote infringer" may not be enjoined from using a trademark that is registered, unless the owner proves consumer confusion in the distant market).

12. See for example, *Data Concepts, Inc. v. Digital Consulting, Inc.*, 150 F.3d 620, 625–26 (6th Cir. 1998) (determining that there was no "relatedness of services" because Data only provided software, while Digital did not); *Hasbro, Inc. v. Clue Computing, Inc.*, 66 F. Supp. 2d 117, 122 (D. Mass. 1999) (failing to find relatedness between Hasbro's CLUE, which is a detective game, and Clue Computing Services, which offers computing consulting to businesses).

See *United States v. Grinnell Corp.*, 384 U.S. 563, 576 (1966) (explaining that a company's national market takes precedence over its regional presence); see also *GOTO.COM., Inc. v. Walt Disney Co.*, 202 F.3d 1199, 1206 (9th Cir. 2000) (distin-guishing a consumer's ability to differentiate between restaurants in "the world of bricks and mortar" and companies in the confusing virtual reality created on the Web).

13. See 15 U.S.C. 1125(c) (Supp. IV 1998) (allowing an injunctive remedy to owners of a famous trademark against a person who uses the mark commercially, which causes the dilution of the trademark).

14. See *Intermatic Inc. v. Toeppen*, 947 F. Supp. 1227, 1233–34 (E.D. Ill. 1996) (stating "regardless of one's view as to the morality of such conduct, the legal issue is whether such conduct is illegal."). Id.

15. *New Kids on the Block v. News America Publishing, Inc.*, 971 F.2d 302 (9th Cir. 1992).

16. 279 F.3d 796 (9th Cir. 2002).

17. See *Playboy Enter., Inc. v. Calvin Designer Label,* 1999 WL 329058, at * 3 (N.D. Cal. 1999) (granting summary judgment for plaintiff and entering injunction); see also 985 F. Supp. 1218, 1218 (N.D. Cal. 1997) (issuing temporary restraining order); 985 F. Supp. 1220, 1220 (N.D. Cal. 1997) (entering preliminary injunction).

18. See J. Thomas McCarthy, McCarthy on Trademarks Sec. 27.13 (3d ed. 1996).

19. See Internet Entertainment Group, 40 U.S.P.Q.2d at 1480.

20. Lawrence Lessig, keynote address to "Building a Digital Commons," Cambridge, MA, March 20, 1999.

21. 141 Cong. Rec. 19312–01 (daily ed. Dec. 29, 1995) (statement of Sen. Leahy).

22. See Anticybersquatting Consumer Protection Act of 1999, 15 U.S.C.A. 1125(d) (Supp. 2000) (imposing civil liability upon a person who uses a protected mark under certain conditions).

23. Anticybersquatting Consumer Protection Act, 15 U.S.C.A. 1125(d) (Supp. 2000).

24. See S. Rep. No. 106–140 2, 7 (1999) (noting that ACPA does not protect "registration, trafficking, or use of a domain name that occurs before the date of enactment"), available in 1999 WL 594571.

25. See id. (stating the purpose of the act). The Senate Report specifically explained the landslide of domain registrations using combinations of Mobil and Exxon after announcement of their proposed merger. See id. (relating that a spectator registered all combinations of the name). In a similar instance, a London computer club attempted to register all possible four-letter names by using an automated computer program.

26. Ron Lofland, "Recycled Domain Names." Available: http://www.webpreda tor.com/nameindex/. (Accessed May 29, 2002).

27. See 15 U.S.C.A. 1125(d)(1)(C) (Supp. 2000) (providing that a court in a civil action, under ACPA, may order the forfeiture or cancellation of a domain name or require the domain name registrant to transfer the domain name to the trademark owner), in 2000 WL 694639.

28. 202 F.3d 1199 (9th Cir. 2000).

29. The Poetry Society is available online at www.poetrysoc.com (accessed February 1, 2003) and www.poetrysociety.org.uk (accessed February 1, 2003).

30. See Christian Anderson, "Approaches to Trademark Challenges Presented by Domain Names," *Client Times* (winter 1999).

31. http://www.wcl.american.edu/journal/lawrev/50/nguyenpp.pdf.

32. See Bus. Wire, Aug. 21, 2000 (reporting that the sales of free.tv, china.tv, and net.tv represent three of the top ten domain name sales in domain history).

11

—◆·❖·◆—

LICENSE AGREEMENTS
IN THE LIBRARY

A library, to modify the famous metaphor of Socrates, should be the delivery
room for the birth of ideas—a place where history comes to life.
—Norman Cousins,
American writer and editor

This chapter will cover:

Four Standard Library Licensing Models

Licensing Associations

The First Sale Doctrine

UCITA—Uniform Computer Information Transaction Act

The study of license agreements is the study of factual detail. This type of
detail is not necessary to commit to memory. However, a familiarity with
licensing, what it can and cannot do, is important for all librarians, whether
or not licensing is an element of their job description. Like many topics in the
law, a familiarity with the topic and a notion of where to find further detailed
information when needed is sufficient. This chapter attempts to provide the
most useful resources.

What is a license? A license agreement is a legally binding contract between
two parties governing the use of an identified product or content for a specified purpose. The licensee is the purchaser, or to make it easier to remember,
the licensee is the "purchasee."[1]

There are driver's licenses, dog licenses, beautician's licenses, mortician's licenses, licenses to fish, licenses to hunt, licenses to practice medicine, licenses to practice dentistry, and licenses to marry. These licenses are bestowed by the state in its power to regulate the activity of its citizens. In their duty to balance the individual freedoms of their citizens with the common good, legislatures require that specific activities be regulated, and a license is the chosen form of regulation. The key word here is "balance." This is the process that is used repeatedly in the law. With license agreements the rights of the vendor are "balanced" with the rights of the user. The state "balances" the need to protect the public with the rights of its citizens to participate in activities as complex and as important as heart surgery and as simple as cutting hair.

In the world of librarianship the licenses with which we must contend come not from the state and city government but from vendors, but like government licenses they restrict freedoms. The freedom that is restricted is the freedom a buyer normally obtains as a result of the purchase of goods. Private entities have the contractual right to regulate the use of their product once it is sold or leased to a library, or to any purchaser for that matter. The library (or the purchaser) has the right not to purchase the product should the licensing agreement be deemed too restrictive. The library also has the right to negotiate more favorable terms for the purchase of the product or to "negotiate the license." Digital content also is almost always subject to licensing agreements.

FOUR STANDARD LIBRARY LICENSING MODELS

Standard library licensing models have been developed and can be used for study.[2] They have been sponsored by and developed in close cooperation with four major subscription agents: EBSCO, Harrassowitz, RoweCom, and Swets Blackwell, which combined offer subscriptions to 20,000 journals. These models are an important resource for the student and professional. They are based on single academic institutions, academic consortia, public libraries, corporate libraries, and other special libraries. These models represent actual licenses that have been negotiated by these companies and because these corporations are international, the models contain optional clauses that vary depending on the country, state, or province where the license is to operate. These models are found on the World Wide Web and updated periodically.

Knowledge of Sections 107 and 108 of the U.S. Copyright Act is essential in understanding the rights of libraries and in negotiating a library license of digital materials. Case law will dictate unforeseen consequences one or both parties did not anticipate in their licensing agreement. The courts' response to protests of unforeseen consequences is "if the (patent) owner did not want this result, it could have drafted the agreement differently." In some license disputes there may be conflicting case law, or no case law. The outcome of license disputes is never certain. Consequently, it is always preferable to nego-tiate a license agreement with specificity.

THREE TYPES OF LICENSE AGREEMENTS

There are three kinds of license agreements that libraries typically encounter. These will be reviewed; while some are negotiated, some are unilateral.

Unilateral License Agreement (The One Under the Shrink-Wrap)

The most common license agreement is one we encounter every day, the unilateral license agreement. Every time we rent a videotape, purchase a CD, or buy a computer game for our children (or ourselves), we are entering into a unilateral licensing agreement by the very act of purchase. We do not take out our cell phone before we reach the check-out stand and attempt to nego-tiate a better deal with the vendor of the product. In fact, we may not even know the complete terms of the license agreement until the product is pur-chased and the shrink-wrap is removed because only part of the agreement is visible through the shrink-wrap.

The concept of removing the shrink-wrap to review the license is a matter we intuitively understand to be forbidden by the seller. The purchase of the shrink-wrapped licensed product (with the partially hidden license) offers a take-it-or-leave-it license agreement. As a society we have voted with out pocketbooks to "take it." How often do parents hand the computer game to the children and state, Now we will review the unilateral license agreement together?

We cannot purchase *Titanic* in video format and sell tickets to watch it at the school auditorium for a fund-raiser for the library unless we gain special permission from the copyright owner, who has the right to earn an income from the public showing of the *Titanic.* We bought it, we own it, it is in our possession and in our VCR, but we bought it subject to certain restrictions, even though in some cases the restrictions were not readable until we opened the package. For this reason these license agreements are commonly referred to as "shrink-wrap" agreements.

Should the library own a product with a shrink-wrap license, its use should be in accord with the licensed agreement. However, the library may wish to use the product in a manner prohibited or not covered by the shrink-wrap agreement. The company may well negotiate terms for use that exceeds the shrink-wrap agreement. This negotiation process can be initiated by either a phone call or letter.

End User License Agreement (EULA)

The second kind of license agreement we commonly encounter is the end user license agreement. This non-negotiable license agreement is typically found on the Web and is entered into by clicking "Agree." This license agreement generally disclaims and excludes any and all implied warranties including ... fitness for a particular purpose. Jonathan Feldman's comments on end user licensing agreements, says it all:

You'd think that if we didn't agree with a software product's licensing conditions or found them incompatible with our needs, we'd look elsewhere. Instead, we blithely ignore the EULAs and use the stuff anyway. For example, there's emergency management agency dispatch software that uses the JRE (Java Runtime Engine). The JRE's EULA says, "Java technology is not fault tolerant and is not designed, manufactured or intended for use ... in hazardous environments requiring fail-safe performance ... in which the failure of Java technology could lead directly to death, personal injury or severe physical or environmental damage." Now that's funny.[3]

Unlike shrink-wrapped license agreements, unilateral Web license agreements can be read completely before being accepted. The duty of the librarian in these instances is greater. Some publicly funded institutions may be limited in those matters to which they are legally capable of agreement. For example, some institutions may agree to venue dispute resolution (the location where you can be sued) only in their home state, whereas the licensor may require the venue for dispute resolution to be in the state that is designated in the license agreement. The vendor may choose a state venue because the law is favorable to them in that state, or merely for convenient. If your school district, institution, or state law requires that all dispute resolution be handled in your home state and it is not the same state designated by the vendor, that is an agreement to which your library cannot agree. Most government agencies have extensive limitations on acceptable terms of agreements.

Companies are also open to negotiation of the terms of this agreement. A library may well negotiate a more appropriate agreement with a EULA.

Bilateral Licensing Agreement

The negotiated two-party license agreement is the one that haunts librarians. This is where their knowledge of the law, of library custom and usage, and of their own bargaining powers comes to the forefront in the guise of those dreaded words, "negotiated license agreement." This is the format in which the rights of the user are, in theory, balanced with the rights of the vendor.

The larger the purchase of the product is, typically, the larger the bargaining power of the licensee (library) will be. Library consortia generally, though not always, have an advantage in the arena of negotiation of a license agreement. The same companies that offer retail shrink-wrap license agreements to the public for the purchase of their product will negotiate a license agreement to large agencies, school districts, or library consortia on a clause-by-clause basis.

There are eighteen standard clauses that typically appear in licensing agreements. Individual clauses may be negotiated, and some clauses are not vastly complicated. Many are straightforward. However, nothing in the law is simple and no contract (or license agreement) can cover every foreseeable contingency. There are historical precedents in the interpretation of some of these clauses and there are no legal precedents in the interpretation of others. Some clauses simply give rise to greater disagreement of consequence, which means the disagreement translates into dollars. Understanding those licenses, which are generally accepted in the library community and in the business community, will enable the librarian to view his or her own license agreements more objectively and potentially negotiate for more favorable treatment or in the event of a failed negotiation, provide a basis for shopping for other products. No one knows the needs of a library's users better than the librarian and the library's staff. These needs must be reflected in the license agreement.

The eighteen standard license clauses are as follow:

1. Parties to Agreement
2. Definition of Terms Used in Agreement
3. Subject of Agreement
4. Grant of Rights Pursuant to License Agreement
5. Licensor Obligation
6. Term and Termination of License Agreement
7. Renewal of License Agreement
8. Fees
9. Conditions of Use and/or Scope of Use
10. Authorized Users
11. Limitations of Liability
12. Governing Law of License Agreement
13. Alternative Dispute Resolution
14. Complete Agreement
15. Assignment of License Agreement
16. Waiver of Clauses of License Agreement
17. Severability of Clauses of License Agreement
18. Audit of Use

A discussion of each clause follows.

Parties to Agreement

Identifying the parties sounds simple, and generally it is. Be certain that the party signing the agreement has the authority to bind the party they purport to represent. The licensor may ask you for information regarding your authority to represent the library and may ask that it be included or attached to the agreement. The librarian also should be certain that the licensor has the authority to bind the licensor. Can a salesman sign for the company or should a corporate representative sign the agreement? If you are uncertain, ask the company and put the answer in writing. If the response you receive from the company is oral or by e-mail, consider responding with a letter that reiterates the answer (e.g., thank you for indicating that Madame X has the authority to bind XYZ Vendor and Supplier Corporation) and be sure to attach it to the agreement. If it is not attached, the letter most likely will not matter in the court's construction of the agreement and may not be a part of the evidence of the case.

Definitions Used in License Agreement

This section defines the terms that will be found in the license agreement to follow. This is an important section. Be certain the terms are consistent with your library's use of those terms. It is a good idea to have each section of your library approve the terms as defined in this section. Not all license agreements use the same definitions for the same terms. Your interlibrary loan department may find glaring deficiencies in the definition of interlibrary loan. History may dictate the manner in which the library defines a material breach of the licensing agreement. Clearly, technical interruption of access to all or a percentage of the content is a material breach. The library may define a time period and/or a percentage for this material breach or may include the inability to contact a representative of the company for repair as a material breach. This is an instance in which the library employees as a community should communicate and collectively determine their definition of a "material breach of contract." If this definition is significantly different from the vendor offered definition this could be an area of negotiation.

Subject of Agreement

The rights the license purports to grant are described in this section. Be certain the agreement specifically states that you will receive the full text of articles—if that is your understanding of the product. If you will receive only abstracts of articles that should be specific in the grant. Define whether the product will have a table of contents, an index, and images. Will the images be in color or in black and white, and are there limitations on the use of the images?

This section should include an agreement on reimbursement should the agreed product be diminished in its content in any capacity during the contractual period. For example, if you are subscribing to several journals, devise a formula for reimbursement or credit toward a future license agreement with the vendor should one journal cease publication.

Grant of Rights Pursuant to License Agreement

The content being granted was described in the previous section, "Subject of Agreement." This section describes the uses your library can make of the content to which you have subscribed. Do not, under any circumstances, presume that specific rights such as printing or copying will be permitted without inclusion and reference in this section. There are standard permitted uses that can be found in virtually all license agreements that are obtained generally from the vendor's server.

It is important to note whether these standard permitted uses apply to images, video, and audio. (It is assumed that you have contracted for images, video, and audio in the previous section.) Often the standard permitted uses apply exclusively to the textual portion of the subject matter. If it has been your experience that your users do in fact download images or other non-textual data, attempt to cover this in both your grant of rights section and your subject matter section. If your users download this non-textual data and it is not covered in the "Grant of Rights" section, your library will be in violation of the licensing agreement.

Typically, license agreements include the following standard rights to:

- Retrieve
- Search
- Browse
- Display
- View
- Download
- Print
- Forward Electronically
- Caching

If you will be using portions of the data retrieved in your library bibliographies you may want to include that right in your agreement. If your faculty will be printing copies for course packets, this should be included in your license agreement. If your faculty will be designating readings from the server for their classes, this should be included in your licensing agreement. If you will be printing articles to be forwarded pursuant to an Interlibrary Loan agreement you may have with other schools, this use should be included in your licensing agreement. If articles from the database will be placed on reserve for student use, this use should be noted. If faculty, administration, or homebound students will be allowed to access the database from a remote site, this use should be included.

Will faculty be permanently downloading data for classroom use? Will some of the information be placed directly on the library or school server? If so, include these uses in the agreement.

Vendors prefer to state the uses that are and are not covered in the licensing agreement. This is best for everyone. It is better for the parties to agree than to have the courts determine the acceptable uses at a later date. Often vendors will include the clause: "All uses not specifically stated herein are excluded from this agreement and are retained by the vendor." This should be a motivation to include all potential uses for the data.

Licensor Obligation

It is natural for the library to presume there will be 24/7 access to the content. Technical support is the heart of the duty of the licensor obligation. Time is of the essence with regard to technical support. Untimely technical support is the equivalent of no technical support. If the data is accessed through a CD-ROM, video, or any other in-house digital format, you might consider making back-up copies to have on location if the current format fails for any reason. If that is not acceptable, you might request the vendor send a replacement format via overnight mail. If there has been a representation that contact will be by a toll free number that should be included in this section of the agreement as should the hours that a representative will be available at that toll free number. Is there a representative on call 24/7 or just nine to five Monday through Friday? If that is not acceptable, you might request overnight mail of replacement format. Any toll-free telephone numbers that can be used to contact representatives of the vendor and their hours of operation should be included in this section of the agreement. Is there a representative on call 24/7 or just nine to five Monday through Friday?

If the data is accessed through a vendor's server, you might consider a penalty clause should the server have excessive and/or extensive periods of inaccessibility. The penalty might be a rebate of fees or a credit toward future use. Generally, these issues are resolved after a period of time and with improved capacity and technology. You might request that any technical adjustments to servers be conducted when the library is not in peak use and that you receive a specified amount of time for notice to technical adjustments to be made to your server.

Schools are required to comply with the Americans with Disabilities Act. (See chapter 12.) Most vendors' now supply content that does comply. Often libraries will include a section that includes this obligation in the license agreement, which states, "Licensor shall comply with the Americans with Disabilities Act (ADA), by supporting assistive software or devices such as large print interfaces, voice-activated input, and alternate keyboard or pointer interfaces in a manner consistent with the Web Accessibility Initiative Web Content Accessibility Guidelines, which may be found at http://www.w3.org/WAI/GL/#Publications."

It is a mistake to presume that online content is consistent with print content. This clause will provide the library with the means of assurance that "online content is at least as complete as print versions of the Licensed Materials, represents complete, accurate and timely replications of the corresponding content contained within the print versions of such Materials, and will cooperate with Licensee to identify and correct errors or omissions."

Return on the library's investment can be calculated most effectively and sometimes exclusively with user statistics and data. This clause assures both the vendor and the publisher that standard statistical data and analysis will be used. "Licensor shall provide to Licensee statistics regarding the usage of the Licensed Materials by Licensee and/or its Authorized Users in conformance with the *Guidelines for the Statistical Measures of Usage of Web-Based Indexed, Abstracted, and Full Text Resources* (November 1998), adopted and approved by the International Consortium of Library Consortia." However, it is important to contract for privacy and protection of user identity in the compilation of this data.

Term of License Agreement and Termination of License Agreement

There is a beginning and an end to all contracts and all licensing agreements. That is their nature. They cover a specific period of time. This section of the license agreement may address issues regarding "automatic termination." Automatic termination of a licensing agreement occurs under specific circumstances stated in the agreement. Standard contractual termination agreements include bankruptcy, failure to make the license payment, and the material breach of the terms of the licensing agreement (who decides what is material—if you do not want it to be the courts define material breach).

In the event that there is no automatic renewal clause or automatic termination clause, the license agreement will terminate at the end of the term of the agreement, which is typically a period of one year. All content agreed to be furnished during the term of the license agreement should be furnished for the entire term of the agreement. Should any content become unavailable during the term of the license agreement, a formula should be reached to compensate the library for the reduced content. Some license agreements permit termination upon notice, which may be other than the stated license date.

When a library terminates a subscription to a journal, it retains all journals to which there has been a previous subscription. With electronic resources, this is more the exception than the rule. If access is by CD-ROM, continued use of the data content past the expiration date should be referred to in this section of the agreement. Backing up online content can be expensive, but if the library chooses that course of action it should be included in the agreement. In some instances libraries may choose to print the content and retain it in print format past the license agreement termination. These are all viable options if a mutually agreed upon course of conduct is reached and recorded in the license agreement.

Renewal of License Agreement

Typically in most licenses agreements there exists a right of renewal, but there is no guarantee that either the content to be renewed or the price of renewal will be the same as the previous agreement.

If the agreement specifies "automatic renewal," then at the end of the user's year typically the contract will be automatically renewed. Automatic renewals vary in application. A two-year contract will typically be renewed for two years, while a one-year contract will typically be renewed for but one year. The fee, however, may change. Notice of fee changes prior to renewal can be an element of the renewal clause. A library may request a ninety-day notice of fee increase, for budgetary purposes. To the contrary, a vendor should be given notice should the library intend not to renew. These notice dates should not be concurrent. Once notice or a fee increase is given to a library, a set time for response to the vendor should be allowed.

Publishers do not automatically notify users of termination dates of license agreements. License termination dates should be calendared so that the library may contact the vendor ninety days prior to termination to initiate a new license agreement.

During the period in which works required a renewal in order to maintain a copyright, most works were not renewed. The effective term limit was, therefore, much shorter than if the entire allowable period was granted in one block of time. It is thought that only fifteen percent of registered copyrights were renewed.[4]

Fees for License Agreements

For new products a trial use of the content may be offered. This trial use may become the basis for the negotiated fee for use. However, initial use may not be indicative of future use once more users become aware of the content's availability.

Essentially fee arrangements include unlimited use, limited use, pay-per-use, or any combination of the three use agreements. Some vendors negotiate fees, some offer various packages for which there is no negotiation, and some neither negotiate nor offer packages. Their one and only package is a take-it-or-leave-it situation.

While subscription fees may allow unlimited use, they may limit the number of simultaneous users. The number of simultaneous users may be negotiated; a library's chief negotiation tool may be that in non-peak times there would be no users of the content.

Subscription fees for limited use may be based on a sliding scale fee that takes into account the size of the institution, the number of users, or the number of pages downloaded. It may also be based on whether or not there is off-site access. If there is only on-site access, the fee may be based on the number of computers with access to the content.

Pay-per-use agreements set a fee for each log-on access or search to the content, or the time of access to the database for both search and access. Downloads may create an additional increment of cost or they may be included in the search and access pay-per-use cost model.

Libraries have an important need to know how their services are being used. This is the section in which a request for monthly or annual statistics for use access should be requested. Some publishers have the ability to provide this data but others cannot. In these instances libraries should secure an agreement to allow them to monitor the use of their patrons so that in the future they will have a basis from which to gauge the importance of the content to their patrons.

Conditions of Use and/or Scope of Use

This section addresses the issue of educational use as opposed to use for commercial gain. The definition section should address and define educational and commercial uses, both as a direct and an indirect product of access to the content. For example, an automotive instructor working on a patented engine application may use the faculty access to content for this pursuit. The engine patent may belong solely to the instructor and not to the institution. Under these circumstances it is conceivable that the access to content may be for commercial gain. An access clause for faculty and staff for both educational and commercial gain would allow such an access. Without such access notice to faculty, staff, and students that access is strictly for educational purposes is important.

Educational uses generally include scholarly and scientific research; critical review and analysis; private (not for profit) use and research; electronic library reserve; conversion to print library reserve; faculty and staff training; community training; class packages in either electronic or print format; and research in the course of the users business or profession (which is a for-profit application) as well as any access by homebound students.

Authorized Users

Authorized users can be a simple matter or a complex matter. If the library is a consortia participant or offers off-site use, then the identity of authorized users becomes more complex. If the library is a single entity with exclusive on-site access, then defining authorized users is generally a simple matter. The key to identifying authorized users is an understanding of who the users will be and communicating that information to the vendor.

Some exclusive on-site providers permit only registered users whereas other on-site providers permit anyone who is on-site to access the content. In K–12 environments this is generally a simple matter with the only difficulty being off-site access. These are issues that can be addressed by negotiation. For a large school district, the number of homebound students becomes relevant. Access by district staff from sites outside the library also becomes relevant. Often access will be restricted by the district's technical capabilities. However, it is never too early to begin discussing increasing capabilities and the potential impact that will have on future negotiations.

Some libraries define their users in their mission statement and their policy. Very few K–12 libraries allow "walk-in" users unless they have chosen to define themselves as a Section 108 library pursuant to the Copyright Act and avail themselves of those benefits and responsibilities. (See chapter 5.) However, some private schools do permit alumnae to use their facilities. These users should be identified in this section.

This section also addresses the use the users make of the content. Yale's Lib-License addresses these issues.[5] You may want to address these uses specifically:

Display. Licensee and Authorized Users shall have the right to electronically display the Licensed Materials.

Digitally Copy. Licensee and Authorized Users may download and digitally copy a reasonable portion of the Licensed Materials.

Print Copy. Licensee and Authorized Users may print a reasonable portion of the Licensed Materials.

Recover Copying Costs. Licensee may charge a fee to cover costs of copying or printing portions of Licensed Materials for Authorized Users.

Archival/Backup Copy. Upon request of Licensee, Licensee may receive from Licensor and/or create one (1) copy of the entire set of Licensed Materials to be maintained as a backup or archival copy during the term of this Agreement or as required to exercise Licensee's rights under Section XIII, "Perpetual License," of this Agreement.

Course Packs. Licensee and Authorized Users may use a reasonable portion of the Licensed Materials in the preparation of Course Packs or other educational materials.

Electronic Reserve. Licensee and Authorized Users may use a reasonable portion of the Licensed Materials for use in connection with specific courses of instruction offered by Licensee and/or its parent institution.

Databases. If the Licensed Materials are a database, compilation, or collection of information, Authorized Users shall be permitted to extract or use information contained in the database for educational, scientific, or research purposes, including extraction and manipulation of information for the purpose of illustration, explanation, example, comment, criticism, teaching, research, or analysis.

Electronic Links. Licensee may provide electronic links to the Licensed Materials from Licensee's Web page(s), and is encouraged to do so in ways that will increase the usefulness of the Licensed Materials to Authorized Users. Licensor staff will assist Licensee upon request in creating such links effectively. Licensee may make changes in the appearance of such links and/or in statements accompanying such links as reasonably requested by Licensor.

Caching. Licensee and Authorized Users may make such local digital copies of the Licensed Materials as are necessary to ensure efficient use by Authorized Users by appropriate browser or other software.

Indices. Licensee may use the Licensed Materials in connection with the preparation of or access to integrated indices to the Licensed Materials, including author, article, abstract and keyword indices.

Scholarly Sharing. Authorized Users may transmit to a third party colleague in hard copy or electronically, minimal, insubstantial amounts of the Licensed Materials for personal use or scholarly, educational, or scientific research or professional use but in no case for re-sale. In addition, Authorized Users have the right to use, with appropriate credit, figures, tables and brief excerpts from the Licensed Materials in the Authorized User's own scientific, scholarly, and educational works.

Interlibrary Loan. Licensee may fulfill requests from other institutions, a practice commonly called Interlibrary Loan. Licensee agrees to fulfill such requests in compliance with Section 108 of the United States copyright law (17 USC 108, "Limitations on exclusive rights: Reproduction by libraries and archives") and clause 3 of the Guidelines for the Proviso of Subsection 108(g)(2) prepared by the National Commission on New Technological Uses of Copyrighted Works.

Typically an electronic reserve clause will limit those users to students, faculty, and staff of the institution. For all electronic reserve access, notice of copyright limitations to the users should be displayed. Further, electronic reserve cannot be accessed by the entire student body, but only by a specific instructor's class and then only for one semester.

Limitations of Liability and Warranty of Product

A warranty is a promise that the licensor (the vendor) makes to the library. Typically a warrantor (the vendor) promises that the information provided is free of copyright infringement and the warrantor is authorized to provide the content. Therefore, in the event that a liability suit is brought against the library for the use of the material, the warrantor will indemnify the library for all resulting litigation costs and damages. This is good news, but you cannot get blood from a turnip. If the vendor is bordering on insolvency, the library will never be successful in recouping its investment capital. Fortunately, lawsuits are rare and it is more likely that the library will receive a "cease and desist" notice to discontinue use of the material subject to copyright.

Governing Law

Governing laws should be analyzed from two frames of reference: the venue, or the location in which the suit if filed, and the jurisdiction or the laws of the state and/or country in which the suit is filed. This clause is not essential and may be the clause that destroys the agreement for governmental agencies. If the contract is silent as to governing laws, often the first person to the courthouse chooses the locale in which the suit will be brought, subject, of course, to a motion to transfer, which is not an easy motion to win.

Generally all libraries that are a part of public institutions require that all governing law clauses be domiciled in the state in which the institution is located. Although copyright law is federal law, many states have their own copyright statutes that may be more restrictive than federal law and offer damages that are at variance with the federal law. Contract law (a license is a contract) is governed by state law, and contract law and the resulting damages vary significantly from state to state. A fact finder's determination of what are good faith and bad faith actions can be governed by extremely different guidelines in different states.

Litigation in a jurisdiction far removed from the locale of the library is intrinsically more expensive. Generally, it is always best to have the venue of the suit (the place in which the litigation is filed) to be the state and the county in which the library is located and often this is the law that governs the school district.

Alternative Dispute Resolution

With alternative dispute resolution, the courthouse becomes the arbitrator of last resort. Other avenues of dispute resolution are required to be accessed first. Even the best of contracts (license agreements) can be ambiguous. One part may understand the contract to mean one thing (advantageous to their position) whereas the other party interpret it completely differently (advantageous to their position).

Negotiations are carried on by the two parties or their respective attorneys. This requires a good faith effort to meet on middle ground. When negotiations fail, mediation attempts to resolve the disputed issues.

Mediation requires the intervention of a third party. Most states have trained certified mediators who are attorneys. Be sure your mediator has no conflicts and association with any of the parties and is trained in intellectual license agreements. Some mediators will also be board certified by their states in contract law or intellectual property law. Find the most knowledgeable mediator pertaining to this area of the law that is available.

Generally, mediation requires the parties and/or their attorneys to meet with the mediator at a neutral location. Most mediators are attorneys (and absolutely choose an attorney), and their conference rooms are the sites of the mediation. The parties will each have their own separate consulting rooms. The mediator will attempt to find the common ground.

It is best if the parties begin mediation with position papers that include the contract, the history of the dispute, and the progress made to the date of the mediation on those historically disputed matters. Position papers are important tools. They should state the party's position as to the status of the law as it applies to the license agreement. The law in intellectual property is not static and not always the same from jurisdiction to jurisdiction. The position paper should also state the facts upon which the parties agree and the facts that are in dispute. Before the law can be applied to the facts, a specific set of facts must be determined. Mediators do not determine what the facts are, or whose version of "the truth" is acceptable.

This saves valuable time and gets the ball rolling more quickly. The mediator then goes from room to room in an attempt to represent the concessions each party is willing to make. Often, the formality of the situation causes parties to become more accommodating.

Mediators generally charge by the day or half day. Obviously, a half day is more economical, and if the parties arrive with position papers and a concise list of four or fewer items for resolution, no more than a half day of mediation should be required. If the items are numerous or complex or the parties have not prepared a position paper, a whole day of mediation (or more) will be necessary. If a half day of mediation is chosen, begin early in the morning and break for lunch with one hour of mediation after lunch. A respite and light meal with the knowledge that only one hour remains to resolve the dispute can be advantageous to both parties.

The last point of resolution should mediation fail, prior to hitting the courthouse doors, is arbitration. Arbitrators are members of the American Arbitration Association (available at http://www.adr.org [accessed February 1, 2003]). Arbitrators go one step further than mediators. Like mediators they must understand the basis of the dispute and understand both parties' points of contention. They then apply the law to the facts and render a decision. This clause will determine whether this decision is binding or whether the parties may then go to court for resolution.

Some law is so straightforward that the court will interpret it in the same fashion as the arbitrator. However, in intellectual property law there are many areas in which the law is still evolving and being created. The attorneys for the parties are in the best position to advise the parties whether the courts might interpret the law differently than the arbitrator has interpreted it.

An arbitrator also renders a position on factual disputes, and this must be done before the law can be applied to the facts. Consequently, there are two areas in which a court may render a finding significantly different from that of the arbitrator: on the facts and in the law and its application to the facts.

Yet a third factor exists in selection of an arbitrator. The arbitrator will be most familiar with the law of their jurisdiction. Attempt to select an arbitrator in the jurisdiction in which the suit will be tried. At each stage of the alternative dispute resolution, valuable information will be obtained for trial preparation. Each party will arrive at the courthouse door with a complete understanding of the other party's position. If there are no factual disputes and a set of facts may be agreed upon, the resolution may be submitted by Summary Judgment. This requires no testimony from the parties, simple written briefs, with sworn attached exhibits, and oral arguments to the court by the attorneys.

Complete Agreement

This clause simply states that the license agreement and all appendices and attachments are the complete agreement between the parties. Any agreements made prior to the signing of the license agreement and not included in the license agreement are not binding and of no force and effect with regard to the license agreement. In fact any prior agreements cannot be introduced into a legal dispute regarding the agreement. This concept arises from the parole evidence rule: In the absence of fraud or mutual mistake, oral statements are not admissible to modify, vary, explain, or contradict the plain terms of a valid written agreement.

Some of the law that governs license agreements is the same law that governs contractual agreements. It is fundamental in contract law that an oral agreement cannot modify a written agreement. For example, if a vendor submits a contract to a library that indicates that visual images found in the database cannot be subject to educational fair use exceptions and may be copied by no one, this contract is binding.

Should the salesperson give you a wink and a nod as you sign the contract, and specifically state that the company would take no action if you infringe upon the copyright, that oral representation is invalid and of no force and effect. The contractual clause is the binding clause. In fact, because of the parole evidence rule, should the school be sued the oral representation will not be allowed into evidence.

If the agreement of the parties is not in the license agreement, there is no agreement and generally most other agreements are not admissible into evidence for the purpose of varying the agreement as signed by the parties.

Assignment

Contracts of a nonpersonal nature may be assigned. Should you contract with a noted artist for your portrait to be painted, that artist cannot assign that duty to another artist. However, contracts of a nonpersonal nature are often assigned. When you contract with a cleaning service to clean the library, the subject of the contract is not personal. Should the business be bought by a large cleaning conglomerate, the original contract continues to be binding upon the purchaser.

If the contract is silent to assignment, should the contract remain binding if either party is absorbed by another party? If the intention of the parties is to the contrary, the license agreement may simply state: Should either party cease to exist the contract will also cease to exist. This is not an optimal clause for a library that must provide content and notice of failure to provide the content to its patrons. However, the alternative, which is a transfer of content provision by a new company, can also be fraught with difficulties. Knowing the content provider is of utmost importance. Always know with whom you have chosen to do business.

Waiver

The desired clause should state: The sole method by which a clause of this license agreement can be waived is by written agreement between the parties.

Watch out! Do not permit one party's failure to enforce a portion of a contract create a waiver, which causes it to no longer be a portion of the contract.

Severability

Severability clauses state that should any part of the agreement be invalid or unenforceable, the remaining portions of the agreement survive and remain in full force and effect. This is not always a feasible position, because some clauses are so fundamental to the contract agreement. For this reason some severability clauses often indicate that only clauses that do not alter the entire agreement may be severed, and the entire license will cease to exist should the removal of a clause make it unreasonable to continue the license agreement in a reasonable manner.

Audit Clause

It is standard procedure for software companies to include an audit clause. The purpose is to allow the supplier to review the actual use of its property. It is not unreasonable for the software licensor to periodically verify that you're using the software within the scope of the license and the number of copies authorized. You have an obligation to pay the supplier for your actual usage if you're using more software than your license allows.

A reasonable audit clause should indicate that the licensor shall have the right, with reasonable notice to the licensee, to audit the licensee's use of the software no more than once each calendar year to ensure compliance with the terms of the license agreement.

If the licensor desires to charge the library for material overuse, should it also agree to a refund for under use. These are addressable issues. "Material overuse" can be defined in percentage terms.

LICENSING ASSOCIATIONS

In order to comply with the U.S. Copyright Law, the use of chapters or journal articles in coursepacks generally requires permission, the use of film clips can require permission, and establishments defined by statute that play copyrighted music are required to secure permission to use copyrighted music.[6] A potential user of copyright information can secure licenses or permission from organizations for the legal use of copyrighted material. Obtaining a license or permission from the licensing organization ensures the user of complying with the copyright law.

American Society of Composers, Artists, and Publishers (ASCAP) collects royalties for copyright holders and can provide a license to use their music.

The Motion Picture Licensing Corporation (MPLC) provides licenses on an annual basis for home use videotapes or videodiscs of public performances.

Movie Licensing USA, a licensing agent for authorized studios such as Walt Disney Pictures, Touchstone Pictures, Hollywood Pictures, Warner Bros., Columbia Pictures, TriStar Pictures, Paramount Pictures, Dream-Works Pictures, Metro-Goldwyn-Mayer, Universal Pictures, Sony Pictures, and United Artists, provides Movie Public Performance Site Licensing to schools for the use of entertainment videos. It licenses the showing of copyrighted movies produced by the studios represented, and used by schools for numerous extracurricular activities.

THE FIRST SALE DOCTRINE

The First Sale doctrine has its roots in contract law where a customer implicitly has a right to enjoy purchased goods without restriction. Unless a licensing agreement provides to the contrary, a patentee (e.g., Microsoft) who permits introduction of its patented article (e.g., Windows) into commerce may lose its rights with respect to the resale of the patented article. If you decide to sell your riding lawn mower, because you have won the lottery and no longer intend to mow your lawn yourself, you would assume you could sell the patented Briggs and Stratton engine that powers the mower, and you would be correct.

The First Sale doctrine may be limited by license. In general, it applies only to patent claims that "read on" the product sold by the licensee.[7] Sale of a machine does not exhaust the patent rights in method claims covering use of the machine.

So you think you will just sell those old computers with their Windows 98 operating system. Windows 98 is not such a bad operating system and someone can still get many good years of use from them. The First Sale doctrine allows you to do just that . . . unless there is a licensing restriction. You purchased the computers and there are no problems associated with selling the hardware, but the operating system can be a whole different matter. Can you sell the operating system, too? Would anyone want the computer without the operating system? Microsoft's licensing agreement permits neither the sale nor the gift of its system with the computer. Microsoft has notified many PC's for Kids–type programs that these types of activities are in violation of the licensing agreement. One solution has been to install Linux-type operating systems on these computers.

Microsoft has a licensing agreement that it routinely and uniformly enforces that does not allow the resale or donation of computers with its software. Because this restriction could not historically be enforced at all times, although Microsoft is willing to bring a lawsuit to enforce this right, Microsoft created a self-enforcing solution by requiring that their software be activated by Microsoft. Users must now activate their products online or experience "reduced functionality mode." RFM means Microsoft has the authority to deactivate your software! This newest concept is referred to as license "leasing" and is becoming more popular, at least with vendors.

However, a library might consider an alternatives to this type of agreements that does not require a license. There has always been a large contingent of computer engineers who believe "software should be free." Open-sourced Linux software, for example, can be found on the Internet. Open-source support services may be an option rather than the use of a proprietary licensed product. For example, Red Hat allows you to pay for support but get free upgrades to source code—without licenses. Linux is a licensed product, but it allows the source code to be modified and is liberal in permitting uses of its software.

Return on Investment Analysis Requires User Data

It is essential that the library have the ability to identify users for the purpose of calculating the true value of the data being licensed to the library. Without actual usage information data, a library can only anecdotally review the patron use of the licensed data. The only cost-efficient and accurate assessment of use of the licensed content is an electronic assessment that documents the actual use of the licensed content. This is vital to understanding the true return on investment of the subject of the license agreement. Vendors often track this information for themselves but do not share that data with the library. Requesting that it be shared and including this agreement to share the usage data in the licensing agreement will help the library determine whether the return on its investment is high or low. When vendors do not have that ability, the library may purchase software to track patron use of the licensed data. It is a good idea to include in the license agreement the fact that the library will use software to track the use of the licensed data.

In analysis of use and users of the content, the concept of patron privacy must be kept in mind. It is a good idea to include the fact that patron identity will not be available should the vendor track the use of the licensed content. No analysis by the provider should in any capacity allow the provider to identify the user. Information about data accessed and time of access is acceptable, however, user identity including home computer terminal identity should be protected. For example, the simple fact that the access was an off-site access should be adequate. Tracking and reporting license use is important for both the publisher and the library. This should be done in a mutually beneficial fashion that completely protects the user's identity.

UCITA—UNIFORM COMPUTER INFORMATION TRANSACTIONS ACT

UCITA (Uniform Computer Information Transactions Act) is a proposed state contract law that will profoundly affect library operations. UCITA will provide the rules that govern licensing of all computer-information products. UCITA places limitations on transactions involving computer information.

This is a model law that is intended for passage in all fifty states. UCITA's primary supporters include Microsoft, AOL, and Reed Elsevier; its challengers include businesses, technology associations, consumer advocates, educational institutions, law professors, and libraries.

Have you ever wondered where the state legislature comes up with these laws? Do they dream them up themselves? Well, obviously, in some instances they do dream them up themselves. But in other cases national committees create proposed model laws for states to consider adopting. Some states adopt these proposed model laws precisely as created by the national committee, whereas others make modifications to or delete whole sections of these model laws. UCITA was adopted as a proposed uniform law in July 1999, the product of a ten-year effort between the National Conference of Commissioners on Uniform State Laws (NCCUSL) and the American Law Institute (ALI), to create a new and consistent legal framework for computer information, transactions, and software.

The goal of UCITA is to legitimize a contractual and licensing basis for computer information. On May 30, 2002, the drafting committee revised the original proposed Model UCITA. The most important change is that donated computers to schools may retain the software on the computer when donated. Essentially, UCITA remains unchanged. However, 2003 has been targeted as the year to promote UCITA to various legislatures around the country.

UCITA takes copyright law and ignores it. It allows contract to govern the use of software instead. UCITA would validate terms in shrink-wrap and clickable online licenses that restrict uses that are permitted under copyright law and negate provisions for fair use, first sale, and preservation. A software vendor or licensor may electronically disable, remove, or prevent the use of computer information through "backdoors" in the software, or hidden shutdown commands activated by phone or other mechanisms.

What Does UCITA Do For Libraries?

An adoption of UCITA would mean that libraries in that state could no longer assume that they can legally loan software or CD-ROMs to library users. License provisions could eliminate the right of libraries to lend products, donate library materials, or resell unwanted materials in the annual library book sale.

License provisions under UCITA could control Section 107 (Fair Use) and Section 108 (Library Copying) of the DMCA (Digital Millennium Copyright Act). These rights of the library and of the patron could be abolished in the licensing agreement by excluding the right to quote from a work, or make a small portion of the work for personal use, or to use the product in a nonprofit, educational setting. These have historically been subject to negotiation but have not been subject to "shrink-wrap" licensing agreements.

Contact Your State Legislator

Most state legislators are not aware of the impact of UCITA on libraries. An educational effort from the perspective of libraries to the legislators is an important function of a librarian. Librarians have the obligation to explain the economic ramifications of UCITA on libraries as well as the importance of full access and use of information pursuant to the law of copyright to the educational community.

For further information, go to http://www.ala.org/washoff/ucita (accessed April 23, 2003) or http://www. affect.ucita.com (accessed February 1, 2003).

CONCLUSION

At the time a licensing agreement is drafted, the parties cannot predict the future and often they cannot weigh the value or relative importance of the licensed content to the library. As users and uses are identified over time, the library will understand better the value of the content to the library and the clauses necessary to accurately reflect its use.

Although some of the rights enunciated in a license agreement may be inferred from Section 107, the Fair Use doctrine, and the privileges found in Section 108 of the copyright law, titled "Limitations on Exclusive Rights: Reproduction by Libraries and Archives," it is best to include any intended rights in the license agreement. It is possible for libraries to copy whole works for certain reasons, to fill interlibrary loan patron requests, and to print and distribute copies pursuant to the Copyright Act, Sections 107 and 108. The more professional course of conduct is to specify the precise uses the library anticipates in the agreement. However, all rights given to a user under the law of copyright may be further restricted by a licenses agreement or they may be extended by a license agreement. It is important to remember the law of copyright may be modified by contract or a license agreement between the parties.

Insightful Web Sites

- The Liblicense Standard Licensing Agreement. Available: http://www.library.yale .edu/~llicense/index.shtml (accessed February 1, 2003). Yale University Library's Web site on licensing digital information for librarians. The Liblicense Standard Licensing Agreement is an attempt to reach consensus on the basic terms of contracts to license digital information between university libraries and academic publishers. It is sponsored by the Council on Library and Information Resources, the Digital Library Federation, and Yale University Library; it represents the contributions of numerous college and university librarians, lawyers, and other university officials responsible for licensing, as well as significant input from representatives of the academic publishing community. The Web site also contains the text of a standard license agreement. This is an important resource for the working librarian and the student.

- International Federal of Library Associations. Available: http://www.ifla.org/V/ebpb/copy.htm. (Accessed February 1, 2003.) Provides IFLA's licensing principles.
- The University of California Libraries Collection Development Committee "Principles for Acquiring and Licensing Information in Digital Formats" (May 1996) Available: http://sunsite.berkeley.edu/Info/principles.html. (Accessed February 1, 2003.)
- Association of Research Libraries. Available: http://www.arl.org/scomm/licensing/principles.html. (Accessed February 1, 2003). The Principles for Licensing Electronic Resources (July 1997), promulgated jointly by the American Association of Law Libraries, the American Library Association, the Association of Academic Health Sciences Libraries, the Association of Research Libraries, the Medical Library Association, and the Special Libraries Association is available here.
- International Coalition of Library Consortia. Available: http://www.library.yale.edu/consortia. (Accessed February 1, 2003.) Made up of roughly sixty-five library consortia and representing over five thousand libraries worldwide, this coalition discusses and updates members on matters of consequence to coalitions.
- ASCAP. Available: http://www.publishers.org/home/index.htm. (Accessed February 1, 2003.)
- Association of American Publishers. Available: http://www.publishers.org. (Accessed February 1, 2003.)
- BMI. Available: http://www.BMI.com. (Accessed February 1, 2003.)
- Cartoon Bank. Available: http://www.CartoonBank.com. (Accessed February 1, 2003.)
- Harry Fox Agency. Available: http://www.nmpa.org/hfa.html. (Accessed February 1, 2003.)
- Motion Picture Association of America. Available: http://www.mpaa.org/home.htm. (Accessed February 1, 2003.)
- Recording Industry of America. Available: http://www.riaa.org. (Accessed February 1, 2003.)
- SESAC Available: http://www.sesac.com. (Accessed February 1, 2003.)

NOTES

1. Webster's Unabridged does not contain this word.

2. Licensingmodels.com, "Model Licenses." Available: http://www.licensingmodels.com. (Accessed May 25, 2002.) Site is authored by John Cox Associates, an international publishing consultancy specializing in licensing and content management but sponsored by Catchword Ltd., an Ingenta Corporation.

3. Jonathan Feldman, Licensing Liability, Network Computing, September 17, 2001. Available: http://www.networkcomputing.com/1219/1219cofeldman.html (Accessed March 3, 2003).

4. See Barbara Ringer, Study No. 31: Renewal of Copyright 187 (1960) (concluding only fifteen percent of registered copyrights were renewed), reprinted in Sub-

comm. on Patents, Trademarks, and Copyrights of the Senate Comm. on the Judiciary, 86th Cong., 1st Sess., Copyright Law Revision (Comm. Print 1960).

5. University Library License. "Standard License Agreement." Yale University Library License site. Available: http://www.library.yale.edu. (Accessed May 25, 2002.) Council of Library Information Resources provides a Web site on "Licensing Digital Information" also referred to as "Lib License," which is a licensing resource for librarians. In this Web site the Council provides a standard licensing agreement for review. Available: http://www.library.yale.edu/~llicense/standlicagree.html. (Accessed May 25, 2002.) "Liblicense: Licensing Digital Information." Yale University Library. Ann Okerson, associate university librarian for collection development management. http://www.library.yale.edu/~llicense/index.shtml. (Accessed March 3, 2003.)

6. In 1995, a bill regarding copyright was introduced in the House and the Senate, and both chambers held hearings. The bill never exited the committee because restaurant and bar owners lobbied Congress for a broader exemption on paying royalties for music broadcast in their establishments. It took three years for the restaurateurs to be successful with their lobbying and win an exemption from the proposed copyright act.

7. *Bandag, Inc v. Al Bolser's Tire Stores, Inc.*, 750 F2d 903 (Fed Cir 1984).

12

——◦•◦——

AMERICANS WITH DISABILITIES ACT
AND THE SCHOOL LIBRARY

If A is a success in life, then A equals x plus y plus z. Work is x; y is play; and z
is keeping your mouth shut.
—Albert Einstein (1879–1955), German-born U.S. scientist,
who had a learning disability and did not speak until age three.

This chapter will cover:

ADD/ADHD Needs for the Diagnosed and Undiagnosed Student

Make Your Library a Source of Positive Self Esteem for People with
Disabilities

Individual Education Plan and the Librarian

Section 504 of the Rehabilitation Act of 1973 and the Americans with
Disabilities Act (ADA) of 1990

Libraries in Public Schools and FAPE

Your Policy is Your Protection from Grievance

Physical Requirements for the Library

What Does Having a Disabled Student Mean to the Librarian?

Americans with disabilities are protected from discrimination by law. What
is a disability? Who has a disability? Can you always see a disability?

Disabilities come in all forms, shapes, and sizes. Mental illness is now a covered disability. Attention Deficit Disorder is a disability. Physical disabilities are
more visible and easy to recognize. Just because a person has a disability is he

or she automatically protected by the Americans with Disabilities Act? No. Just because they document that disability and the school district agrees that the student has that disability, is the student covered by the Americans with Disabilities Act? No. Because a student has not been officially documented with a disability, should librarians not recognize that some students need just a bit of extra attention and help? Never.

I have never met a librarian that did not want to be fair and that was not sympathetic to disabilities. But like everything in life, resources are limited. However, it does not always take additional resources to address the disabled student. Under Section 504 of the Rehabilitation Act and the ADA, educational personnel only need to provide accommodations for limitations that can be directly connected to the disability. However, compassion and fairness motivate most librarians to do more.

School librarians have compassion and a sense of humanity that was not created by statutory regulation. No one had to pass the Americans with Disabilities Act for librarians to understand that certain students need special considerations in their library. In addition to observing the laws pertaining to disabilities, there are a multitude of wonderful acts a librarian can take to include all students, including those with diagnosed disabilities who are protected by law and those with undiagnosed disabilities who are not protected by law.

ADD/ADHD NEEDS FOR THE DIAGNOSED AND UNDIAGNOSED STUDENT

There will be ADD/ADHD students in all classes whether they have been designated as disabled or not. A general sensitivity to their needs should be a cornerstone of any school library. These students generally have these clustered symptoms:

Inability to screen out environmental stimuli. Stimuli such as sounds, sights, or smells, may distract them from their focus. For example, it may be hard for them to focus while sitting near a high-traffic area or a fan.

Possible solutions: Always provide a quiet study area and quiet computer area. Privacy screens in the computer area help the students as do study carrels in quiet corners of the library.

Inability to concentrate: These students display restlessness, have a short attention span, are easily distracted, or have a hard time remembering verbal directions.

Possible solutions: When providing them with aid in research, break large projects into smaller tasks; provide them with frequent breaks to stretch or walk around; and give them research information in writing. You may follow up in a few days to determine if they understood the directions.

Lack of stamina. Their medications may make them drowsy.

Possible solutions: For these students putting their head down on a desk and napping may not be wrong. However, be sensitive. They may also be ill. In this instance, the librarian is certainly authorized to inquire of the disability officer of the effects of any medication being taken.

MAKE YOUR LIBRARY A SOURCE OF POSITIVE SELF-ESTEEM FOR PEOPLE WITH DISABILITIES

How do you make your library a source of positive self-esteem for the disabled student? Try to make your library a place where students with disabilities can be self-sufficient. For example, wheelchair-bound students are frustrated at not being able to browse the stacks. Make the aisles sufficiently wide for them with both ends open so they do not have to back out of the aisle. Although the law requires an aisle width of thirty-six inches, forty-two inches is strongly preferred because young students do not have the same strength that adults have and cannot manipulate their wheelchairs with the same sense of ease and control.

Have a computer terminal that is wheelchair accessible. Be sure that students with disabilities may enter or exit the library with a minimal amount of aid and preferably none. Use students with disabilities as aides and other students will begin to view them as more valued. This function increases their social interaction and social skills and improves their self-esteem. Give the disabled student aide the opportunity to share their expertise and pair them with abled students, particularly when it is the disabled student who is leading the way. Collaboration and teamwork projects including the disabled is an important opportunity for the disabled student. Note all these activities in your library policy.

Give a disabled student a section of the library to "monitor." Let them do all the reshelving for this area and be the "expert." For some students, for example, this might be the sports section. They could then be asked to share their knowledge of this section with other students who have an interest in this area. As they master the sports area, they may move on to master other areas in the library and possibly the entire library. For students who are involved in no extracurricular activities, this can be a very important element of their school life. It not only gives them a familiarity with the library and a confidence in their library skills but also builds their social skills and sense of accomplishment.

Libraries are not just for reading. Involve disabled students in library work. This creates an outlet for their services that is not always present in other school activities. Encourage student aides with disabilities to help conduct and participate in library-sponsored activities such as a chess club. Make an effort to include these students in as many aspects of running the library as possible. Encourage them to showcase their interests by putting together exhibits, displaying their collections and artwork, and building their own bibliography Web pages. Let your student staff feel special and know they are an important contributory member of your library and in doing so, give them the library to treasure for the rest of their lives.

Doing What We Do Best: Reading Lists

Librarians can promote a positive self-image for the disabled student through their collection. It is important to include a good collection about disability in both fiction and non-fiction genres. When building such a collection, keep in mind that it is important for disabled students to see themselves portrayed in literature in an understanding, empathetic, yet realistic manner, not in a sappy, overly emotional, unrealistic scenario. The faculty also needs a collection addressing the educator's needs and duties where disability is present.

Educate students on diversity. Disability is a part of life. Librarians have always had reading lists on specific topics. Provide these reading lists to your faculty, to your disability therapist, and to disabled students and their families. Include these readings in reading lists for the general student body.

Easter Seals and the American Library Association (ALA) developed a program titled AccessAbility @ your library, a reading initiative for people of all ages—and abilities—to discover the true value of diversity and inclusion, acknowledge individual differences, and celebrate the personal accomplishments of people with disabilities.[1] Central to the program is a list of ALA-recommended books for children and adults—all featuring characters with disabilities. "The books on our list tell entertaining stories about how people who happen to have a disability have accomplished their personal goals, whether raising a family or climbing Mt. Everest," said James E. Williams, Jr., president and CEO of Easter Seals. "We see many of these same kinds of accomplishments every day at Easter Seals, whether it's learning how to overcome and live with a physical disability or learning how to speak and read. We hope these stories will connect with people on an emotional level and make an immediate impact on their lives."[2]

Having videos available for faculty use can also be an important part of the library's services. A video about the life of Helen Keller would be appropriate for grades four through nine. A video and teacher's guide are available at http://www.disabilityresources.org/DRMlibs-ala.html (Accessed March 3, 2003).

INDIVIDUAL EDUCATION PLAN AND THE LIBRARIAN

As a school librarian you will not be entitled to know the details of the disability of a specific student, nor will the faculty members. This information is protected by law. Only those with a "compelling reason" to be informed of the details will have access to the documentation of the disability. There will, however, be circumstances that present a "compelling reason" for a librarian to understand the nature of a specific student's disability.

Your school district should have a person who documents disabilities and a committee that creates an "individual educational plan" that is tailored exclusively for the disabled student once a disability is determined to exist. This plan is provided to the teachers and should be provided to the librarian. You should have close communications with your disability officer each year to evaluate the accessibility of your library, its services and policies. For a smaller school district this can be handled on a case-by-case basis. It is not uncommon for families of the disabled to become involved in the implementation of the plan.

Although the librarian cannot access the details of the disability, the librarian should be able to discuss the needs of the student and begin to understand the nature of the special services the librarian will be required to provide. In some districts the family makes a specific request of the district to accommodate the needs of the student. In order to anticipate needs as well as streamline library services and accommodations, the librarian may file with the disability officer of the district those accommodations that can routinely be made available to the disabled. The librarian should strongly consider being placed on the Individual Educational Program Committee for students. This will provide the librarian with valuable information in structuring the library facilities, services, and policies to address the needs of the disabled students. [It can also inform collection development and instruction.]

Disability-related information must be treated and handled as medical information: collected and maintained on separate forms and stored in secure files with access limited to members of the disability services office. The information cannot be shared with other people outside the school. Even within the school, people not in the disability services office can only access the information with permission of the family or if there is a compelling reason to do so.

Faculty, and this should include librarians, should be informed of the existence of a verified disability and the need to accommodate the disabled student through the IEP. However, in an attempt to create new accommodations, it may be necessary to discuss with the student, the family, or the disability officer of the district the nature of the limitations of the disability. This could be construed as the "compelling reason" a librarian might have to understand the details of the disability. Compassion and discretion are the guiding concepts in this area.

STANDARD USED TO DETERMINE AN ADA DISABILITY

The standard used by the disability director of your school district to evaluate a disability should be a comparison of the performance of the disabled student with the average performance of a student in the general population. If a student with ADHD were performing as well as average children in their grade level, notwithstanding the disability, they will not be designated as disabled. This comes as a complete surprise to many parents. If the student does not have to do significantly extra work to achieve at this level, there may be a finding that there is no substantial limitation in learning. Your school district may not uniformly find all students with the same limitations to be disabled. The key to finding a disability is that the student cannot achieve at the level of their peers as a result of their disability or the student must participate in significant additional work to achieve at the level of their peers. In education terminology, there must be a "gap" between potential and achievement caused by the disability.

More succinctly put, substantial limitation must result from the physical or mental impairment being claimed by the student and the family. In determining whether the substantial limitation requirement is met, the disability director will consider the nature and severity of the impairment, the duration of the impairment, and any long-term impact of the impairment. The standard used to determine whether a physical or mental impairment results in a substantial limitation is average performance level in the general population, not the optimal performance level for a person. Libraries of larger school districts should build these considerations into their policies and systems and libraries of smaller school districts should do their best to accommodate students.

The courts have routinely placed decisions regarding the choice of educational methodologies in the hands of educators.[3] Parents of students with disabilities do not have a legal right to compel a school district to use a specific methodology or provide a specific program in educating their children, as long as school districts offer a free acceptable public education.[4] A concise statement of the case law regarding educational methodology was provided by the U.S. Court of Appeals for the Fourth Circuit in *Barnett v. Fairfax County School Board* (1991), which stated that "while a school system must offer a program which provides educational benefits, the choice of the particular educational methodology employed is left to the school system" (p. 350). However, this will require the librarian to consider how to best adapt the library facilities to learning disabled and physically handicapped children.

SECTION 504 OF THE REHABILITATION ACT OF 1973 AND THE AMERICANS WITH DISABILITIES ACT (ADA) OF 1990

Section 504 of the Rehabilitation Act of 1973 and the Americans with Disabilities Act (ADA) of 1990 are major federal legislative acts that are designed to protect the civil rights of individuals with disabilities. The intent of these two laws is to prevent any form of discrimination against individuals with disabilities. It creates by law an equality between two persons who are equally qualified. Section 504 applies to entities that receive federal funds, and the ADA applies to virtually every entity except churches and private clubs. Unlike the 1973 Rehabilitation Act, Section 504 and the ADA provided no funding for public schools. They do, however, protect the rights of students in public schools.

Public Law 94–142, the Education for All Handicapped Children Act, passed in 1975. This was the federal legislation that initially resulted in major changes in the way schools served children with disabilities. This law is now called the Individuals with Disabilities Education Act (IDEA). It was accompanied by federal funds and was initially the focal point of schools in serving children with disabilities.

Section 504 and the ADA use a different definition of disability and a different approach to eligibility than does the IDEA of 1990, resulting in many children who are not eligible under IDEA being protected by Section 504 and the ADA.

What Is Section 504?

Section 504 is civil rights legislation for persons with disabilities. It prohibits discrimination against individuals who meet the definition of disability in the act, and it is applied to entities that receive federal funding. The primary objective of Congress in enacting Section 504 was to "honor the requirements of simple justice; by ensuring that federal funds not be expended in a discriminatory fashion." Section 504 is a relatively simple part of the Rehabilitation Act. It states:

"No otherwise qualified individual with a disability shall solely by reason of her or his disability be excluded from the participation in, be denied the benefits of, or be subjected to discrimination under any program or activity receiving Federal financial assistance." (29 U.S.C.A. Sec. 794)

Schools must afford students with disabilities with equal opportunities "to obtain the same result, to gain the same benefit, or to reach the same level of achievement" as students without disabilities. Section 504 applies only to entities that receive federal funds. Most public schools receive substantial federal funds through their participation in various federally supported activities, and as a result, they must comply with the provisions of Section 504.

What Is the ADA?

Like Section 504, the American with Disabilities Act (ADA) is civil rights legislation for individuals with disabilities. Unlike Section 504, the ADA applies to almost every entity in the United States, regardless of whether it receives federal funds; churches and private clubs are the only two entities that are exempt from the ADA. Therefore, private schools that are not associated with a religious organization have to comply with the provisions of the ADA; these schools may be exempt from Section 504 because they do not receive federal funds.

Title I of the ADA prohibits discrimination in employment areas. Title II deals with state and local governmental entities, including schools. Title III targets public accommodations, including hotels, restaurants, department stores, grocery stores, and banks. In all cases, entities covered are required to make the reasonable accommodations or modifications necessary to ensure persons with disabilities access to goods and services.

The Definition of Disability Under Section 504 and the ADA

The definition of disability under Section 504 and the ADA is significantly broader than the definition used in the IDEA. Under 504 and the ADA, a person is considered to have a disability if that person (1) has a physical or mental impairment that substantially limits one or more of such person's major life activities; (2) has a record of such an impairment; or (3) is regarded as having such an impairment.[5]

The Rehabilitation Act defines a physical or mental impairment as (1) any physiological disorder or condition, cosmetic disfigurement, or anatomical loss affecting one or more of the following body systems: neurological, musculoskeletal, special sense organs, respiratory, speech organs, cardiovascular, reproductive, digestive, genito-urinary, hemic and lymphatic, skin, and endocrine; or (2) any mental or psychological disorder, such as mental retardation, organic brain syndrome, emotional or mental illness, and specific learning disabilities. The last part of the definition is similar to the one round in the IDEA. However, the first part, although including some of the categories found in the IDEA, goes well beyond those specific areas in defining disability.

To be eligible for special education under the IDEA, a student must have a categorical disability that results in the student's needing special education. Section 504 and the ADA, however, require that the person have a physical or mental impairment that substantially limits one or more of the person's major life activities.

Major Life Activity Defined

Section 504 and the ADA define a major life activity using a very functional approach. Major life activities include a wide variety of daily activities, but for school-age children this major life activity is learning. Other life activities include: caring for oneself, performing manual tasks, walking, seeing, hearing, speaking, breathing, and working. Federal court cases have added additional major life activities, including sitting, stooping, reaching, and eating.[7] Basically, any function that is performed routinely by individuals is considered a major life activity.

Individuals need not currently have a physical or mental impairment in order to be covered under Section 504 and the ADA; they may be covered if they have a record of having such an impairment or if they are simply regarded as having such an impairment. These two categories are generally not the focus for school-age children; they are more likely to deal with individuals in employment or community situations.[8] Still, there may be instances when children are protected under Section 504 and the ADA because of their being regarded as having an impairment or their having a record of such an impairment.

Just because a child is referred for consideration for Section 504 and ADA services does not mean the child will be determined to be eligible. Referral is simply a first step in the process. Often, parents think that if they bring the school a diagnosis from a physician stating that a child has a particular disability, such as ADD/ADHD, the school will have to serve the child under Section 504 and the ADA. This is simply not the case. A diagnosis by anyone is only part of the referral. Although physicians and other health professionals may make various diagnoses, school personnel make the eligibility determination. Parents can always contest the decision through due process hearings, but the determination regarding eligibility rests with the school. After a child has been referred, either by school personnel, which includes the librarian, or parents, the school is obligated to consider the referral. A group of knowledgeable people should come together to decide whether they think the child is eligible. Most schools have a committee that addresses this issue. Schools do not have to evaluate a student who has been referred if school personnel do not believe that the child is eligible under Section 504 and the ADA.[9]

FAPE—Free Appropriate Public Education

Section 504 and the ADA protect disabled children from discrimination and provide them with the right to a free, appropriate public education (FAPE). Schools must provide procedural safeguards to children and their families while providing services and protection. Students with disabilities should be allowed to participate in all activities that are available for students without disabilities. Equal access to the library, its services, and its facilities is an element of a free, appropriate public education. But how far does the library have to go in providing these services? Must they install handicap-accessible electric doors, which would be an expense greater than five years of acquisitions? The answer is no. The library must provide facilities, services, and programs to the disabled student that would not cause an "undue burden" to the library. Clearly, if reasonable modifications for a reasonable expenditure of time and or money can be made, then they must be made.

Libraries must do numerous things to meet the requirements of Section 504 and the ADA. For the most part, these actions are based on common sense and treating individuals with disabilities fairly. If schools approach the implementation of Section 504 and the ADA using these guidelines, then most instances of potential discrimination can be dealt with simply and without a great deal of expense. This can be as simple as having a student worker assigned to the library to retrieve books or browse shelves for a student in a wheelchair or it can be as complex as redesigning your Web site. Communication with the family of the student is important. Ask them to tour the library and provide specific advice regarding barriers.

Section 504 defines FAPE as the provision of general or special education and related aids and services that are:

- designed to meet individual educational needs of persons with disabilities as well as the needs of a nonhandicapped person are met, and
- based on adherence to procedural safeguards outlined in the law. (§ 104.33[b])

A free, appropriate public education for disabled students can include education in general education classes, education in general education classes with supplementary aids, and special education and related services outside the general education setting. Libraries may offer specialized one-on-one training for students with special needs. Arrangements can be made for after-school sessions or release during specific classes. The specific actions that libraries must take in order to comply with the FAPE requirement of Section 504 and the ADA vary with each child. In most situations, simple, inexpensive accommodations and modifications are sufficient. In order for an educational program to be appropriate, it must be designed to meet the individual needs of students.

IDEA defines related services as services that are necessary to enable a student to benefit from special education. Related services under Section 504 and the ADA are required for children who do not receive any other special education services or interventions.

Education with Peers

Section 504 and the ADA, like the IDEA, require that students with disabilities be educated with their nondisabled peers, to the maximum extent appropriate, while meeting the needs of the students with disabilities. This is part of the FAPE requirement of Section 504 and the ADA. Schools should always place students with disabilities with their nondisabled peers, unless the school can demonstrate that the student's education program cannot be achieved satisfactorily, with or without supplementary aids and services, in the general education setting.

Accommodations to Educate Students with their Peers

Providing accommodations for students protected under Section 504 and the ADA is one way schools can provide an appropriate education. Just as an appropriate education is based on an individual student's needs in IDEA programs, accommodations provided under Section 504 and the ADA are determined on an individual basis. Although schools do not have to develop Individualized Education Programs (IEPs) for students served under IDEA, they do have to develop individual plans for students under Section 504. Section 504 does not specify the contents of the plan, but the plan must be designed to meet the needs of individual students, including specific accommodations and modifications that are necessary to meet the FAPE requirement.[10]

The Office of Civil Rights (OCR; 1989a) described the following specific requirements for schools regarding Section 504:

Undertake annually to identify and locate all children with disabilities who are unserved;

Provide a "free appropriate public education" to each student with disabilities, regardless of the nature or severity of the disability. This means providing regular or special education and related aids and services designed to meet the individual educational needs of disabled persons as adequately as the needs of nondisabled persons are met;

Ensure that each student with disabilities is educated with nondisabled students to the maximum extent appropriate;

Establish nondiscriminatory evaluation and placement procedures to avoid the inappropriate education that may result from the misclassification or misplacement of students;

Establish procedural safeguards to enable parents and guardians to participate meaningfully in decisions regarding the evaluation and placement of their children; and

Afford children with disabilities an equal opportunity to participate in non-academic and extra-curricular services and activities. (p. 8)

LIBRARIES IN PUBLIC SCHOOLS AND FAPE

After a child has been determined to be eligible for Section 504 and ADA services and protections, an individual written plan must be developed. Schools should have Section 504 and ADA accommodation plans for teachers to use. The disability director does not always include the librarian in the plans. In these instances it is the duty of the librarian to make their inclusion standard procedure and to include their library's policies and capabilities in the plan. These plans should be simple and easy to complete, yet able to include the important information that will enable school personnel to implement the necessary accommodations to meet individual needs.

Training programs for general education teachers for disabled students should include librarians. Students with disabilities who are protected under Section 504 and the ADA but are not eligible for IDEA services must be afforded a FAPE through a designated process. This includes referral, evaluation, program planning, placement, and reevaluation. Schools should establish policies that spell out steps that should be taken to provide these services. Library policies should include FAPE considerations. Schools can use the same process they use with IDEA, or they can develop a set of procedures that is specific to students who are protected by Section 504 and the ADA.

Librarians and the Referral Committee

If the referral committee deems it likely that the child is eligible for Section 504 and ADA services, then the school must conduct its own evaluation to determine whether the student is eligible for Section 504 and ADA services and what services would be required to ensure a FAPE. The evaluation requirements for Section 504 and the ADA differ from those found in IDEA.

Observations, anecdotal information, and judgments are considered legitimate sources of assessment data. Norm-referenced, standardized tests are not required as part of the evaluation. If data from these sources are considered necessary to make eligibility decisions and decisions regarding accommodations and modifications, then they should be used. If school personnel believe that a medical evaluation or another evaluation from a specialist is needed in order to make an eligibility decision or to determine accommodations, then the school is obligated to obtain the evaluation and pay for the evaluation.

Accommodations to consider include seating arrangements, testing modifications, homework modifications, the use of readers or taped materials, and accommodations in attendance policies. For the most part, accommodations for students with disabilities are inexpensive, commonsense modifications that help give students equal access to learning and extracurricular activities. Good teachers have used these types of accommodations and modifications for years.

Discipline

Students can definitely be disciplined; rules and standards can be applied to these students just as they are applied to nondisabled students. The important thing to consider is that students served under Section 504 and the ADA have an equal opportunity to be successful with classroom rules and behavioral regulations. In order to ensure this with some students, a behavior intervention plan may be necessary. Disciplinary procedures for students under Section 504 and the ADA are similar to those under IDEA. Expulsion or suspensions of ten or more days are considered a change of placement and require the same procedural requirements as the IDEA. Therefore, before a student can be suspended or expelled for more than ten days, a manifest determination must be made. If a manifest determination shows no relationship between the behavior and disability, then the student can be disciplined as any other student. If a manifest determination shows that there is a relationship between the behavior and disability, then the student cannot be expelled or suspended; the school should consider the appropriateness of the current program and consider appropriate changes.

Visually Impaired and Blind Students

Braille computer terminals are an obvious compensatory path for blind students. Braille books are another. You can obtain books from your state libraries for the blind. A list can be found at the Web site of the National Federation for the Blind (available at http://www.nfb.org/states/library.htm [accessed February 3, 2003]). Generally state libraries for the blind provide special four-track tape players for books on tape and their selection is generally comparable to large public library, although they do not carry school textbooks. They generally give priority to schools and students who books assignments. The books are sent via standard mail for a period of ninety days with no postage due to the school. The libraries typically also have Braille and large-print books and a large assortment of magazines on tape, as well as large-print periodicals, audio books, and audio-described videotapes. Most state libraries will have a referral librarian on staff who will be able to discuss special equipment needs of specific disabilities and do further research for you if your specific situation has not already been researched. In order to access these services it is generally necessary for the student and the school to register with the State Library for the Blind.

EIES (Electronic Information and Education Service) of New Jersey offers a fully searchable, dial-up TeleReader service providing full-text recordings by volunteers of articles from a selection of local and national newspapers and magazines.

The American Action Fund for Blind Children and Adults is a service agency that specializes in providing blind people with help that is not readily available to them from government programs or other existing service systems. The services of the American Action Fund for Blind Children and Adults are planned especially to meet the needs of blind children, the elderly blind, and the deaf-blind.

The American Action Fund for Blind Children and Adults has offices in Baltimore, Maryland, and Tarzana, California, and volunteer workers throughout the country. The Tarzana office houses a free lending library of Braille and *Twin Vision*® books for blind children. Books are sent postage free to borrowers wherever they live. They publish and distribute to deaf-blind persons a free weekly newspaper in Braille. The Action Fund also distributes free Braille calendars to blind and deaf-blind people on a nationwide basis. The Kenneth Jernigan Library for Blind Children provides free service at 18440 Oxnard Street, Tarzana, California 91356. They can be reached by phone at (816) 343-2022. The web address is: http:// www.actionfund.org (Accessed March 3, 2002.)

The National Organization of Parents of Blind Children can also be a resource for information on helping blind students (NOPBC). Mrs. Barbara Cheadle is president of NOPBC. You may contact her by mail at 1800 Johnson Street, Baltimore, Maryland 21230; by phone at (410) 659-9314, Extension 360; by fax at (410) 685-5653; or via e-mail at bcheadle@nfb.org. The web address is http://www.nfb.org/ (Accessed March 3, 2003).

Braille printers and large-type keyboards can be connected to a computer already equipped with software that offers voice activation and Braille-text translation. Print materials can be scanned for magnified on-screen display and a synthesizer can read this same material aloud. The same equipment can double as an automated coach in spelling, phonetics, and word definitions. A tabletop-lighted magnifying system and handheld magnifiers in a range of strengths allow those with low vision to read print materials.

With a little effort a whole new world can be opened for the low-vision and the blind student and the librarian as well.

Auditory Processing Deficits

Providing for children with auditory processing deficits (APD) can be done with little or no expense. All libraries should be prepared to manage APD students. For these students some environmental modifications will be necessary. These children may be involved in remediation (direct therapy) techniques and compensatory strategies. For therapy and compensatory strategies the librarian might identify and suggest readings appropriate for these children. This reading list could be delivered to their therapist, parents and/or students themselves. As always, compassion and discretion are the watchwords. These children do not want to be made to feel inferior to their peers. In fact many APD students have gone on to accomplish great feats. John Chambers, president of CISCO corporation, was an APD student.

Environmental modifications allow the students to focus on learning. Sitting in groups may be distracting to these students. Consequently, libraries should contain some carrels to allow these students to block out intruding auditory and visual distractions. Traffic noise distracts these students as can something as minute and unobtrusive to a non-APD student as the buzz of a fluorescent light. Their carrels should be tucked away in a quiet corner of the library.

When addressing the ADP child your face should be visible to the child. You should speak without moving and deliver information in small increments.[11] Because children with APD often do not understand directions or instructions, discretely monitor them to evaluate whether learning and comprehension are taking place. Some children with APD can repeat verbatim an entire message; it is like a tape running through their head, and yet they do not comprehend its meaning. Deliver a written summary of your instructions and repeat your instructions in a rephrased manner one last time. If the child does not appear to understand, gently and discreetly determine their comprehension of your instructions. You might follow up their comprehension at another meeting.

If your presentation includes video and audio, understand that many children with Integration Deficit have, by definition, difficulty integrating multi-modal cues. When provided with visual, tactile, and auditory information all at once, these children may become more confused than they would have been if the information had been presented through only one modality. Children with Integration Deficit often do far better when information is presented sequentially; that is, when the message is first delivered verbally, then visually, and then tactile cues (such as touching the actual object) are added.[12]

It is important to understand the special needs of specific students. When presenting education information on library use, it is important to be sensitive to these various learning deficits that exist in diagnosed and undiagnosed students.

It is useful to pre-teach key vocabulary and critical concepts by presenting them in writing through the special needs therapist before these students arrive at the library for instruction. This allows the student to already be familiar with the words and ideas that will be presented. They also will be able to hear and understand your presentation rather than puzzle over the new concepts and lose the content of your presentation.[13]

YOUR POLICY IS YOUR PROTECTION FROM GRIEVANCE

It is wise to develop a policy directed toward handling disabled students so that it may be relied upon should a grievance be filed by parents who feel that their child has been discriminated against under Section 504 and the ADA. Hopefully, this position of discrimination will not include your library or its resources.

A grievance can be initiated with the school or by filing a complaint with the Office of Civil Rights and requesting a due process hearing. It may also be initiated by the filing of a suit in federal court. Complaints have to be filed within 180 days of the reputed violation. Complaints are filed with the U.S. Department of Education and should be sent to the Office of Civil Rights of the Department of Education in the region where the school district is located. If parents file a complaint regarding Section 504 and ADA services, the school district must have in place an impartial hearing procedure similar to the one required by the IDEA. This opportunity must be afforded parents if they choose an administrative appeal rather than immediate court action.

Generally, a grievance will identify area deficiencies of the school that do not meet the student's needs. A librarian cannot set school or school district policy. Your library policy should include a procedure by which the librarian is informed of students determined to have disabilities by the disability officer. With the disability officer and student therapist, discuss the best method that the library and its staff may accommodate the student. This should include accessibility of each form of media in the library. Your instructional capacity should address specific teaching methods best suited for the individual student. The chosen approach for the student should be documented and a copy kept in the library, a copy sent to the student's therapist, and a copy sent to the disability officer. For each activity in which a nondisabled student can engage in the library there should be a means for a disabled student to engage in that same activity. The engagement may not take the same path but alternative paths can be devised.

The librarian can determine if the intensity of the library services is sufficient to address the student's need. However, this is an element that will be reviewed in a grievance procedure. Try to take the perspective of the parent of the student. Have you done all you can to provide library services to this child that are equal to a nondisabled child?

In order to comply with the ADA and Section 504, the special needs educator needs to collect meaningful data to monitor student progress and document program effectiveness. Check with this educator each January to evaluate the library services provided to the student to that date and request feedback on additional services you might provide. Document this request both in your library and in the student's file in the disability office of your school district and in the student's individual educational program. Ask that you be advised of the student's progress as monitored through their IEP so that the library might upgrade its services to the disabled student. The IEP will be carefully scrutinized in litigation involving the determination of a FAPE. If the librarian is involved in the IEP, include meaningful goals and objectives for library skills, with criteria for their mastery. This could be as simple as being able to locate a book in the card catalog by title or as complex as a student aide being capable of reshelving books. Adequate notice to parents to attend IEP meetings is an essential element of an IEP. Failure to provide adequate notice will usually render a student's IEP illegal. Take the opportunity to discuss the parents' goals for the student's library skills. This could be one of the more important skills the student takes away from their public school education. Consider working with the public library to encourage the students to generalize their library skills.

The IEP should include present levels of performance. Interviewing the parents and speaking with the student is the librarian's first opportunity to evaluate the student's existing library skills and to develop measurable annual goals, which may be the same as those for nondisabled students.

Because an IEP must address both the academic and nonacademic needs (e.g., social development, communication) of a student, consider whether the student could work as an aide in the library to strengthen his or her social and communication skills. The assessment and instructional strategies must be linked in the IEP. Every area of identified need must have a corresponding measurable annual goal. In your library policy, include the library's approach to disabled students and its role in IEPs.

Having a student aide retrieve books from shelves for students in wheelchairs accommodates that disability. Hearing-impaired children are often fitted with listening devices. Include these capabilities in your policy. Also have a policy of involving disabled students in library work. Some students that are not mainstreamed, but visit the library as a group, may be given special duties, such as reshelving the books used by the students during their visit. The library can also provide pre-vocational skills for learning-impaired or disabled students. Many library tasks can be converted into other vocational applications once the student begins job searching.

PHYSICAL REQUIREMENTS FOR THE LIBRARY

If you are fortunate enough to be involved in building a new library or are involved in the renovation of an existing library, the school's contract with the architect should specify ADA construction compliance. Barrier-free design is an important element of ADA compliance.

The ADA provides certain guidelines for the creation of a barrier-free design. The guidelines are outlined below, but remember these are but the minimum required by the federal government. Some states have more stringent guidelines. Children often are not as adept as adults when maneuvering their wheelchairs. Although their wheelchairs may be smaller, they may need more room to maneuver if they lack physical strength or coordination.

An open, barrier-free library is not only required by law, it also creates a more inviting and functional environment for everyone, including the librarians. Book trucks, for example, are easier to maneuver in an open space. A spacious environment is intrinsically more appealing.

Wheelchair accessibility requires special design considerations for the library such as the following: An adult wheelchair requires thirty inches in width at a minimum, and many motorized wheelchairs are wider. A U-turn in a wheelchair requires at a minimum seventy-eight inches by sixty inches. A right or left turn requires thirty-six inches by thirty-six inches. All doors must be a minimum of thirty-two inches wide. Thresholds must be beveled so the wheelchair may roll over them with a minimum of ease and must be no thicker than one-half-inch tall. Door handles must be operable with one hand and placed at a height of no more than forty-eight inches from the floor. Elevator access must be available for all floors. If carpet is used, the maximum pile length is one-half inch to allow the wheelchair to roll easily along the floor; it must be firm and have a no-cushion backing or pad.

Aisles between books stacks must be at least three feet wide; however, a forty-two-inch width at the narrowest portal between shelves is strongly recommended. A wheelchair-bound student cannot reach above five feet or below twenty inches for access to materials.

Five percent of all workstations must be wheelchair accessible; this includes fixed seating, tables, and carrels. Knee space must be twenty-seven inches high, thirty inches wide, and nineteen inches deep. Workspace must be twenty-eight to thirty-four inches above the floor. Children twelve and under in wheelchairs require a minimum height of twenty-four inches. Height-adjustable carrels often provide the best option, particularly in middle school where students come in all sizes.

The circulation desk must have a handicapped-accessible area with a countertop that is at least thirty-six inches long and a maximum of thirty-six inches above the floor. If students must sign their names in order to check out books, there must be a space no more than thirty-four inches above the floor to allow access. Light switches must not be placed over forty-eight inches from the floor and lounge areas should have wheelchair space.

Signage must also meet ADA guidelines. Signs for permanent rooms must have tactile lettering of a minimum of one-half-inch thick. The lettering must be between five-eighths of an inch and two inches tall, and must include grade 2 Braille. They must be mounted on the same side of the door as the door handle, forty-eight to sixty inches from the center of the sign to the floor, and far enough to the side of the door frame that a person reading the sign at a distance of three inches from the door will not be hit when the door opens. Signs must have a nonglare finish and sharp contrast between the colors of the letters and the background. Overhead signs must have letters at least three inches high, and must be hung a minimum of eighty inches above the finished floor.

As with many laws pertaining to the library, the librarian may be the most knowledgeable person of the laws that affect the library design. Contact both your state and the federal offices for the latest requirements and be certain that the design complies with the minimum regulations, noting that these change from time to time. Also, some local building codes may have restrictions and guidelines with which the library must comply. When planning evacuation routes and procedures be certain these, too, consider the disabled.

If you are planning a new library, be aware of shelving depth, which is required to be ten inches for standard shelving, twelve inches for reference and picture books, and fifteen inches for multimedia books. The required table height for grades K–1 is 20–22 inches; grades 2–4 is 24–26 inches; grades 5–12 is 27–29 inches. Table height for the wheelchair accessible adult is 28–34 inches, preferably adjustable, and for K–5 it is 26–29 inches in height. Seat height from the chair to the table for K–1 is 8–10 inches; for grades 2–12 it is 10–11 inches.

WHAT DOES HAVING A DISABLED STUDENT MEAN TO THE LIBRARIAN?

Having a disabled student requires understanding the disability. Be open. The larger the world we embrace the larger our world becomes. Review your school district's policies and evaluate their application to your library. Include all your activities with the disabled in your policy. If you have a monthly showcase of the bibliographies of the disabled student staff, mention this in your policy. If you display the collections of the disabled student staff, mention this in your policy. Describe how the disabled student staff contributes to the functioning of your library.

The inclusion of these activities as an integral part of your library program in your policies serves not only as a written documentation of your attitude of affirmative inclusion of the disabled, but also it will be a reminder to those that you work with and those that succeed you of the library's priorities.

A useful resource is the Association of Specialized and Cooperative Library Agencies (ASCLA), which is a division of the American Library Association. ASCLA's Libraries Serving Special Populations (LSSPs) section has separate forums on Library Service to People with Visual or Physical Disabilities, Library Service to the Deaf Forum, Library Service to the Impaired Elderly, Library Service to Developmentally Disabled Persons, and Academic Librarians Assisting the Disabled. The Americans with Disabilities Act Assembly is a committee of ASCLA that facilitates communication among ALA units and other groups concerning the Americans with Disabilities Act.

Another resource, the American Library Association's Office for Literacy and Outreach Services (OLOS), supports and promotes "literacy and equity of information access initiatives for traditionally underserved populations." These include new and nonreaders, people geographically isolated, people with disabilities, rural and urban poor people, and people generally discriminated against based on race, ethnicity, sexual orientation, age, language and social class. OLOS maintains an outreach listserv.

NOTES

1. Reading List Courtesy of Easter Seals AccessAbility Program. Available: http://www.easterseals.org. (Accessed March 3, 2003.)

2. "AccessAbility @ Your Library." Available: http://www.easter-seals.org. (Accessed March 3, 2003.)

3. D. Gorn, *What Do I Do When . . . The Answer Book on Special Education Law.* (Horsham, PA: LRP Publications, 1996).

4. *Lachman v. Illinois State Board of Education,* 852 F2d 290 (7th Cir. 1988).

5. Rehabilitation Act, Sec. 706[8].

6. P.A. Zirkel and J.M. Kincaid, *Section 504 and the Schools* (Horsham, PA: LRP Publications, 1994).

7. E. Hartwig, "Not Every ADD Student Is Covered Under Section 504," *Section 504 Compliance Advisor* 4 (2000): 4.

8. Ibid.

9. R. Wenkart, "Comparing the IDEA with Section 504," *Special Education Law Update* 9 (2000):1–4.

10. H. R. Turnbull and A. Turnbull, *Free Appropriate Public Education,* 6th ed. (Denver: Love, 2000).

11. Teri James Bellis, *When the Brain Can't Hear* (New York: Pocket Books, 2002).

12. Ibid.

13. Ibid.

13

EMPLOYMENT LAW
IN LIBRARIES

If you wish success in life, make perseverance your bosom friend, experience your wise counselor, caution your elder brother and hope your guardian genius.

—Joseph Addison

This chapter will cover:

Contractual Employment

At-Will Employees

Implied Contract

Wrongful Discharge for Public Policy Reasons

Protected Class

Promissory Estoppel

Employee Evaluation

Job Interview

In education it is typical for employees to have contracts that govern their employment with the school district. It is not uncommon for library employees to be hired, supervised, promoted, and at times fired by the librarian. Often these employees do not have contracts and are known as "at-will" employees. At-will employees serve at the pleasure of the employer or at the employer's will. The librarian may even be an at-will employee.

One labor commentator noted at the middle of the twentieth century:

We have become a nation of employees. We are dependent upon others for our means of livelihood, and most of our people have become completely dependent upon wages. If they lose their jobs they lose every resource, except for the relief supplied by the various forms of social security. Such dependence of the mass of the people upon others for all of their income is something new in the world. For our generation, the substance of life is in another man's hands.[1]

There are decisions we make that affect the very fabric and core of our lives. Work is one of these. Work has the potential to shape the fashion in which we approach our lives. Much of our identity is expressed through our chosen work; it influences our world perspective, provides us with friends, determines where and how we will live, and creates opportunities for us and for our children. We organize our lives, from the smallest of things such as when and what we will eat for lunch to where we will live and where our children will go to school, based on employment. To a certain extent the job a person chooses transforms nearly everything about that person. Without work, health insurance may not be available; without work, lives may become less full; without places to work, whole towns or neighborhoods may disintegrate. Employment is a huge part of our lives and of our society.

Because employment is so important to the preservation of the family and of society, and because jobs may be a family's most valuable asset and the basis for their survival, there are laws that govern employment. In the relationship between employer and employee, U.S. society has addressed the complex interdependence between individuals and the increasing ability of those in positions of power (employers) to harm the powerless. Federal and state laws have addressed this imbalance.

CONTRACTUAL EMPLOYMENT

School boards approve the contracts used in their districts by professional educators. Generally there are three separate types of contracts:

- **Probationary contracts** are typically given to all certified professional employees new to the district. The contracts cannot exceed a term of one year but may be re-issued for two additional terms—and for a fourth year if the board is in doubt of an employee's performance.

- **Term contracts** are for a fixed period of time generally not to exceed five years. Employees hold these contracts until they resign, are returned to probationary status in accordance with statute, or until the contracts are not renewed or terminated by dismissal.

- **Continuing contracts** are similar to tenure and continue indefinitely. An employee remains on a continuing contract until the employee relinquishes the contract, is released or discharged for "good cause," or is returned to a probationary contract, which is typically covered by state statute.

The education code or statute of your state typically governs the education and/or certification and credentials required of its principals, classroom teachers, counselors, and any other full-time professional employees, which can include librarians and nurses. This code or statute generally defines whether a specific category of employee will be hired for a probationary period, term period, or be given a continuing contract. In some states librarians must have teacher certification and have taught for a number of years, whereas in others this is not a prerequisite.

In some states this policy is governed by statute, in others it is governed by the state board of education, and in yet others it is governed by individual school districts. The education code or statutes generally hold that districts are not allowed to offer a contract of any kind to categories of personnel other than those listed.

Some boards of education or state statutes require teacher certification for all administrative positions, except for assistant principals, principals, and superintendents; some do not. Positions such as administrative supervisor, special education director, curriculum director, librarian, gifted and talented coordinator, and vocational supervisor, among others, may not require teacher certification. This gives districts more discretion and flexibility in hiring to meet local needs. However, often employees in positions for which certification is not required are not entitled to a contract, which means they are at-will employees.

At-will employees may be paraprofessionals, auxiliary personnel, teachers with school district permits, and any noncertified administrators or professionals, such as the business manager, transportation director, or technology coordinator. In some instances, the librarians may be an at-will employee and in others they will have a contract. The librarian may be in a position of being both the employer and the employee. Consequently, it is important to understand the law from both perspectives.

AT-WILL EMPLOYEES

The employment-at-will rule provides that the employment relationship, absent a contract to the contrary, is "at will," meaning that either the employer or the employee can terminate the relationship at any time for any reason, even for no reason, without legal liability attaching.

Federal and state statutes in some instances protect employees from discharge when they have done nothing wrong. The key here is "in some instances." In many instances, the employer is entitled to hire and to retain persons with whom they and their coworkers can work. The federal and state employment discrimination laws limit the ability of employers to discharge employees if that discharge is motivated by the employee's status as a member of a defined protected class. Many attempts have been made in the last decade to broaden the scope of these enumerated protected classes, but they have failed.

Our country has cherished the right of employers to run their own business and to hire those persons that will best serve their interests. The legal doctrine of at-will employment is doctrine that embodies the concept that the employee serves at the will of the employer. Employers can legally change the terms and conditions of employment at will. Employers can dismiss employees at any time for any or no reason, without notice or severance pay. Most employment in the United States is contingent employment with no legally guaranteed terms or continuity.

More narrow protections come from statutes prohibiting discharge, for example, for jury service, filing workers' compensation or OSHA (Occupational Safety and Health Administration) claims, and testifying in court.[2] Common law limitations on the ability of the employer to fire at will arise from both contract and tort law.[3]

IMPLIED CONTRACT

Statements in employee handbooks and oral promises made during the interview or during the initial period of employment have been found to constitute implied contracts limiting the employer's ability to fire without just cause.[4]

The significance of an implied contract exception to the at-will doctrine has been minimized in recent years, however, because of employers' attempts to state clearly, usually in the contract if there is one as well as in a prominent location in the employee handbook, that the employment relationship is an at-will relationship.

WRONGFUL DISCHARGE FOR PUBLIC POLICY REASONS

The courts have infringed upon the employment-at-will doctrine by carving out a niche for "public policy." For example, an employee cannot be fired for refusing to give false testimony. This would be "against public policy." To discharge an employee for this reason has been defined to be a wrongful discharge. The terminated employee can recover from the employer if the court determines that the firing violated public policy and was a wrongful discharge.

In one of the earliest reported cases discussing public policy in the employment context, *Petermann v. International Brotherhood of Teamsters Local 396*, the court held the employer liable for firing an at-will employee for refusing to commit perjury. Such a firing was deemed to have violated public policy by an attempt to encourage untruthful testimony. Employment-at-will doctrine developed rapidly after the Petermann decision and has broadened its scope.[5]

PROTECTED CLASS

It is unlawful under federal law to discriminate between persons with regard to the hiring of that person, the terms of employment, training, promotion, advancement, firings or working conditions because of age (persons over 40); disability; race or color; national origin; religion; sex; and pregnancy. These limitations do not apply if there is a bona fide occupational qualification that is required for the job.[6] For example a pregnant employee would not be the proper employee to participate in the heavy lifting of relocating a library from the first floor to the second. Discrimination would be appropriate in this instance. A blind employee would not be able to participate in non-Braille shelving.

ADA Protections

The Supreme Court has concluded that the protections of the Americans with Disabilities Act, at least in the employment context, should be reserved for those individuals who "as a group, occupy an inferior status in our society, and are severely disadvantaged socially, vocationally, economically, and educationally."[7] This description does not extend to protect individuals who, no matter how unfortunately, are prevented from holding the particular job they prefer as opposed to being unable to work in any meaningful way.

The purpose of the ADA[8] is to allow individuals who, because of their disabilities, are prevented from or hampered in participating in the mainstream of American life. It was aimed at an "insular minority," not a broad majority. The ADA protects persons who have

- a physical or mental impairment that substantially limits one or more of the major life activities of such individual;
- a record of such an impairment; or
- are regarded as having such an impairment.

Thus, to understand and apply the Act's provisions to real-life circumstances, one must determine what is meant by "physical or mental impairment," "substantially limited," and "major life activities of such individual." The Act provides no definitions of these terms. However, the Equal Employment Opportunity Commission (EEOC) has attempted to address this omission by way of regulation.

The Americans with Disabilities Act of 1990 (ADA) specifically refers to 43 million disabled Americans with the potential of "160 million under a 'health conditions approach,' which looks at all conditions that impair the health or normal functional abilities of an individual."[9] Likewise, the court noted that there were more than 100 million Americans with vision impairments,

28 million with impaired hearing, and 50 million with high blood pressure.[10] It found these numbers far larger than the 43 million specifically articulated by Congress in the Act.[11] Therefore, the court concluded that any legislative history was irrelevant and the intent of the Act, as written, required consideration of mitigating and corrective measures in determining whether an individual was "disabled" for purposes of the Act.[12]

These numbers are significant. They give us a key to understanding the scope of the disability envisioned by the Congress in its enactment of the ADA.

PROMISSORY ESTOPPEL

An equitable doctrine, promissory estoppel, has been asserted under circumstances similar to those giving rise to tort claims for fraudulent inducement.[13] Promissory estoppel can be applied even though no contract exists if three requirements are met:

- a promise is made upon which the promisee reasonably relies,
- the promisor reasonably should have expected the promisee to rely on it, and
- enforcement of the promise is the only way to avoid injustice.[14]

Even though, because of the nature of the at-will employment relationship, the at-will employee cannot assert contractual breaches upon termination, the lack of a contract allows claims for promissory estoppel. Do not promise an employee an inducement to take a job and then fail to honor that promise.

EMPLOYEE EVALUATION

School libraries are flexible environments. If someone is not pulling his or her weight, the consequence is manifested in many different areas and it may be difficult to document this deficiency. Documentation is the key to fairness.

Staffing Adequacy

First, in employee evaluation, it could be helpful to determine how your library is staffed as compared to other school libraries of the same size. Is your staffing above or below the national average? This might help in a decision regarding the reasonableness of expectations of the staff.

The U.S. Department of Education, National Center for Education Statistics (NCES), Schools and Staffing Survey, Library Statistics Program (http://nces.ed.gov/surveys/libraries [accessed February 3, 2003]) can give guidance of the statistical norms in this area. The data provide a national picture of school library collections, expenditures, staff, technology, and services. The library media specialist questionnaire provides a national profile of the school library media specialist workforce. Federal surveys of school library media centers in elementary and secondary schools in the United States were conducted in 1958, 1962, 1974, 1978, 1985, school year 1993–1994, and school year 1999–2000.

The "Schools and Staffing Survey, 1999–2000: Overview of the Data for Public, Private, Public Charter, and Bureau of Indian Affairs Elementary and Secondary Schools" was released in June 1, 2002. This report provides comparisons of key estimates across four sectors, as well as comparisons across different types of schools, such as community type, region, school level, and school enrollment within each sector. The 1999–2000 Schools and Staffing Survey (SASS) data is presented through tables of estimates for traditional public, private, public charter, and Bureau of Indian Affairs (BIA) schools, school library media centers, public school districts, and the principals and teachers that work in these schools. Data are available by state for public schools and by private school affiliation and NCES typology for private schools.

Job Description

Each job should have a written description that enumerates the specific responsibilities of that position. This should be updated annually and should be an honest reflection of all the tasks of that expected position. This is an important tool not only for the employee and as the basis for an employee evaluation, but it also aids the head librarian in effective library management. There are scientific methods of determining the actual use of an employee's time, and there are anecdotal methods.

There are several Web sites that can guide you in crafting or updating a job description model. The Washington Library Media Association (available: http://www.wlma.org/Professional/responsibilities.htm [accessed February 1, 2003]) maintains an excellent and extensive bibliography, which outlines many Web sites that will be an aid in structuring job descriptions for your library.

Only with this job description can a fair and accurate evaluation be made of the employee's performance on an annual basis. Evaluating an employee's performance on set and communicated criteria is the only fair way to promote, demote, or dismiss an employee.

Typically a librarian media specialist in a school library will:

- Develop a curriculum for student instruction and faculty instruction;
- Participate in the administration responsibilities of the library;
- Participate in instruction of students;
- Participate in reference support to the students;
- Participate in curriculum support for the faculty;

- Participate in circulation activates;
- Provide access to technology;
- Aid both students and faculty in the use of technology;
- Weed the collection;
- Participate in cataloging activates;

These are the sorts of categories that may be found in school library job descriptions. Certainly some librarians will be better with interpersonal skills and others will be better with administrative and technical tasks. Using this type of task itemization will serve as a tool for performance evaluation and perhaps a tool to assign those tasks to an employee that is best suited to perform them. The important point here is to have a criterion by which the employees can be judged on a consistent and uniform scale and document the results.

JOB INTERVIEW

The law relating to what may and may not be asked during a job interview is simple and based in courtesy and common sense. However, it is essential to understand that during a job interview questions may not be asked for the purpose of discriminating on the basis of race, color, religion, sex, national origin, birthplace, age, or physical disability. Any question asked during the selection process must be related to the job.

This rule applies to all questions posed throughout the entire employment process, whether in the application form, during the interview, or in any testing materials administered. You may believe that staffing the library entitles you to know whether an employee is planning on becoming pregnant in the near future, or whether childcare is likely to become a problem. The question cannot be asked in that fashion. Rather it can go only so far as to determine whether the potential employee can work the hours that the job requires. Although you cannot ask whether the employee has any disabilities, you may certainly inquire as to whether they can perform all the tasks normally expected in that position.

The qualities of a good library media staff person can be found at the Washington Library Media Association Web site (http://www.wlma.org /Professional/jobdescriptions.htm [accessed February 1, 2003]). This is an important departure point for an interview. Interview a prospective employee to illuminate whether they have these qualities.

Consider the following interview questions:

- Would you describe yourself as a lifelong learner? How do you participate in lifelong learning?
- Do you consider yourself to have leadership skills? Give me an example of your personal leadership qualities and how they were used.

- What experience do you have in management? Which would you prefer to manage: people, a program, a collection or a budget? Why?
- Tell me about your research skills.
- What are your favorite resources within and outside the library?
- What is the most beneficial educational trend you have observed in the last three years?
- What is the most detrimental?

This is not intended to be a sample of a "legal" interview. Rather, this is an example of a portion of an effective "legal" interview. These types of questions will elicit much more than facts; they will elicit the applicant's attitude, ability to interact with the world, and perspective of his or her role in the world and in the library. Good interview skills can be learned and can elicit all the information ever needed to form an opinion of the potential contributions the applicant can make without venturing into areas protected by law.

INTENTIONAL INFLICTION OF EMOTIONAL DISTRESS AND EMPLOYMENT TERMINATION

In some states a suit can be brought for the intentional infliction of emotional distress that occurs in conjunction with an employment termination. Generally, in these states to establish a cause of action for intentional infliction of emotional distress in the workplace, an employee must prove some conduct that brings the dispute outside the scope of an ordinary employment dispute and into the realm of extreme and outrageous conduct. Only in the most unusual of employment cases does the conduct move out of the 'realm of an ordinary employment dispute' and into the classification of extreme and outrageous.

The mere fact of termination of employment, even if the termination is wrongful, is not legally sufficient evidence that the employer's conduct was extreme and outrageous under the rigorous standards set in most states.[15]

CONSTRUCTIVE TERMINATION OR DISCHARGE

Constructive discharge occurs when an employer makes conditions so intolerable that an employee reasonably feels resignation is their only option. The courts will find constructive discharge on an objective basis, not a subjective one. That is, the court will objectively examine the conditions of the work situation and evaluate whether a "reasonable person" would have found the working conditions so onerous, so humiliating that a "reasonable person" would have no alternative but to resign. Generally, the court will not take into account the employer's state of mind. Consequently, the employee does not need to prove that an employer subjectively intended to force the employee to resign.

Derogatory comments resulting from disciplinary proceedings do not constitute constructive discharge. Nor do unfavorable work evaluations support a constructive discharge claim. Humiliation or embarrassment stemming from a transfer to a different position within a school district is not significant enough to support a claim for constructive termination.

LIABILITY FOR EMPLOYEE CONDUCT AND THE USE OF COMPUTERS

Employers who provide employees access to computers and the Internet in the workplace provide employees with not only the medium but also the opportunity to commit illegal activity. The courts may hold an employer liable under the theory of *respondeat superior* if it is determined that the employee's acts were within the scope of employment. The court may also hold an employer liable under the doctrine of negligent retention if the employer did not remedy illegal or wrongful activity when the employer knew or should have known of its existence in the workplace.

To reduce the risk of liability, the employer should adopt strict and defensive computer- and Internet-use policies and procedures prohibiting illegal and wrongful computer and online conduct. By doing so the employer also puts the employee on notice that the employer may be monitoring its employee's activities.

CONCLUSION

Most school employees have a contractual relationship with the school district. However, the library also may have at-will employees. These employees do not have a contract governing the terms of their employment and may be fired at will. Unfettered dismissal is not acceptable. Dismissal of a protected category of employee must be for just cause.

NOTES

1. Lawrence E. Blades, "Employment At Will vs. Individual Freedom: On Limiting the Abusive Exercise of Employer Power," *Columbia Law Review.* 67 (1967): 1433–34.

2. See Elletta S. Callahan, "Employment at Will: The Relationship Between Societal Expectations and the Law," *American Business Law Journal* 28 (1990): 455.

3. David J. Walsh and Joshua L. Schwarz, "State Common Law Wrongful Discharge Doctrines: Up-Date, Refinement, and Rationales," *American Business Law Journal* 33 (1996): 645.

4. See, for example, *Toussaint v. Blue Cross & Blue Shield of Michigan,* 292 N.W.2d 880 (Mich. 1980); *Small v. Springs Indus.,* 357 S.E.2d 452 (S.C. 1987). See also Stephen F. Befort, "Employee Handbooks and Employment-At-Will Contracts," *Duke Law Journal*

(1985): 196; *Berube v. Fashion Centre Ltd.*, 771 P.2d 1033 (Utah 1989); *Finley v. Aetna Life & Cas. Co.*, 520 A.2d 208 (Conn. 1987); *Eales v. Tanana Valley Medical-Surgical Group*, 663 P.2d 958 (Alaska 1983). An express contract specifying a fixed duration for the employment, of course, by definition negates the employment-at-will relationship.

5. 344 P.2d 25 (Cal. 1959). Petermann sued for breach of contract, and not for the tort of wrongful discharge, arguing that public policy should prohibit an employer from firing an at-will employee for truthfully testifying. The court found for Petermann on the contract claim. Nevertheless, the court's discussion of public policy in this case laid the groundwork for the development of the tort of wrongful discharge. See *Green v. Ralee Eng'g Co.*, 960 P.2d 1046, 1048 (Cal. 1998).

6. 42 U.S.C. 2000 (e)21.

7. *Kessler v. Equity Management, Inc.*, 572 A.2d 1144 (Md. 1990).

8. See 42 U.S.C. §§ 12111–12117 (1994). Title I's prohibition against employment discrimination states: "No covered entity shall discriminate against a qualified individual with a disability because of the disability of such individual in regard to job application procedures, the hiring, advancement, or discharge of employees, employee compensation, job training, and other terms, conditions, and privileges of employment." 42 U.S.C. § 12112(a) (1994).

See 42 U.S.C. §§ 12131–12165 (1994). Title II states: "Subject to the provisions of this sub-chapter, no qualified individual with a disability shall, by reason of such disability, be excluded from participation in or be denied the benefits of the services, programs, or activities of a public entity, or be subjected to discrimination by any such entity." 42 U.S.C. § 12132 (1994).

See 42 U.S.C. §§ 12181–12189 (1994). Title III provides: "No individual shall be discriminated against on the basis of disability in the full and equal enjoyment of the goods, services, facilities, privileges, advantages, or accommodations of any place of public accommodation by any person who owns, leases (or leases to), or operates a place of public accommodation." 42 U.S.C. § 12182.

9. See *Sutton v. United Airlines*, 119 S. Ct. 2148 (1999) at 2148.

10. See id. at 2149.

11. See id.

12. Although not discussed by the court, further support for this conclusion is found in the congressional findings incorporated into the Act. For example, 42 U.S.C. § 12101(a) (6) states, "People with disabilities, as a group, occupy an inferior status in our society, and are severely disadvantaged socially, vocationally, economically, and educationally." This description hardly seems applicable to the plaintiffs in *Sutton*, who admittedly, like tens of millions of other Americans, have normal vision with the use of eyeglasses or contact lenses, and who are trained as commercial pilots. Further, § 12101(a) (7) describes individuals with disabilities as "a discreet and insular minority who have been . . . relegated to a position of political powerlessness in our society." Again, this description hardly fits the plaintiffs in *Sutton*.

13. See Cortlan H. Maddux, Comment, "Employers Beware! The Emerging Use of Promissory Estoppel as an Exception to Employment at Will," *Baylor Law Review* 49 (1997): 197.

14. Restatement (Second) of Contracts § 90 (1981).

15. See the Eighth District Court of Appeals, El Paso, Texas. "Texas Eighth District Court of Appeals—Writing on Causes of Action for Wrongful Termination." Available: http://www.8thcoa.courts.state.tx.us/. (Accessed June 30, 2002.)

14

POLICIES AND PROCEDURES—
A DIFFERENCE
WITH SIGNIFICANCE

The execution of the laws is more important than the making of them.
—Thomas Jefferson, 1789

This chapter will cover the following topics:

- The Distinction Between Policy and Procedure
- Library and School Goals Reflected in Policy
- Library Policy in Defense of Library Decisions

There is no substitute in life for experience. This reality hits most of us when we first graduate from school and find that all the jobs we really want require "experience." That's when we turn to our mentors, our parents, our professors, and even our peers with the question: How can I get experience if I cannot find a job that does not require experience? So we dig our heels in a little deeper, set our sites a little lower, and begin on the long and often lonely road of our private and personal quest for experience, truly believing our path of experience is ours alone. And to a certain extent it is ours alone, but much of our professional experience has a commonality. This experience that we are acquiring has been acquired by those who have preceded us, by those around us, and around the world in library science. Suddenly, we are in the swim of things and doing more than treading water. Somewhere down this path of experience, the quiet recognition comes: "I am experienced." We find, much to our surprise, that with this experience we have a shared understanding of the world of library science, and very much of what we have learned was not a product of our education.

Our education simply opened the door to the world of library science. Once we walked through that door we were on our own to continue to learn and continue to grow in our profession. There was no course about libraries and the law in library science school. We were able to pick up snippets of the law at seminars and in professional journals, but in the back of our minds was the burning question of accuracy. Was the legal insight we obtained five years ago correct then? Is it correct now? Experience has been our teacher in the area of legal education. Anyone who has the job of managing a library has a job as responsible and as varied as any corporate chief executive officer (CEO). You are responsible for the faculty, the students, your staff, and your inventory. That inventory comes in a variety of ever-changing formats, some of which has an extremely brief shelf life (pun intended).

Hopefully, most of the topics that have been covered in this text are topics with which the librarian has had some experience. Experience will guide the librarian in developing policies for the librarian's faculty, students, and community. Smaller schools typically require fewer policies, and issues are often handled on an informal basis. Larger schools have extensive policies.

THE DISTINCTION BETWEEN POLICY AND PROCEDURE

Technically, there is a significant distinction between policies and procedures. Policies explain why the library has chosen a certain approach. Policies are general in tone and guide the library and the librarians toward an ideal for the library. Policy statements are public documents and state the library's goals and its purpose; they establish the direction of the library. It is the library's policy that should have the capacity to resolve conflict. Policies are flexible statements and should not be changed routinely.

Procedures are grounded in the library's policies. Procedures are the methods by which the policies are implemented. Whereas policies are flexible statements that are changed infrequently, procedures are less flexible statements that may be reviewed and changed on a regular basis. Whereas policies are public, procedures are private. Procedures are the internal guidelines for the library.

LIBRARY AND SCHOOL GOALS REFLECTED IN POLICY

When developing a library policy, the goals of the institution should be paramount. The goals of the library should parallel those same policies. Some issues seem so fundamental that they are often forgotten in the development of policies. Each policy on each issue should establish which staff position is responsible for each duty. For example, the position responsible for employment interviews should be established. The position responsible to receive subpoenas or to make collection decisions should be established.

The collection program policy will never be more important than when angry parents address the school board regarding specific materials. If you have specific policies governing your collection and these policies are consistent with the institution's policies it should be the policies that prevail, and not emotions of fear and anger. It is a good idea to incorporate your institution's policies directly into your own policies.

Your policy should require evaluation of the policies periodically and specify the parties to participate in this evaluation. Your policy should also provide for an orderly means of addressing complaints. If your policy requires all concerns regarding the library to be first addressed to the library, this will allow for the simplest and most immediate solutions. Create a library committee to address these issues, and only when they are irresolvable at the library level should they be addressed at a higher level.

Involving teachers in library committees is important to the sense of community in a school. Their input in material selection is crucial. Involving student representatives in library policies is of equal importance. They bring fresh insight and often are more current on technology than the adults. Involving their parents adds yet another dimension—the reality factor. Many schools are considering summer access to the library and evening hours. Parents can provide the feedback necessary to understanding whether proposed or existing policies are feasible for your community.

However, it is important to understand and implement the distinction between policies and procedures. Broad input and support in policy development is crucial to the success of the library. The more people that have a "stake" in the library, the more people will support the library. Procedures, however, belong to the library alone. Thoughtfully and artfully draft your policies omitting procedures. Standard procedures are crucial to the functioning of a library, but they must be in the domain of the librarian.

Today, for example, librarians face the very real threat of child pornography coming into their library. This is contraband as illegal as heroin, and it is only a mouse-click away. The FBI may decide to track a school library's computer activities because of a patron's actions wholly unrelated to school. Tracking a computer with the FBI's program *Magic Lantern* may not identify the student using the computer. For that information the library's records might require access. Suddenly, how a library retains records of students using specific computers becomes relevant.

Free speech has always been a flash point issue in the library. Filters do inhibit free speech and free access, but our society has determined that we do in fact have a "compelling interest" in protecting our students from pornography.

Libraries are at the center of copyright issues. Students routinely pirate music from the Internet and are preconditioned to believe that if it's on the

Internet, it's theirs for the taking, or cutting and pasting. Students access research from the Internet before they access print materials. Many Internet sites have a biased presentation, and the students often do not have the experience to detect this bias. Students mistakenly believe the Internet will provide all the information obtainable on a specific subject and that the print world will have no greater resources. The role of the librarian is to provide the policies that govern Web site selection and to inform the student that print resources will enhance the information obtainable on the Web.

At times it is difficult to distinguish policy from procedure. The best criterion is to simply ask yourself, Is this a matter that should be decided by the librarian because it impacts the day-to-day functioning of the library (i.e., procedure) or is this a direction in which the library should be moving (i.e., policy)?

Never before have so many legal issues focused squarely on the library. It is naïve to think that your library will be the library that escapes critical scrutiny. Hopefully, it will be. However, it is important to be prepared for public, critical scrutiny of every action your library takes and some inaction. Be prepared to defend acts of commission and acts of omission.

LIBRARY POLICY IN DEFENSE OF LIBRARY DECISIONS

Your best defense will be your policy. Your policy should reflect the school's policy and support the school's goals. Incorporating these policies and goals into the library's policies is an excellent starting point in creating or updating your library policy. The American Association of School Librarians reaffirms the Library Bill of Rights of the American Library Association. This is an excellent starting point for your school library's policies and objectives.[1]

Consider each topic found in the chapters of this text and decide whether your library should have a formal policy on this issue or whether it should be handled informally. It is fundamental that all school libraries have a policy that respects all state and federal laws of copyright by students and faculties. The devil here will be in the details. The school library is in the heart of fair-use territory. Perhaps the first procedure and the easiest step in supporting this policy is to place the "Warning Concerning Copyright Restrictions" notices at each copy machine, whether your library is a Section 108 compliance library or not. A thornier issue will be the decision to adopt in whole or in modified part the "Guidelines for Classroom Copying in Not-for-Profit Educational Institutions with Respect to Books and Periodicals," also known as the "Classroom Guidelines." If these are adopted wholesale, the decisions must then be made as to whether an appeal process for exceptions to these guidelines will be adopted and whether a single person or a committee will determine its outcome. The decision to create a committee review will itself ensure a lengthy process and a very minimal number of requests for exceptions to the Classroom Guidelines. The more difficult it becomes to make exceptions to the Classroom Guidelines the stronger they become.

A school policy might be adopted to create approved bibliography pages for Internet sites for specific topics of study. The procedure will determine whether this bibliography will be created by committee, by the librarian with suggestions from the faculty, or by the faculty alone. Guidelines for Web site selection could become part of the procedural process in selecting informative and unbiased Web sites to be reviewed on an annual basis for modification of content.

A school policy regarding the privacy and confidentiality of students' records should be extended specifically to the library. The library procedures will determine whether the identity of students using particular computers will be maintained by record and how long these records will be kept. The length of time could be either a procedural decision or a policy decision. A record retention policy of retaining a student's records for the period of time plus one year that they are enrolled in the school would create a procedure by which these records were periodically purged. If the school policy regarding subpoenas and court orders requires that they be forwarded to the school district's attorney, the school library policy should be the same.

The policies and procedures for media and print selection have historically been the flash point for many school libraries. Today the school library media center functions as an integral part of the total educational process. Its program supports the fundamental learning experiences for each student. It serves to enrich and support the curriculum; to provide materials in many formats on all difficulty levels; and to provide materials with different points of view. The librarian's procedures for selection should consider the scope of the library's entire collection and consider student needs, interests, and requests along with recommendations from administrators and teachers. Librarians should continue to use their vast resources of professional selection aids.

With the broad range of media materials available, age appropriateness must be determined and a person to whom review of this appropriateness is determined must be designated. The video rating system should be created and implemented. Most school libraries already have in place a procedure by which citizens, staff, or students may challenge materials, which includes a review of the challenged material.

In many school districts, the library policies are school board adopted and apply throughout all the libraries in the district. These broad policies are implemented by different procedures and guidelines in different schools. Individual libraries or levels of libraries may have different policies. Elementary and secondary schools' policies may vary. Larger libraries may have distinctly different guidelines and procedures from their smaller counterparts.

CONCLUSION

Your policies, procedures and guidelines should make your day-to-day life simpler and be your greatest ally in times of conflict—which will inevitably come. No difficult job is ever accomplished without conflict. They key is to handle the issue fairly, openly, and with the ability to examine the intrinsic fairness and legality of your chosen position.

NOTE

1. American Association School Librarians Position Statements. Available: http://www.ala.org/aasl/positions. (Accessed July 3, 2002.)

INDEX

About the Author

LEE ANN TORRANS is an attorney in Texas who, after practicing for ten years, returned to school for her Masters in Library Science. She has written several articles on copyright and choreography and frequently lectures on that topic.